To Rhyme...
Or Not To Rhyme?

TEACHING CHILDREN TO WRITE POETRY

Sandy Brownjohn

Hodder & Stoughton
A MEMBER OF THE HODDER HEADLINE GROUP

British Library Cataloguing in Publication Data

A catalogue for this title is available from the British Library

ISBN 0 340 61148 0

This edition first published 1994
Impression number   10   9   8   7   6   5   4   3   2   1
Year   1999   1998   1997   1996   1995   1994

Typeset by Wearset, Boldon, Tyne and Wear
Printed in Great Britain for Hodder & Stoughton Educational, a division of Hodder Headline, Plc, 338 Euston Road, London NW1 3BH by St Edmundsbury Press, Bury St Edmunds, Suffolk.

Contents

SECTION 2

SECTION 3

Dedication

For Emily, Helen and Jessica

Foreword

This book by Sandy Brownjohn will interest all teachers of
English. The writing she has drawn from her young pupils over
the last years has been remarkable – and often astonishing – for
its quality and inventiveness. One important part of her method
is a repertoire of verbal classroom games. In these chapters she
describes these games, and shows how they can be used
productively. Whatever is going on here, it is certainly worth very
close examination by all English teachers.

A first reaction to Sandy Brownjohn's success is sometimes a
negative one: her results are so striking that we might feel,
automatically, there must be something wrong with them, or
with her methods. We might even feel it is not natural that such
young children should write with such sophistication.

But have we any notion of what would be natural? I think
most of us would hesitate to call the situation in any classroom
'natural'. We actually have no idea what any child's real abilities
are – we only know they are much greater than the child ever
brings into play. And we have no idea, either, what kind of
teaching would engage these hidden real abilities and bring
them to full flower. I know – I have felt it myself – the teacher's
pang of despair when he glimpses a pupil's real potential, and
realises there is no way of catching hold of it and developing it.
Few teachers, if any, know how to do such a thing. It is beyond
what ordinary educational methods are designed to deal with,
and even, in a way, beyond what our society can accept. One is
amazed to read how the Kazars are said to have executed any of
their members who showed unusal intelligence, yet we have all
felt our natural human resistance against superior cleverness,
even in those we are trying to teach.

My own view of the contrast between a child's hidden abilities
and the ones he or she shows in class was sharpened by an
experience I had while teaching in a secondary modern school.
There was no question, in that school, of the children deriving
any academic advantage from their home background. Two or
three times a week I took a class of backward boys. I'm not sure
how they were singled out, but our lesson was meant to be
maths. It always began with a laborious mass recitation of the

viii ◆ *To Rhyme Or Not To Rhyme?*

multiplication tables, and was then filled up by anything I could invent. It seemed to me that all these boys were bright enough, but were simply non-survivors in the extreme climate of the classroom. None of them could give the answer to 3×3. After a hesitant wrong guess, there would be a free-for-all of wrong guesses, until some random hit got it right.

Seeing how perversely they avoided the correct answer, it struck me that what they lacked was not so much mathematical ability as confidence in their own brains. I explained this to them as a slight temporary flaw, and persuaded them that mathematical ability is equal in all people, because it takes its instructions direct from the physical chemistry of our body, which is a phenomenal genius and always gets everything miraculously right. My story was quite long, with digressions about the subconscious mind, but it evidently persuaded them that all they needed to do, when I gave them a mental sum, was to trust the first thing that came into their heads. 'Your real brain is moving so fast,' I assured them, 'that if you hesitate even for a second you'll miss it. It will have gone past like an express train through a station. Then you'll have to catch the next slow stopping one along and that will be wrong.' I asked them to yell out an answer – without thinking – as soon as I gave them the sum.

For the remaining ten minutes of the lesson, it worked. I asked simple multiplications (I wrote the answers out on paper first – the highest was 19×19 – so that I could seem to be in on the gift of instant certainty), and every answer jumped back at me correct. I wondered if I had chanced on some revolutionary teaching method. By the end of the lesson the boys were wildly excited – and bemused. Neither they nor I knew what to make of it. Our problem solved itself, however. By the next lesson, the miracle was over. Their idea of their own limitations had moved in the night, and sealed off the escape route I had opened, and was now on guard. I was never able to open it again.

I've often remembered those boys, because in the act of writing, especially of writing verse, one is always convinced that what appears on the page is only a distorted fraction of what, somewhere or other inside us, wanted to appear, and would have appeared, too, if only we knew how to listen to it more subtly and widely and deeply, and record it more boldly. The progress of any writer is marked by those moments when he manages to outwit his own inner police system which tells him what is permissible, what is possible, what is 'him', or tells her what is 'her'. Writers have invented all kinds of 'games' to get past their own censorship. Dickens had to wear a certain ring. Hart Crane played jazz at top volume. Schiller invented free association.

'Inspiration' is a poor word for those occasions, and perhaps in most cases a wrong word. One thing such times have in common is a willingness to relax expectation, and to experiment, to let flow – a willingness to put on masks and to play.

Which brings us back to the games which Sandy Brownjohn uses in her writing classes. Her pupils produce what they want to produce: startling poetic combinations of words and ideas, startling complete patterns of poetic sense. But these effects are really incidental. These writers are simultaneously doing something else, something which must be much more valuable to them. They are practising techniques of self-exploration and productive play, by which I mean free, searching play of the mind among its galleries of memory, imagination and perception.

It is a multiple, unselfconscious exercise of what has come to be known as lateral thinking. Though it is applied here, in an intensive way, to imaginative writing, it is at bottom the same technique which is becoming popular, because so successful, in the brainstorming creative idea sessions of working scientists, engineers, and in all activities that depend on flexible adaptation to new facts and needs, and a steady influx of new and better solutions. It is a natural technique, too – it is the one the brain itself uses in subconscious work and in sleep, to solve the problems of daily life.

And as a system it is based on assumptions quite opposite to the minimal expectations of our educational system. It is based on the confidence that we have an inexhaustible capacity for producing the answers to problems, and that there is only one problem, how to tap that capacity at will, and that we have answers to that problem too.

But the incidental fruits of Sandy Brownjohn's method are also very great. Reading her account of her methods and practice, we can see that while her pupils are focusing all their excitement on the one ambition, to write their poem, they are becoming, in the process and almost unwittingly, sophisticated verbalists, with large vocabularies which they use with discrimination and zest; they are becoming both skilled manipulators of sentence structure and phrasing, and strongly motivated critical readers. In making their bid for the three minute forty second mile, so to speak, they are running four minute miles just for training. Most of the aims of English teaching have been encompassed in the single task.

In all this, no teacher will fail to give Sandy Brownjohn her due. It is a remarkable personal achievement for her, to have fitted so many novel approaches together, and to have brought off, year after year, such a triumph of sheer teaching. But even when we have given full credit to her skill in locating the hidden ability in a wide variety of young individuals, there still remain those practical solid tools of her methods, which are for anybody to use.

Perhaps they leave us with only one problem, the old problem. Once children have come so far, so fast, where else can they go, in English lessons? How can this beginning be hung on to and developed? Surely everything that has been uncovered in this way will soon be smothered by conventional English teaching. What kind of English teaching will not smother it? That problem still has to be solved, but it is one which in most schools has not yet been consciously tackled.

But whatever comes afterwards, these early exercises, this precociously developed ability, in lateral thinking in words, imaginative ideas and perceptions, can only be good. The pupil has been given a whole kit of techniques for opening his or her own mind, quite apart from that pleasure and confidence in the uses of language, and a taste for literature. This is as crucial as the teaching of memory and recall, and of concentration in productive effort – two fundamental, essential skills without which education cannot properly start (without which it becomes little more than institutionalised baby-sitting).

These 'games', which Sandy Brownjohn has collected here, seem to me the most serious kind of business.

Ted Hughes

Introduction

To Rhyme Or Not To Rhyme? contains the material from my three previous books for teachers – *Does It Have To Rhyme?*, *What Rhymes With 'Secret'?* and *The Ability To Name Cats* – together with many new ideas for teaching children to write poetry. The order of chapters from the original books has been reorganised to coincide with the 'scheme' described in my 'Credo' which appears here at the beginning. The book now offers a three-tier approach for teachers, with the ideas set out in an ascending order of difficulty based on either the forms and techniques offered or the advanced nature of the material. It is not envisaged that teachers will work through the book from start to finish, but I hope they will be able to dip in and find something to stimulate them and their pupils.

I have resisted the temptation to rewrite chapters, except where references needed to be updated; although I continue to learn about the process of teaching children to write, I still believe what I wrote when much younger and am content to let it stand. I hope the ideas gathered together here will inspire other teachers to take confidence and enable them to tap the well of talent that undoubtedly exists in all their classes.

Sandy Brownjohn

Acknowledgements

The following poems all won major awards in the W H Smith Young Writers' Competition between 1976 and 1993:

'Window' by Steve Webber; 'Ship in a Bottle' and 'Jack-in-a-Box' by Miles Greene; 'Suburbia' by Ben Owen; 'The Making of the Tiger' by Nadya Kassam; 'Alcohol' by Helen Alexander; 'The Photograph' by James Souter; 'The Postcard', 'Three Faces' and 'Ambition' by Jonty Leff; 'Today I Start School' by Fidel Asante; 'The Tree of Knowledge' by Lucy Head.

The following were prize-winning runners-up: 'The Making of the World' by Nicholas Midgley; 'My Religion' by David Stallibrass.

Many other poems were highly commended.

A number of poems were part of an entry which won a major school award in The Poetry Society/World Wildlife Fund Competition in 1986. Many poems appeared in the booklets *Crossing Lines* (1978) and *Second Crossing* (1980), Fitzjohn's Imprint, and were the subject of a Radio 4 programme called 'Crossing Lines'.

Chapter 77, *Learning Poems by Heart*, first appeared as an article in *Junior Education* (May 1980, Vol.4, No. 5).

All the poems in this book were contributed by children from the following institutions, and are gratefully acknowledged: Belsize Young Writers (BYW); Fitzjohn's Primary School; ILEA Young Writers' Workshop (YWW); Pearse House Children's Writing Courses (PH); St. Alban's School, Herts (St.A). (These acronyms are used in the book to indicate which institution children belonged to: any name without an acronym following it indicates a pupil from Fitzjohn's Primary School.)

The author and publishers would also like to thank Wes Magee for permission to reproduce a stanza from his poem 'Up On The Downs'.

Section

I

CREDO

This chapter is intended to be an attempt to clarify why and, to some extent, how I teach children to write poetry. There will not be a lot of theorising, I suspect, as this is not my way, and the chapter may not be of any use to anyone. However, because occasionally one or two critics have questioned the validity of my methods and the authenticity of the children's work, I felt I should like to try to explain what in some cases is the unexplainable.

MY TEACHING STYLE

At the risk of being self-indulgent, I will start by giving some background on myself and my style of teaching which must obviously have something to do with what goes on. Educated at grammar school and university, I always had an ear for music and languages. I adored Latin, and my degree is in German. English I did not study further than O level. I mention all this because I have been told that I was perhaps lucky not to have had a more formal critical training in English, and certainly my approach has not been too bound by convention. Latin has probably been the most interesting and useful subject to have studied in some ways. I constantly draw the children's attention to the roots of words and encourage them to think of others which come from the same stable. I think this actually helps children remember words and how to spell them, too. The children laugh at me sometimes over my Latin references but many of them have made a point of taking the subject up where possible when they go on to their secondary schools.

I do not mean to say that all this is not possible without Latin. It is the pure love of the sound of words that is important. One only has to listen to a very small child who has just heard a new word – and who perhaps does not even know what it means but just likes the sound of it and walks around saying it over and over again – to realise the power of words. It is no accident that one of the most popular projects for five and six year olds is dinosaurs. The names are so wonderful and immensely, excitingly long. Who would not want to say Tyrannosaurus Rex, Diplodocus, Triceratops, *et al.*, and yet, how many people, if asked, would say that such words were suitable for children of that age? It is actually surprising that we have not renamed these creatures in simple terms – we do with so many other things. Big King Lizard does not somehow have the same cachet.

We forget all this as we grow older, and teachers often take the magic out of learning, from the best of motives, by not using the proper names for things. Just pause for a moment and write down a list of ten words whose sound you enjoy, irrespective of meaning, and say them out loud to yourself. Isn't it quite fun? Foreign languages can enhance this effect. There is a magic about sound and repetition which can give a feeling of power and release.

To me then, this enjoyment of, and playing with, language is essential if one is ever going to use words to good effect. Over the years, I have evolved a loose system which has three tiers covering the three terms of a school year. If I had the choice, I would spread the system over a longer period, but changing classes each year has forced me to rush through selected material. I am constantly on the lookout for new ideas, or new ways of presenting the material, because I become bored with the same thing year in and year out. If I cannot feel inspired by an idea I will not be able to enthuse children. Conversely, if I become excited about an idea, I know I will be able to carry the children with me. Whenever an enthusiast waxes lyrical about a subject, he or she exudes an energy and fascination which draws people like a magnet. One element of my teaching style is certainly inspiration combined with personality.

However, nobody can work in this gear all the time so the other elements needed are good organisation and high expectations. I have always tried to know why I am teaching a particular thing, where it is leading, or what it is designed to do for children. I do not think I did this so much when younger and certainly, in the past, the understanding has followed *after* the practice. I think one always has to do a thing for a while before a fuller understanding gradually dawns. I am a firm believer in 'learning by doing' alongside a well-informed practitioner, or, failing that, with access to books, etc. to which one can turn when ready.

I have learned about writing poetry by doing it myself. I have learned about teaching children to write poetry by trying out forms, techniques and ideas that interested me; and all of this by chance because a girl in one of my classes wrote something rather extraordinary. This happened to coincide with my admitting to myself that, try as I might, I just did not seem able to obtain good writing from children using the old methods. All I received, more often than not, were 30 odd pieces all ringing the changes on the selection of words we put on the board during our discussions.

This is the poem which came out of a very mundane lesson on spells written at the time of Hallowe'en.

— ◆ —

Hellebore and Witches Broom,
Come swift and silent as the tomb,
The deathly graveyard is your doom.
Silver dagger stained with blood
Call the gods named Lok and Wod.
Evil circle now is formed,
Ancient ritual now be performed.
Tie the victim with head well back,
Sharpen the knife and slowly hack,
Hold the blade up to the moon,
With evil face chant spell of doom.
Steel the blade right through the throat
Chanting wildly spell of goat,
Take the head and slice the brain,
Swiftly scatter hemlock grain.
Lay the cauldron between two gravestones,

Call the devil in implacable tones,
Jet of fire, Heaven and Hell,
Call the devil with this spell.
Flame of fire, burning heat,
Drain the blood from leg and feet,
Tear the flesh and take the toes,
Call nine bats and three black crows.

Fire dies and cauldron goes,
Away go bats and three black crows,
Lok and Wod; and now we part
But next Hallowe'en again we'll start.
Graveyard silent, body gone.
A cold dead body in every tomb.
A shadow darkens across the moon,
And one lone witch in steady flight
Helping evil to win the night.

Sarah Simpson   October 1974

Along came this talented girl, and a book called *The Poet's Manual and Rhyming Dictionary* by Frances Stillman[1]. Here was a revelation! As someone who enjoyed Latin prose at school and loves solving crosswords and puzzles, I was excited beyond measure by all the poetic forms and techniques set out so clearly in this book. My O level knowledge was limited to sonnets (Shakespearean), ballads and not much more. Naturally, I began to experiment in my own writing and, because my mind was taken up with it, I used this obsession in my teaching.

I relate all this as it might be useful to others. With no accepted formal training in English outside O level, I managed purely out of interest to begin to make sense of how to teach poetry. It took a few years for me to stand back from the initial excitement and be able to draw some conclusions. I am still learning.

Basically, what I discovered was how to demystify the whole process. So many teachers are willing and even desperate to

---

[1]Stillman, F. (1966), *The Poet's Manual and Rhyming Dictionary*, Thames and Hudson

come to grips with teaching poetry-writing but do not know where to start. They feel they should be able to do it because we all speak English and can write, etc., but this obscures the fact that some specialist knowledge *is* required. By the time they reach this conclusion they have lost heart and become defensive. The whole subject seems so vast and is beset by so many preconceived ideas that teachers suffer from an increasing lack of confidence, if they think about it at all.

The best way I have found of helping teachers to overcome this problem, because it was the way I found for myself, is to break the subject down into small, easily assimilated parts; each is one idea, one technique or one form. In other words, I separate all the individual details which go to make the whole. Every part understood is a part conquered. Eventually, with this layer-upon-layer approach, the confidence gained by success will enable teachers to strike off on their own from this solid base and to come to their own understanding of what it is all about. I do the same thing with the children. I think this is how all teaching should be done. It is our job as teachers to give our pupils a thorough knowledge and practice in basic techniques, thus building up a bank of experience on which they can call in future when appropriate. This does not mean that we must do it in a dry way. Wherever possible, we must make the learning fun. We always remember experiences which made us laugh, or frightened us to death. I prefer to 'make 'em laugh', though it has to be said that when necessary I can frighten with the best of them.

I am obviously a 'personality' teacher with all that that entails, including a need not to feed too many of my own ideas to the detriment of the children's developing powers of invention and judgement. I like to question things and I choose what I do and when I do it, and what, if any, books I wish to use. Following a scheme of any kind without deviating from it or questioning it is anathema to me. I just do not believe anything is perfect. I have strong opinions and I think I have very high standards, but I know I do not always succeed and am not always right! No two people can teach in the same way but I hope that, by setting out ideas I have tried and things I have learned, other teachers will be encouraged to have a go, too. Everyone will bring his or her own personality to bear and adapt methods to suit the situation. In the second part of this chapter I will try to set out my three-tier scheme, with observations along the way.

To sum up this section:

- Previous knowledge and experience is not necessary.
- A love of words and playing with them *is*.
- A willingness to practise the techniques oneself is essential.
- No amount of reading the theory will teach you.
- Start with simple ideas/techniques and build up slowly.
- The whole will take shape in time – and sooner than you think.
- Poetry, like any other art form, is also a craft.
- The teacher's job is to give the tools to shape the inspiration.
- If you are enthusiastic you are on a good wicket.
- A sense of humour goes a long way.

THE SCHEME

First Part

I begin with a set of assumptions based on my experience over many years, and they form the rationale behind the exercises offered for use with any class in the first term. These assumptions are as follows:

1   That children need to be allowed to rediscover, or be given the opportunity to use, a love of playing with language just for its own sake.
2   That they need plenty of practice in manipulating words so that they can feel in control of them, rather than allowing the words to take control.
3   That the best way of encouraging this is to present them with games and exercises which highlight individual types of words, and which they can enjoy using without having to cope with the demands of producing a sustained piece of writing about something dear to their hearts.
4   That they may have spent many years writing lengthy pieces

which have taken all their energy merely to complete in the time allotted, without the opportunity or incentive to think carefully about the words being used.

5   That they need some basic experience of the grammar of language in order to experiment with its limits and potential.

6   That they need to discover that the dictionary is a treasure chest and a useful 'friend', rather than a book of correction and a nuisance to have to consult.

7   That, above all, writing is not a chore. It is fun and a route to self-fulfilment. It will bring confidence and satisfaction in the way that any task wrestled with and overcome will do.

The sort of exercises I have used are: collections of words; alphabet games highlighting nouns, adjectives or verbs; simple sentences employing different prepositions; word games, both oral and written; tongue twisters; spoonerisms; jokes making use of puns which rely on homophones; anagrams; sayings; similes; collective nouns; and any kind of language which gives a chance to laugh or experiment. The emphasis is on making words do what you want them to do, finding new words with which to play, inventing new expressions from old conventions, seeing the funny side of things: for example, 'His eye fell on the box in the corner' (literally?).

(I have set out many of these 'games' in *Word Games*[1], a book which arose from a series of BBC school radio programmes and which I put together with the producer, Janet Whitaker.)

Working sometimes as a whole class, or in small groups, or individually, the children spend much of the first half term – and sometimes longer – on these types of activity. There is really no age limit, up or downwards, for this kind of work. All that needs to be varied is the approach and presentation.

Once I feel that children have relaxed and become enthusiastic about writing sessions, I move them along a little by introducing more poetry-orientated exercises. Among them would be: 'Kennings'; 'Alliteration'; 'I'd rather be . . . '; 'I saw a

---

[1]Brownjohn, S. and Whitaker, J. (1984 and 1994), *Word Games*, Hodder & Stoughton

peacock'; 'Acrostics'; 'Places and Details'; 'I should like to . . . ';
list-poems of various kinds; 'The Furniture Game'; 'Similes';
'Belly like a Bream'; 'Last Will and Testament'; 'Gifts'; and other
stimuli for writing which have a recognisable framework in
which to fit ideas.

All of these exercises enable children to write without having
too many demands put on them. The form/framework is set and
is one problem fewer to think about. The subject matter is not
too vast but allows children to be quite sure of the task before
they embark upon it. This also takes the pressure off. In many
cases they are required to write only one sentence/phrase at a
time, thus giving them breathing space and a chance to break
concentration without losing the thread. This is very important.
If the task seems too daunting, many children will give up
halfway, or even before they start.

Note: There are two important extra points to be made in this
section, the keynote of which is confidence-building:

1 I have found that typing out the children's work and putting
   it into a large class poetry book does almost more than
   anything else to encourage children and give them
   confidence. A reasonably high standard must be applied,
   though, if entry into the book is to mean anything of lasting
   value.
2 I have also found that children are relieved of an added
   pressure if I make it clear to them that I do not expect them
   to write something marvellous each session. I say that I
   consider three pieces of high quality writing produced by a
   child during a year to be very acceptable. In fact, as the year
   progresses, one raises the level of expectation so that three
   pieces would be very good indeed.

What happens is that, far from using this as an excuse not to try,
the children are encouraged. They realise that nobody can
succeed all the time and that not to do so is not being a failure.
The freedom this brings can be exhilarating. Trying too hard is
almost the same as not trying enough – both lead to
disappointment and can reinforce a sense of failure which is
completely counterproductive. We, as teachers, must try to exert

the right pressures, not the wrong ones.

Second Part

In the second term some specific poetry techniques and forms can be introduced. By now, we hope the children are quite at ease with using language properly and taking a pride in their work. They are ready for some more concentrated teaching to give them the language tools necessary for writing proper poems. Incidentally, it is worth saying that although I concentrate on poetry, this language practice automatically improves the children's prose too. As long as the children are not satisfied with just writing the first thing that comes into their heads, all their writing will improve.

Among the things that figure in this term's work are the following: syllabic forms, such as haiku, tanka, cinquains, renga, naga-uta, and the children's own invented forms; rondelets; sonnets; metaphor; rhyme (full, half and internal); rhythms of different kinds; repetition; running on lines; pattern poems; alliteration and assonance.

In the chapters dealing with these forms, I describe what I hope they can do for the children. Basically, I believe that the job of a teacher is to provide the tools for shaping thought on paper so that it can be communicated in the best possible way to others. I think it is important to vary the writing tasks for children as much as possible, so that there is no room for boredom, and to allow everyone to find something that appeals. Every new challenge could be the one that sparks a child off. Once started on the road, most children will continue. It is the getting started that is crucial. All the exercises introducing these techniques/forms are designed to help a child build up a bank of knowledge which can be drawn on at will in future writing. I think of the lessons as opportunities to practise getting to know the possibilities, of flexing the literary muscles – as the literary equivalent of musical scales, mathematical tables, artistic techniques or keep-fit exercises.

Third Part

In the third term, the children are fairly well-versed in the craft of writing and I consider the teacher's rôle to be to throw out ideas for subjects and to allow the children the luxury of time to write. It is now that the groundwork of the previous two terms comes to fruition. With their newly-acquired confidence with language, the children often do not even want ideas, but for those who do we can present a variety of subjects in ways which may capture their imaginations. These would include such things as: 'Ship in a Bottle'; 'Shells'; 'Pictures and Jack-in-the-Box'; 'Shadows'; 'Mirrors and Reflections'; 'The Creation of the World'; 'The Seven Ages of Man'; 'Faces and Places', among others. At this stage all we really need to do is initiate the discussion and help to enthuse. Where necessary, we can contribute thoughts to widen the scope of possibilities for poems, and then we can leave the children to write.

In the first stages we will have given children help in how to set out their poems and how to cut out superfluous words, and encouraged them to be specific in their choice of language. You may find that, at the start, you need to go through their pieces with them, suggesting where they might end one line and begin another. Usually, you only need to do this a few times before they understand what is required and can then do it for themselves. The easiest way to approach this problem is to read the work aloud and feel where a breath is needed or an idea ends. Later, a more sophisticated use of line-breaks can be employed, for example, to highlight a word or phrase by isolating it on one line. Much of this boils down to personal taste and is learned almost by osmosis. Seeing what other people in the class do, and reading published poems, obviously helps, too.

In class, you can be available for any technical assistance, or as an arbiter if a child cannot decide which word or phrase seems better. Offer advice, if asked, but be very careful not to suggest exactly what to write. Children must be led to make their own decisions – and by this time they rarely want any interference at all. Confidence brings with it a certain arrogance, which is not a bad thing as long as it does not take over completely. Take the work home to read at leisure, when you can give it your full attention. Tell the children this, and they will appreciate it. If you regularly type out their poems for the class book they know you really do care, and they soon lose that need for an immediate response in the lesson. Having queues of children seems to me a waste of everyone's time. It is far better that they use the time available to write and that you are free to give help where it is really needed. After you have read the poems at home, you could often make time to talk to children individually about their work on a subsequent occasion, when they receive a considered opinion which is more useful. Anyway, the child who comes out after only ten minutes, saying he or she has finished and wanting praise, is probably only showing that lack of confidence which this scheme is designed to combat.

Throughout the Year

I have specifically dealt with the actual writing in this chapter, but many other things are happening all the time.

'The Poet-tree', as described in Chapter 72, helps to encourage children to read poetry. Often you can fill in five minutes by reading a poem purely for pleasure. The children, too, can take turns to choose poems to read out loud to the class. They often prefer their teacher to read out their poems when these enter the class book, and this book is left around the room for children to consult during a reading session or when they have finished some other work. There is no doubt that they can learn an enormous amount from each other this way.

At some point during the year, I have always tried to bring in one or two published poets to visit the class and read their own poems. This means that we would have prepared for the occasion by studying some of the poems, and the children always enjoyed these visits. Meeting people who believe poetry is important and who make their living from it helps to give it a higher profile. The chance to ask the author what he or she actually meant by a particular line is a rare opportunity and, I believe, of great value. The children and the poets meet on the same ground, as fellow practitioners, and both can derive so much from the experience.

From time to time I have also entered the children's work for poetry competitions. Without dwelling here on the pros and cons of such things, I find, on balance, that the advantages outweigh the disadvantages. If the children (or the school) receive prizes it must be encouraging for everybody, as long as we do not allow others to think they have failed. Competitions serve as a guide for us, as teachers, on the level of achievement for which we should be aiming in the children's work. The published winners will not always impress us, for there is bound to be dissent at times over the judges' choices; but, as a general rule, we can learn from these, and they can be a means by which we can measure our own standards. If they force us to question how we are teaching (something we should be doing constantly), they will have served a purpose. Are we raising our expectations? Are we maintaining standards? If the work we are receiving from children is nothing like the standard of others, where are we going wrong? How can we approach it differently?

CONCLUSION

In all our teaching I feel it is incumbent on us to encourage children to set their own targets, make their own decisions, be their own critics. We set the framework and provide the back-up while guiding the children towards their own autonomy. This is not an easy way to teach and demands a constant review of methods, and of levels of achievement. It is not an excuse to opt out of organisation; in fact, it requires more. And it demands a thorough knowledge of the subjects one is teaching in order to be able to move children on, according to their readiness and ability. However, all this can be done by being only one or two steps ahead of the children, as long as the underlying philosophy is solidly understood. I always think that one golden rule plays a very important part here: namely, never ask the children to do something that you could not, or would not, attempt yourself. This does not mean that you must be able to do it well. There are obviously some things we can teach by knowing the theory, even if we cannot do them ourselves, either through physical or other disqualification. But, as I stress elsewhere, in order to teach poetry, I believe teachers should try writing themselves so that they know what to expect and can present the task sympathetically. The children can differentiate between teachers who know what they are talking about and those who do not. That they are more likely to listen to one who does is obvious. I hope that by breaking down the subject of poetry-teaching into easily understandable parts I can help other teachers to become 'experts' in their classes and discover the joy of introducing children to the highest literary art.

I teach children to write poetry because I enjoy it – both the poetry itself and the teaching. Poetry is only one aspect of my life, but it is crucial. Moreover, I find I have almost unlimited patience when teaching this subject, because there is such excitement in helping somebody grapple with the problem of trying to express an idea. It seems to be more real than teaching in other areas (though I am sure this feels true for others in different disciplines also). Language fascinates me and I revel in its possibilities.

I have seen so many children grow in confidence and self-esteem through poetry-writing. I try to write myself and know the satisfaction to be gained from time spent exercising the mind in manipulating and bringing together words and ideas towards some kind of near-perfect conclusion. It never *is* perfect, so the need to write grows with each attempt. The 'perfect' creation is always just out of reach, but hovers tantalisingly and spurs one on.

Reading and writing poetry helps me to understand myself, clarify my thoughts and see things in new ways. It keeps the mind alert and also satisfies that basic urge we have to create something unique. In such ways as this poetry is crucial to me, as are the arts generally, and this is why I feel they are so important for our development and our quality of life. I should like to feel I have been able to pass some of this on to the children I have taught.

Whether they go on writing poetry through their lives or not, these children will retain something of that love for words. There will be times when they turn to poetry for comfort or enjoyment, as we all do, and many of them will write secretly for pleasure or to help them make sense of situations they encounter. Their level of consciousness will have been raised and something of the discipline of language will remain. This must be good for its survival and ensure that it will go on developing in rich and exciting ways.

Note: Since writing this 'Credo', I have left teaching and now work freelance. I still teach poetry-writing to groups of children, but not as a class teacher.

2

POETRY

GAMES

I see the teaching of poetry-writing to children as the teaching of skills and techniques almost as much as the use of original ideas – a love of language and the excitement of exploring its possibilities, of making it work for you. Children are capable of writing with a high degree of sophistication and control if they are encouraged to do so, and we should beware of those who say it cannot, or should not, be done – they merely wish to keep children 'childish', or save themselves some effort. We must not underestimate what children can do.

To achieve this takes time and enthusiasm. Haphazard or half-hearted lip service to teaching poetry will lay no foundations. It is a constant building on layers of knowledge and practice that brings the rewards.

I make no apology for mentioning the teaching of grammar in connection with some of the poetry games. I feel it is important; and good writing, in the end, should be correct in grammar and spelling. Teaching it this way is not only more enjoyable, but also more relevant. Reading and writing poetry – being steeped in poetry – incidentally introduces and reinforces many aspects of English teaching. I would almost go as far as to say that most necessary skills in English can be taught through poetry at this level.

The following games represent only a few of the ways that can be used to encourage children to think about the meaning of words and to use them adventurously. They are fun to play and can be considered as 'warm-up' exercises before a lesson or as a lesson in itself. It is not a good idea to play more than one (or perhaps two) in one session. Some of these games can lead directly into poems, as will be seen.

THE EXQUISITE CORPSE

This game is a version of Consequences and was played by the Dadaists and Surrealists; indeed, it is the surreal quality of the sentences produced which particularly appeals to adults and children alike. There are various ways of playing this game, but the result is always of the same kind.

Each child has a piece of paper on which are drawn several columns. The headings of these can be as follows:

Adjective/Adjective/Noun/Verb/Adjective/Adjective/Noun

or *Adjective/Adjective/Noun/Verb/Adverb/Adjective/Adjective/Noun*

In other words, the column headings stand for the main parts of speech required to make up an interesting sentence. Some work will have to be done to explain the grammatical terms, but the children will soon learn them by playing the game. Because children often have difficulty in understanding each other's handwriting I usually find the following method of play most successful.

Each child writes down five different adjectives in the first column (it is best to use lined paper as this will help later): five seems to be about the right number. The paper is then folded back so that the first column cannot be seen. Now five different adjectives are written in the second column. This is folded back, and five nouns are written – and so on until each column has been filled. When completed, the paper is opened out and the resulting sentences are read across the page with definite or indefinite articles inserted where appropriate. Prepositions can also be added and verbs can be put into the required tense and form.

The sentences usually have a bizarre quality which appeals to the children and they occasionally produce a phrase or a whole line that is quite remarkable. These can often be used in future poems. It is these fortuitous combinations of words that can help to show children that poetry does not have to be 'long words', but can be simple words put together in an unusual way.

As will be obvious, the game can also be played a whole line at a time, with each person writing a word in a column, folding it back, and passing the paper on to the next person (more like the game of Consequences).

ADVERBS

This is a simple game involving some drama work and can be used to give a clearer understanding of what adverbs are and how they work.

The children sit in a circle while one person leaves the room. Those left behind decide on an adverb on which they all agree (e.g. 'gloomily'). The person outside is called in and must try to guess the adverb. Each child in the circle is asked in turn to illustrate an action in the manner of the adverb. The children might be asked to do simple tasks, like doing up a shoelace, dancing, playing football, writing a letter. While acting them out they must attempt to convey the spirit of the adverb. This forces them to think hard about words and their meanings. Equally, the person guessing has to work at understanding the hints offered.

THE FURNITURE GAME

This is another guessing game for a group of children. One person thinks of someone (preferably in the group) but does not say who it is. The rest of the group must guess the name of the person by asking certain sorts of questions. As examples: What piece of furniture is this person? What time of day? What kind of flower? What sort of weather?

The one who has chosen must answer immediately with whatever first comes into his or her head. The answers will give the clues as to who it is. Children are quite remarkable at guessing the names.

This game can be an aid to introducing similes and metaphors since the children are seeing others as totally different things. It can also be carried out as an individual exercise where each child writes about someone in the class using the same criteria.

— ◆ —

(a) This person is a lampshade.
   She reminds me of a tom cat
   And her colour is a sharp mauve.
   She reminds me of an ashtray
   And if she were a clock she would be at 3 a.m. all the time.
   She is a large glass of sherry,
   A mean aunt,
   A double X film,
   And the element fire,
   And she would like the sun to be dedicated to her when she dies.
(b) He's a plump Jaffa orange
   And pink pyjamas with white stripes.
   He's a restless labrador jumping onto a sofa.
   He's a wig flying down a laundry chute.
   Placed by the pines and the river he'd be a contented moose.
   He's a wooden fence with lots of holes
   And smoke without fire.
   He's a bouncy beachball,
   A brightly coloured clown.
   If placed in the sky on a Sunday night he'd become a U.F.O.
   He's an Action Man of Robinson Crusoe.
(c) She's an anxious kingfisher,
   She's purple.
   If placed in a raging river she becomes an aluminium canoe.
   She stands out to the world as a dining room table.
   She's the cold of Alaska and the warmth of Italy,
   She's a fox
   And a five bar gate.
   She's Irish coffee and also vodka.
   If she were a boot she'd be trampling down the rubbish.
   She's a country pub in Dorset
   And she's the sprinter who works for her crowd.

LEXICON SENTENCES

This is a game for one to about eight people. A pack of Lexicon
cards (or their equivalent, e.g. Kan-u-go) and a scribe is all that

is needed; or, if playing alone, a child will have to write down the results himself. There are many variations of this game and scoring can be introduced if it is thought necessary. Take out 'X' and 'Z', and 'Q' is 'wild'.

(a) Each player is dealt five cards and the pack is placed face down in the centre of the table. (Players may look at their cards.) The player on the left of the dealer starts by laying any card from his hand face up on the table. He says a word beginning with that letter, to begin a sentence. He then replenishes his hand from the pile in the centre.

The next player plays a card face up on the first card and says a word, beginning with her letter, which will follow the previous word and help to build up a sentence. Each player adds to the sentence in turn. At any point a player can say 'Full stop!' and begin a new sentence. You are allowed to pass, but the fun is in using your ingenuity to find a word each time. The game continues until all the cards are used up.

This game is best played fast: you should not have to think too long about a word. Obviously there is a chance of some very interesting phrases and sentences emerging from this communal effort, but probably its chief value lies in the exercise of thinking quickly of words and linking them to what has gone before.

(b) Another variation is to lay a certain number of cards face down on the table in a formation, e.g. four rows of eight cards. The second and fourth line might be expected to rhyme. The first card is then turned over and a word said which begins with this letter. The same is done for the next seven cards while the scribe writes down the line as it emerges. This is now the first line of the poem. The same procedure is followed with the next three lines and, if rhymes have been decided on, every attempt must be made to achieve them. (A reminder about the sort of words more likely to have a number of possible rhymes may be necessary here. If all else fails, you will have to cheat!)

Both of these games involve using words in a novel way which can be fun; at the same time, the children will be increasing their ability to produce words and, we hope, enlarging their vocabulary by learning from other members of the group. A fast reaction can often result in providing words which, though ordinary in themselves, combine to give a phrase of startling originality: the kind of language we are looking for in poetry.

TELEGRAMS

This is a well-known word game which is similar to the lexicon games mentioned above. Most of us probably know S.W.A.L.K. (Sealed With A Loving Kiss) which was put on the backs of envelopes to boyfriends or girlfriends in *much* younger days. There are others, often spelling names of towns or countries, as in the examples used to such effect by Alan Bennett: B.U.R.M.A. and N.O.R.W.I.C.H.

This game consists of printing out the name of a town, county or country, and making up a message, the words of which begin with the letters that spell the name. Teachers can make up their own examples. You might think of it as an exercise in mnemonics!

QUESTIONS AND ANSWERS

This can be introduced as a game, although I feel it goes beyond that and can lead to some interesting poems. It can be approached in two ways.

(a) Each child writes down five questions of any kind. The children then swap books and each proceeds to answer the questions he or she has received. The children should be encouraged to be inventive in both questions and answers. The results can be read out round the class, and the best can be collected together as a poem. There will probably be a mixture of serious and humorous combinations.

(b) The same results can be obtained if a child writes and answers his or her own questions. However, there is often marginally more success if the first method is used. Someone else's slant when answering your questions can introduce a more exciting and unexpected element.

— ◆ —

What is the sun?
– The blushing face of the universe.
Where does the sky begin?
– Just above the smoke of the factory chimneys.
Where does Nature part?
– In the middle years.
How do you cut the air?
– With the wind.
What's inside a hill?
– Things to come up in the future.
When is the end of time?
– When the last cuckoo sinks into Hell.

How does a window see?
– Through another window.
What does a policeman do when he's alone?
– Learns to be a man.
How does the moon cry?
– With a hanky in his hand.
Why do dogs have four legs?
– They had to put their hair somewhere.
Is life a dream?
– Mine is.

Written by children aged 10 years

PREFERENCES

This game is played with two teams. One team is the 'Hates' and the other is the 'Likes' (or 'Loves'). A subject is chosen to which people may have strong reactions, either positive or negative, and the teams line up opposite one another. They then take it in turns to shout to each other about the subject in the following way.

Let us take the subject of holidays – not perhaps, on the surface, something that children might dislike, but worth a try. The first member of the 'Loves' might shout – 'What I love about holidays is that that I can go swimming every day.' The first member of the 'Hates' might reply – 'What I hate about holidays is that it always rains.' The second member of the 'Loves' – 'What I love about holidays is being able to stay in bed.' The second member of the 'Hates' – 'What I hate about holidays is having to stay with Auntie Jean.'

This continues with every member of each team contributing a line when it is his or her turn. Other subjects that might be interesting are Spiders, Jelly, Winter, Neighbours and Mirrors, and of course anything else you care to try. It may be necessary for the groups to discuss the subject first of all to allow each team member to write down his or her line. This ensures that everyone has a different thing to say and also makes the final effort run freely without awkward pauses.

It is quite good to write all the lines down to make a poem. The particular benefit gained from this exercise is the practice it gives in thinking about a subject in as many different ways as possible (see also Chapters 24 and 29, pages 112 and 132). This will provide the children with a useful approach to writing their poems later. It can help to give depth and more interesting angles so that they do not all write the same thing – rather boring if you have to mark them! (See Edwin Morgan's poem 'A View of Things' which can be found in *Junior Voices, the third book*[1].)

PREPOSITIONS

This is another game which provides the added bonus of teaching some grammar in a painless way. It is best to have some discussion as to what prepositions are and to write on the blackboard all the prepositions the children suggest, e.g. before, behind, beside, round, under, over. The game can then be played in two ways.

(a) Making a communal poem
A subject is selected, e.g. 'my head' or 'the window', and each child writes one line beginning with a preposition. The sort of

---

[1] Geoffrey Summerfield (*ed.*), (1970), *Junior Voices, the third book,* Penguin

lines written might be as follows: 'Inside my head are caves I can't explore', or 'Below the soft sand is the dead water'. The children then read the lines one after the other, producing an instant poem.

One of the great benefits of this game is that the children are made aware of all the different angles you can take on a particular subject. It should help them to look at something in greater depth and, of course, it highlights a particular part of speech and should both heighten their awareness and extend their use of prepositions.

(b) Making individual poems
The second way of using prepositions is to ask each child to write a poem either using the same formula as above, or using the prepositions as a stepping-off point for the poem.

The Window

Outside the window there are impressions,
These are impressions of the outside world.
Inside looks outside and outside looks in.
My range of sight has grown because of this.

Next to the window there are some curtains,
These curtains are ready to block my view.
From outside it seems to be a mirror
When these curtains are drawn from the inside.

Inside the window there is one big piece
Made of all the colours of the spectrum.
The dark blue of night, the turquoise of day,
The green of the grass and the red of blood.

Throughout the window there is life and death
Showing the life of the outside beings.
Outside the people just look in at us,
It is more than just glass. The curtains close.

Alex Gollner

Looking at the World

Behind my back the world spins like a top,
My back faces towards a life and death.
You, in front of me, are behind me too.
The world's behind me, I am behind myself.

Beneath my feet the ants are making a maze,
Down by the earth's core lava forms and erupts,
It melts, cools, and is the rock it once was.
Like gushing water my feet run madly.

Over my head man builds a concrete jungle
For us to be born, to live and die in.
Far away the sun shines hot and brightly,
But here I sit staring, staring at you.

Michael Corti

Behind my Head

Behind my head time passed by in haste,
Throughout the turning of my head it ended.
Without time I grew old hair and wrinkles.
Through my life time started and finished.
Behind my head the wood rotted far away,
Across one leg lay a decaying white rose,
Outside, the woodworms chewed at my case.

Richard Ball

Prepositions

Behind my head lives sadness without life,
Between my head swims a paradise world,
Around my head lie clouds dizzy from the wind.
Far from my head are shadows melting quickly,
Beside my head stands another head
Reflecting.

Catriona Ferguson

LUCKY DIP

This game can be used as a warming-up exercise or as a whole lesson. The children make up perhaps ten lines of poetry; these are written down, with a space between each one. The lines may hang together as a poem in its own right, or they may be ten completely separate lines. It is important to ensure that the lines are legible if the game is to work. The lines can be of any length, but the game works best if they do not exceed one line of writing. (Sometimes it may be useful to stipulate a certain length or rhythm.)

The lines are then cut up and folded. These are collected in a hat or suitable container and mixed around. Each person will have put ten different lines into the pot, and each one then dips in and takes ten lines out.

This *is* a lucky dip, and it is possible that children will draw out one or two of their own lines, but this does not matter. What follows is rather like a jigsaw puzzle, as everyone moves the lines about and tries to create a poem from them. Tenses of verbs may be changed and odd link words may be omitted or added where necessary (e.g. prepositions, conjunctions). This can also be played with a variation which allows each person to add in two new lines wherever these would help the sense and run of the poem.

The value of this game is mainly to exercise the mind in playing with, and thinking about, words. It is fun to do and children enjoy the challenge it presents. Having to write ten lines quite quickly in the beginning is useful practice and often produces good lines which children may want to keep and work from later. Trying to make sense of ten random lines can also result in interesting phrases or groups of lines which, again, could be taken up later on. This can be a good way of showing that chance is one element in the writing of poetry. These fortuitous combinations of unlikely or disparate thoughts and ideas can create a memorable image and throw new light on to a subject. There are no new themes in poetry, all poems are really treating the same concerns of man – the art is to find the new angle, or different ways of saying the same thing.

BRAN TUB

This is similar to Lucky Dip and might even use some of the lines written for that game. The Bran Tub is really an ideas pot and can be left around the classroom and used at any time. The children are asked to write a number of separate lines which are then cut up and collected in the pot. If they have a few isolated good lines in an otherwise mediocre poem they might like to put these in too. However, if a child is attached to his or her own line and feels possessive about it, he or she must keep it for themselves. The pot is now available for anyone to dip into and find an idea for a poem.

This time the children only take one line which attracts them and they use it somewhere in the poem they write. They should be allowed a little time to sift through until they find a line which fires their imagination, but with plenty to choose from this should not take too long. It may be that more than one child will use the same line – all lines should be returned to the tub. It may also be that once the line has served its purpose of setting the child writing, it may not appear in the poem at all. Children like the feeling that the writing stimulus comes from amongst themselves, but if they have a pride in their work they will probably not want someone else's words in their own poems. It is also a well known fact that many people begin writing about one thing and find, as they proceed, that the poem is creating its own impetus and very often results in being about something totally different. The original stimulus was necessary but can then be discarded. It has tapped the imagination and set it loose to meander off on its own.

MIME THE RHYME

This game can be played in odd moments, or used specifically to accustom children to think of rhymes before writing some poems where rhyme will be used. It can also help those children who are not quite sure of true rhymes and seem to have some difficulty in hearing them.

A small group (perhaps four children) is sent out of the

room. While outside, they think of a word, preferably one for which there are a number of rhymes. For example, they might choose the word 'bed'. They return to the room and tell the class that their word rhymes with, let us say, 'bread'. The class then has to guess the original word.

This is done by thinking of words that also rhyme with 'bread' and miming those words. Some of the words they might mime would be 'dead', 'lead', 'red', 'fed', 'head', 'shed', and so on. The small group watches and must identify the word being mimed. If it is not the original word they must say, 'No, it is not . . . ' (here they say the mimed word). If the group cannot guess the word being mimed, it loses a point to the class. The group gains a point for every mime guessed correctly. This is continued until the group is forced to say, 'Yes, it is "bed".' If the word 'bed' were mimed as someone lying down to sleep, it is perfectly legitimate for a member of the group to say, 'No, it is not "sleepyhead",' even though it is fairly obvious that the mimer meant 'bed'. This is where ingenuity can come in. As long as the word rhymes, and could be said to represent the mime, it must be accepted and the class must think of another way to mime 'bed'.

This game gives children valuable practice in thinking of many different rhymes for a word instead of choosing the first one that comes to mind. If they are to use rhyme in their poetry it is essential that they use it properly. Too many poems are spoilt by bad rhyme. What a poem is trying to say is the most important thing and should not be lost through the use of ridiculous rhymes. Children will also become aware that some words have few rhymes, and that using them might result in forced writing which spoils the poem.

RHYMING CONSEQUENCES

This is a game that can be played with children once they are used to using rhyme; they should probably have played Mime the Rhyme quite often before attempting this.

Each child has a piece of paper and something with which to write. Everyone writes a line that will begin a poem. These are passed round the circle so that each child has the line written by the person on his or her right (or left). The next step is for the children to write a second line which rhymes with, and follows on the sense of, the first line they have received. They then write a new (third) line continuing the subject but not rhyming, and fold the first two back out of sight. The papers are again passed on and, seeing only this new (third) line, the children must write a line that rhymes and follows on the sense of the line they have visible. These two are also folded back and a new (fifth) line is written, etc. This process continues until the poem is felt to be long enough – probably about twelve or fourteen lines, ending on a rhyme.

The fun comes when the poems are unfolded and read out. Points to emphasise before playing this game are that handwriting should be as clear as possible and end of line words should be chosen carefully to allow for someone else having to rhyme with them. There are very few words that have no rhymes, but there *are* some (what rhymes with 'secret'?), and also there are plenty of words that have perhaps only one or two rhymes, some of which children would be unlikely to know.

PERSON, PLACE, WEATHER, TIME

I first heard of this game being used by the novelist and poet Russell Hoban, and it has proved very successful on all levels, with both adults and children. It can give rise to poems or prose pieces and can be used simply as a game, or more often as a full session which can be repeated any number of times, as the ingredients always change. No preparation is needed, spontaneity is all-important.

Choose four children; one will be 'person', the second 'place', the third 'weather', and the fourth 'time'. The first one is asked to think of a person, real or imaginary, in fact or in fiction. There must be a few details, perhaps concerning the age of the person, the sex, state of mind, or clothing. The second child thinks of a place, again with some details of description but excluding time and weather conditions. The third thinks of a type of weather, and the fourth sets the time, perhaps the year, season and time of day. Each child thinks of these things quietly, without reference to any other, for a few minutes at the most. Then they each tell the class what they have imagined. The four elements combine to produce the bones of a story, albeit sometimes rather surreal.

Everyone then has ten to fifteen minutes *only* in which to write something. This may contain all the information given, or it may derive from only one part of what was said. It may, indeed, contain nothing that was mentioned but be about something that was sparked off by one of the things said. It is essential, however, that the time allowed for writing is limited. There are occasions when children should not be rushed and there are times when it is better to get something down quickly. Both practices should be encouraged, as they open up different facets of the imagination. Interesting things can emerge from this exercise and children can always polish and organise their thoughts later if they have something they wish to work on.

When the time is up, everyone reads out what has been written. It is fascinating for the whole class to hear what others have done. The pieces always vary so much and yet they originated from the same stimulus. The different styles, the various points that have been taken up and expanded upon, help to show how the same subject can be dealt with by different people, the wealth of possibilities that exists in the treatment of any one thing.

The four elements which gave rise to the following poems were – 'Queen Victoria' at 'Trafalgar Square' at '9.30 pm' in '1666' and it is 'raining'. All the poems take as their starting points only one aspect of the original 'story'.

— ◆ —

Nelson

The water is rippling gently,
The music begins.
My lions do not tire but guard me forever.
Here I stand reminding people of a war,
My only eye beginning to go blind,

My only arm breaking off,
My memory beginning to stick.
Kismet or kiss me? I don't know.
The words echo through my mind
Fading gently.

Jason Sewards

The Plague

The wooden house darkens in silence,
A red cough slowly becomes black,
Roses are laid across his grave
With a white cross waiting

Tony Reed

Drought

I am punishing the earth for its liking of the rain.
I shall make the earth rotate at my mercy.
I can do this
For I am the sun, hater of wetness,
Maker of light, radiator of the skies.

Zak Hall

9.30 pm 1666

The rattle of carts on the cobblestones,
The smoke rising from the chimneys,
Dogs barking at the horses.
Through an open window I see a man writing
His quill quivering as it scratches the paper,
The man writing his diary.
The flame flickers as all his thoughts
Of the day are recalled
And caged on the page.
His coded shorthand multiplies
As it eternally grows.
He strains his eyes in the candlelight.

Ben Owen

Trafalgar Square

My name is Nelson,
Admiral of the Navy,
Standing on the crow's nest looking out to sea.
Eternally crippled by a strait jacket of cement,
Writing my fixed bearings in the ship's log.
Up to the top! cried a pigeon,
What can you see?
I see no ships
But I see the smog.

Ben Owen

PICTURE QUOTES

This game was described to me by Miss Anne Bourn Harvey as
something she used to play at school. It is a game for children
who have had more exposure to poetry than a beginner. It
demands some shared knowledge of poems and is played as
follows.

Somebody thinks of a quotation and draws a picture of it on
the board. Everyone else has to guess the quotation. Since no
teacher would probably be encouraging children to write
without also exposing them to reading and listening to poetry,
this game could be played with most classes. They could even try
illustrating lines from their own poems which the rest of the
class knew. The example that most amused me was of a girl who
chalked a smudge on the board and then proceeded to rub it
out. This was to illustrate 'Out, damned spot!'

TALL STORIES

This is a game of invention and performance. Two teams are
needed and both sides must use their imagination and
vocabulary to invent the sort of exaggerated accounts of
incidents that one can often hear over the public bar. It draws its
inspiration from those people we all know who, when they tell a
story, always make a performance out of it. Facts are readily

twisted for dramatic effect, and everything they tell you makes their lives sound interesting.

The children are asked to imagine that something has happened but they are not told what it is. Each child in one team then writes down a sentence or two beginning with the words, 'It was so funny I . . . ' The members of the other team do the same but begin with the words, 'It was so awful I . . . ' When they have finished both teams stand in a line facing each other and take it in turns, alternating team to team, to deliver their sentences. The result is usually very entertaining as it switches from mood to mood, each person trying to outdo the ones before.

EXAMPLE

— ◆ —

Team 1 It was so funny it made Groucho Marx look like Margaret Thatcher.

Team 2 It was so awful I wished the ground had swallowed me up and not even spat out the bones.

Team 1 It was so funny even the birds were laughing so hard they fell out of the trees.

Team 2 It was so awful that Anne Boleyn rejoiced since she'd only had her head cut off.

Team 1 It was so funny that I laughed for a whole year and got into the Guinness Book of Records.

Team 2 It was so awful, I cried so much that they had to draw a new ocean on all the world maps.

And so it goes on.

3

Collections

I t is well worth spending time with a new class encouraging them to collect words that fall into different categories. We often ask children to do too much, too soon: having to produce a sustained piece of writing can be too difficult for children to do well before they feel completely comfortable with words. This may sound slightly strange, but I think most teachers will recognise the problem. It is very often the case that the words seem to be in charge of the children, rather than the other way round: witness the restricted range of vocabulary used in children's poems and stories. Children tend to play safe, and certain words occur over and over again, giving rise to bland, often boring, pieces. Vocabulary extension and confidence-building are of paramount importance at an early stage – we want children to have the courage to branch out and say exactly what they think, in the best way possible.

VERBS

Nowhere is children's lack of boldness with words more evident than in the choice of verbs, and in particular, the verbs associated with 'speaking' and 'moving'. Look at any cross-section of writing from school pupils and you will notice a comparatively small range of verbs. 'Said' is by far the most frequently used of the verbs of speech, and 'went', 'walked' or, perhaps, 'ran' are the most frequently chosen verbs of movement. However, there are well over a hundred verbs of speaking or communicating, and in excess of three hundred verbs of moving, whether this be to convey movement from place to place (like 'meander', 'sidle' or 'shuffle') or small movements (like 'twitch', 'blink' or 'shudder').

Making a class wall thesaurus for each of these verbs is time well spent and will help to improve children's writing substantially. Collect as many ways of speaking as possible, first by asking children to suggest ones they know, and later by encouraging them to use thesauruses and dictionaries – or to ask at home – to add to the growing collection. It is probably best if you write down all the suggestions on the board or a large piece of paper. Afterwards you can all decide on how you wish to make the collection rather more permanent. Possibilities include mounting a display on the wall or on the windows, or hanging the words as mobiles from the ceiling.

Children write out the words in black felt tip on slips of paper which are then stuck at angles (*not* in serried ranks, as these are harder to read) on to a large chart, perhaps with a painted open mouth in the centre. If you make mobiles, words might be grouped by like meanings, e.g. 'ask', 'demand', 'request', 'beg', 'question', 'plead'. You might set a number at which you aim – say, one hundred and one ways to speak – or use the tried and trusted ploy of saying, 'I wonder how many you can find?' It never fails!

After this kind of exercise, whenever children are writing, they are likely to be more adventurous by choosing words from these home-made thesauruses. It is well known that children take greater note of something in which they have been involved – since *they* found the words, they feel they *belong* to them. They will also have a better understanding of where they can be used; and if, every time you looked up, you were confronted with a wealth of possible verbs, the chances are that you would be keen to use them.

This exercise works just as well with verbs of movement and is highly recommended. You can follow this with a piece of writing which uses up as many verbs as possible. It is advisable to spend a little time sorting out some of the verbs into sets, as part of the planning. For example, do some of the verbs rhyme (e.g. 'shift', 'drift', 'lift'; 'curl', 'swirl', 'twirl'; 'smash', 'crash', 'lash', 'dash', 'clash')? Do some of them alliterate, that is, begin with the same sounds (e.g. 'scatter', 'scamper', 'scramble', 'scratch'; 'hurtle', 'hurry', 'hamper', 'hoist')?

First, compose a piece as a whole class, so that everyone understands what to do. Later, children can work in pairs, or on their own. The subjects that I have found to offer the most scope are: The Flood, The Hurricane, The Snow, The River, The Breeze, Sunshine, Rain or Hail. The idea is to use as many verbs as possible to describe the progress of the subject, incorporating examples of alliteration and rhyme (both end-stop and internal – see Chapter 47, page 189). The following give some idea of the possibilities.

— ◆ —

The Flood

It floods the land with swooshing and slopping,
It twists, swerves, ripples and wrinkles,
Entranced so deeply in itself.
It wanders around tackling the wind,
Forcing and flicking itself over the land.
It pursues and pulls to string itself along,
Stripping itself free of the force of the wind.
It twists and twirls, unravelling itself,
Marching maliciously and viciously.
As it pounces on objects
It strolls forcefully around them
Until it embraces them eagerly in its strong power.
It glides into houses and smashes up furniture,
It sinks slyly into cushions and cloth
While it thrusts chairs into the power of its hold.
It races upstairs, swerving round corners,
Collides into doors but then punches them open.
As it prances and dances it follows the road,
Whirls and slides down the river banks
And sinks into the flow of the river
Where the ripples in the water die down.

Lucinda Wright (BYW)

The Breeze

The breeze wrapped round the ring of the trees,
Rustling the leaves and leaping between the branches.
It stepped, skipped and skidded across the town centre
And pushed and pulled at the picnic food.
The breeze bounced, bobbed and burrowed
Deep into dark, damp cellars.
It washed into windows, waving and mild,
It flew into flats, floating and furrowing,
Gliding, gushing and gulping the garden greens.
Managing to meander into meadows,
Full of mole hills and mules,
The breeze covered every corner
And heaved at every hedge.
It flustered every field
And shook the shed made of wood.
But at last the breeze died down
And disappeared.

Lisa Kramer (BYW)

The Hurricane

It crashed down the door and entered the theatre,
Whizzed past the box office and bustled into the foyer.
Dodging the tables and chairs
It careered down the corridors and off backstage.
It squashed the dressing-room doors,
Darting and squeezing between costumes.
It hurried into the workshop, passing between bits of timber,
Whistling, whirling, curling round furniture and pillars,
Then headbutted through the stage door
And into the vast space of the stage,
Sending flaps crashing to the ground;
Shaking, quaking, stripping the walls,
Jolting and jerking around.
Then it slowly died down to a little breeze
And quietly evacuated the building.

Charles Johnson (St.A)

OTHER COLLECTIONS

Homophones (homo = same, phone = sound)
Words that sound the same but are spelt differently, e.g. 'queue',
'cue', 'Kew'; 'hymn', 'him'; 'write', 'right', 'rite'.

Palindromes
Words which read the same backwards as forwards, e.g. 'level',
'peep', 'madam', 'minim'.

A man, a plan, a canal – Panama

Words spelt in the same order as the alphabet
No double letters, e.g. 'an', 'buy', 'city', 'ghost', 'first'; and, the
longest in current use, 'chintz'.
With double letters, e.g. 'lorry', 'abbey', 'bellow'.

Mirror words
Words that spell a different word backwards, e.g. 'drab' – 'bard';
'flog' – 'golf'; 'stop' – 'pots'; 'meet' – 'teem'.

Rhyming compounds
e.g. 'huggermugger', 'pellmell', 'humdrum', 'abracadabra',
'pooper-scooper'.

Vowel-change compounds
e.g. 'dillydally', 'flipflop', 'pitterpatter', 'singsong'.

Homonyms (homo = same, onoma = name)
Same words, different meanings, e.g. 'bow' (as in 'ribbon' and
'violin'), 'stick' (as in 'adhere' and 'twig'), 'lie' (as in 'lying
down' and 'telling an untruth').

Heteronyms (hetero = different, onoma = name)
Same spelling, different pronunciation and meaning, e.g. 'bow',
'refuse', 'wind', 'entrance', 'close', 'live'.

Spoonerisms (named after the Reverend Spooner)
The transposing of initial sounds between two words, e.g. 'A
shoving leopard' instead of 'A loving shepherd'; 'Hoot from the

ship' instead of 'Shoot from the hip'; 'Well-boiled icicle' instead of 'Well-oiled bicycle'.

N.B. Spoonerisms should make proper words; 'Chish and fips', for example, is not acceptable.

All these collections can be gathered by children working in small groups. As well as giving children much enjoyment, it will be clear that such work cannot but help their spelling and widen their vocabulary. Children can be encouraged to consult dictionaries, thesauruses, any other books – and people, including those at home. The main aim, however, is to let children play with the raw material of their later writing, and to become used to handling words. This way they will gain in confidence and become better able to cope with the demands of writing more sustained pieces in the future.

Don't forget jokes – a very under-used resource. Children usually have joke books they can bring into school. Many jokes rely on puns (using homophones or homonyms), spoonerisms or other wordplay, e.g. 'What do you call a cat that has eaten your Christmas dinner?' 'A duck-filled fatty puss!'

The

Minister's Cat

It is always worth digging out old word games that one used to play as a child. Games are fun to play and are a means whereby a child can learn to handle language, extend vocabulary, and just enjoy the sound of words; all this is achieved outside a formal setting such as a grammar exercise. I do not suppose these games were ever envisaged as starting points for poetry writing, but they are, in fact, a fruitful source of ideas for encouraging children to write. Too often teachers expect children to produce what amounts to highly sophisticated work without having given them the chance to play with language. The results are frequently disappointing because the children are trying to cope with too many demands, and consequently they fail to be in control of the medium. We must allow children to experiment and play with words so that they cease to be afraid of them and can begin to make use of these tools properly.

Many of the chapters of this book have their origins in games, and I hope it will be clear that much more is being taught than might at first appear to be the case. These games are a serious part of teaching – but the children do not know that! As with many word games, The Minister's Cat was originally intended to be played orally and is, perhaps, best introduced that way to children. It is principally about adjectives, but it also reinforces the order of the alphabet. Names of cats come into it, too.

To play the game, everybody stands up, preferably in a circle, and the first person says the following words:

'The minister's cat is an . . . cat and his (her) name is . . . '

An adjective beginning with 'A' is said before the word 'cat', and a name is given, also beginning with 'A'. The next person has to repeat the words, but this time supplying an adjective and a name beginning with the second letter of the alphabet, 'B'. This pattern is repeated through the whole alphabet and when 'Z' is reached the process starts again. The aim is to follow on as soon as the person before you has finished. If there is too long a gap at any point that person is out and should sit down. The person left standing at the end is the winner. No adjective or name can be repeated during the course of one game (if it is, the person doing so is also out). Cheating with 'X', however, is allowed: words that begin with the sound EX are acceptable, for example, 'EXceptional cat named ECCentricity'.

After playing this game orally, it can be turned into a writing exercise which will give each child the opportunity to think about what he or she wants to say. I always encourage children to use dictionaries in this exercise and to be adventurous in their choice of adjectives. Obviously, there must be dictionaries available which explain what part of speech a word is (an adjective is usually marked 'a.' or 'adj.'). By looking up words, children will be familiarising themselves with the way dictionaries work and learning, incidentally, what a treasure chest the dictionary can be. They will not be so frightened of referring to it later on when they come to write more sustained pieces. It is a marvel of modern living that the dictionary, luckily, is in the same order as the alphabet which the children need to follow for this game!

The following pieces were written by children aged nine, using dictionaries. The children took a fairly long time (the alphabet is so long) but enjoyed doing it, as I think the results show.

— ◆ —

The Minister's Cat is . . .

an affluent cat and his name is Alexander
a belligerent cat and his name is Brutus
a casual cat and her name is Camilla
a discernible cat and his name is David
an extinct cat and his name was Egbert

a feckless cat and his name is Fred
a gusty cat and his name is Gandalf
an habitual cat and his name is Humphrey
an impractical cat and her name is Ingrid
a Jewish cat and his name is Joseph
a knowledgeable cat and his name is Kenneth
a meticulous cat and her name is Melissa
a namby-pamby cat and his name is Neil
an octogenarian cat and his name is O'Mally the Great
a perfunctory cat and his name is Peterson
a quotidian cat and his name is Quentin
a Rabelaisian cat and his name is Robin
a sadistic cat and her name is Suzette
a translucent cat and her name is Theresa
an unattainable cat and his name is Uranus
a velvet cat and his name is Valerian
a winsome cat and her name is Wanda
an execrable cat and his name is Xanadu
a youthful cat and his name is Yorick
a zealous cat and his name is Zebedee

The Minister's Cat is . . .

an abject cat and his name is Antoine
a bald cat and his name is Brian
a calamitous cat and her name is Caroline
a demoniacal cat and his name is Damian
an erroneous cat and his name is Eric
a fallible cat and his name is Flabby
a geographical cat and his name is George
a haggard cat and his name is Henry
an infernal cat and his name is Ivor
a juicy cat and his name is Jaffa
a knobbly cat and her name is Kelly
a laconic cat and his name is Leonardo
a majestic cat and her name is Moonreed
a narrow-minded cat and her name is Natalia
an obdurate cat and her name is Octavia
a paltry cat and his name is Paddy

a quiescent cat and her name is Queenie
a rapacious cat and her name is Rebecca
a secular cat and his name is Sylvester
a tawdry cat and his name is Tweedy
an ultramarine cat and his name is Urquhart
a vapid cat and his name is Victor
a wistful cat and her name is Winifred
a xiphoid cat and his name is Xavier
a yearning cat and her name is Yowler
a zestful cat and his name is Zorba

ALPHABETICAL

VERBS

When children are beginning to write, it is important that we, as teachers, do not place too many demands on them at one time. Even established writers will say that poems often fail to achieve, or turn into something totally different from, what they originally intended. It is not generally understood just how complex the business of producing good writing is, nor is it appreciated just how much skill is required to present ideas to the best advantage. I consider that it is our job to provide opportunities for children to learn techniques (the effects one can create with the tools – words), in ways which are fun for them, through what I call exercises. I do not expect earth-shattering pieces of writing to come from these exercises themselves, but, of course, occasionally this does happen. That is a bonus. What I seek to do is to provide the children with a bank of techniques which they will be able to use when they have a subject about which they really need to write. In other words, I hope they will assimilate the various techniques so that when they have something to say they will not be floundering around trying to make sense of their ideas, or giving up altogether at the sheer enormity of the task, or, worse still, presenting something bland and unimaginative which passes, but is time-wasting and paper-filling.

The alphabet offers a recognisable framework within which children can play with language, and, incidentally, learn some grammar along the way (which should be a method of satisfying most schools of thought in the education lobby). It also provides a good reason to use dictionaries again, which I feel is very important. Children should come to regard the dictionary as an old friend, and not shy away from it or be afraid to look things up. It helps if a teacher is prepared to show a class that he or she needs to check words every now and then. I love having *The Shorter Oxford*[1] (two volumes) in class and frequently enjoy looking up derivations and meanings, as well as spellings on occasion. I also like to have a wide selection of different dictionaries available to cater for every level of ability.

I have already talked about using adjectives in The Minister's Cat (see Chapter 4, page 41). Another obvious possibility is to go through the alphabet highlighting nouns, as in the traditional rhyme beginning 'A was an Archer who shot at a frog'.

Verbs, in many ways, are more exciting. They are the words that make things happen. Children's writing is frequently not very adventurous when it comes to verbs. Too often they settle unquestioningly for 'get', 'went', 'had', 'said', 'like', etc. So an exercise that places emphasis on choosing interesting verbs can alert them to the power they can wield.

The following exercise, by chance, yielded an unexpected lesson in writing. Compiling a list is a technique in itself and has been used to good effect by many a poet, for example, Anthony Thwaite in his wonderfully crafted poem, 'On Consulting "Contemporary Poets of the English Language"'. Lists must never be too short, or the effect is lost. However, if they are too long and without variation they do not work either. The alphabet is about the right length to build up a picture, when used as in the examples below. If the children choose a title as a theme for their list, what actually results is a vivid description of a particular place, occurrence or scene. The sort of titles they might consider are: 'A Day at the Seaside'; 'The Market'; 'At the Football Match'; 'On the Picnic'; 'In the Playground'; 'At the Party', etc. In the following examples, only the letters of the alphabet have been used to denote people, but these could be replaced by actual names beginning with the appropriate letters. As before, cheating is allowed with the letter 'X'. Some parts of the following poems are fairly simple and thus draw attention to the verbs giving a particular effect. In others, the lines are expanded to create a fuller picture of the scene.

---

[1]The Shorter Oxford Dictionary (1993), Oxford University Press

A Day at the Seaside

A attempted to climb the cliffs,
B built a sandcastle,
C covered her feet with sand,
D dozed under his paper.
E emitted yells of surprise at the water's temperature,
F finished in a rockpool,
G got sand in his eyes,
H hurled stones at the sea.
I injured his knee,
J jumped off a boulder,
K kicked his football into the sea,
L licked his stick of rock,
M mounted a donkey.
N noticed an ice cream stall,
O outran her brother in a race,
P paddled at the edge,
Q quacked at a seagull,
R ran away from the waves,
S splashed about in the shallows,
T tilled the sand with a plastic fork,
U unearthed a small crab,
V volunteered to buy them an ice lolly each.
W waded out up to his middle,
X eXplored the caves,
Y yawned a lot and slept on a towel,
Z zoomed about untiringly.

Natalia Poncé

The Picnic

A asked to go somewhere else,
B bribed someone for a sandwich,
C caught a wasp in a jar.
D departed early.
E enticed a bird to sit on his finger,
F fought with the school cat,

G glowed with heat.
H hit the girl in front of him,
I ignored the teacher,
J jumped over a puddle,
K kept his sweets to himself.
L looked daggers at his girlfriend,
M memorised the alphabet.
N nagged the teacher for more food,
O offered to help wash up afterwards,
P pulled out the drinks.
Q quaked at the sight of a tree.
R ran so fast he won the race,
S sacrificed his sandwich to a bird,
T tumbled over the food basket,
U upheld the idea for games,
V ventured into the woods.
W wailed that he wanted to go home,
X eXamined a snail crawling,
Y yawned tiredly,
Z zipped down the hill.

Guy Higginson

A Day at the Seaside

A arranged seashells,
B bathed in the sea,
C caught a crab,
D dug a hole.
E enveloped himself in sand,
F fell in the sea,
G groped for his towel,
H hoarded the hamper,
I instructed a fisherman to move,
J jumped off a cliff,
K kicked a beachcomber,
L lectured a lifesaver.
M marooned his friend,
N navigated the coast,

O offended a coastguard,
P punctured the beach ball,
Q quaffed all the drink,
R rode the rapids.
S shooed seagulls,
T teased a dog,
U undermined the pier,
V vacated the best part of the beach,
W wept for home.
X eXtracted fossils from rocks,
Y yowled when he stepped on a jellyfish,
Z zigzagged as he climbed a cliff.

Jesse Scott

The Picnic

A admitted that he had eaten five eggs,
B brought the sandwiches,
C curried the chicken,
D drank the lime juice cordial,
E exchanged some crisps for a toffee.
F fought over the ham and tongue,
G grabbed a sausage,
H handed out the napkins.
I interfered in the girls' quarrel,
J joked cheerfully,
K knocked a glass over,
L laughed, long and loud.
M moaned having eaten too much ice cream,
N nibbled a biscuit,
O opened a box of chocolates,
P passed the anchovies.
Q quietened down and slept,
R rocketed up, having sat on a bee,
S stood all the time.
T took some soup,
U understood everyone's feelings about the stale bread.
V vaulted a gate to retrieve his napkin,

W worried that he was going to miss the chicken.
X eXcited his dog by pointing out a rabbit in the distance,
Y yelled as he brushed against a stinging nettle,
Z zoomed all over his piece of drawing paper.

Rachel Bosanquet

(*Note*: do any of the above remind you of a school outing?)

I'd Rather

Be . . .

This is another party game which is normally played orally; it is a good introduction to rhyming and to the necessary knowledge that, although many words in English have a number of rhymes, some do not. It also requires the player to consider pairs of words that go together in some way, whether in expressions like 'knife and fork' or 'home and dry', or combinations which are opposite in meaning, such as 'dead and alive' or 'thick and thin'.

The game is played by any number over two, and each person takes it in turn to supply a line on the pattern 'I'd rather be . . . than . . . '. The second word of the pair establishes the rhyme for that round: all the other second words must rhyme with it. If a player cannot do this, he or she is out until a new round begins. It is obviously advantageous to start, as you can then set the rhyme. Unscrupulous players will, if they are so inclined, choose words for which there are few or no rhymes. This knowledge will come with practice and is a useful lesson for would-be poets, as well as good practice in using rhyme when it matters less than when writing serious pieces. No rhyme may be used more than once in a round. The opening stages of a round might go something like this:

I'd rather be hot than cold
I'd rather be young than old
I'd rather be bought than sold
I'd rather be asked than told
I'd rather be silver than gold
I'd rather be a daffodil than a marigold
I'd rather be a front page than a centrefold
I'd rather be a fortress than a stronghold

and so on, until somebody cannot complete another line. Then the game is over and the last person to supply a rhyming line is the winner.

In a game like this, the lessons to be learned about handling language and concepts are very valuable for future writing. As with all these games, because they are fun to play, children will learn easily without realising they are doing so, but we can see the results of their new-found confidence with language very soon in their other writing. The games also give children a chance to experiment at a stage when it is not quite as crucial to find the right word as it will be later. Rhyme always presents pitfalls in poetry. We are naturally drawn to it because of its effect and sound (akin to harmony in music), but very few children can use it properly without much practice. Games provide a safety net and will help to prevent a child from letting rhyme take over at the expense of the meaning of a poem.

As with all the games I use, this one can also be employed as a writing exercise, when children can work at a more leisurely pace using dictionaries. There are possibilities of some very interesting juxtapositions of ideas which are of great benefit to the beginner, and also good fun for the more experienced writer.

I'd rather be an honest man than a knave,
I'd rather have a six-foot beard than shave,
I'd rather disobey than misbehave,
I'd rather spend it all than try to save,
I'd rather live at home than on the ocean wave,
I'd rather be cremated than buried in a grave,
I'd rather live in a house than in a cave,
I'd rather play with teddy than be brave.

Rachel Meyers

I'd rather be heavy than light,
I'd rather be a plane than a kite,
I'd rather be peaceful than fight,
I'd rather be the day than the night,
I'd rather be depth than height,
I'd rather chomp than bite,
I'd rather be a flea than a mite,
I'd rather drink Castlemaine XXXX than Miller Lite.

Thomas Ludgrove

I'd rather be alive than dead,
I'd rather stay here than go to bed,
I'd rather be blue than red,
I'd rather be a body than a head,
I'd rather be starved than fed,
I'd rather go my own way than be led,
I'd rather be butter than bread,
I'd rather be single than wed,
I'd rather be me than Fred,
I'd rather be brave than dread,
I'd rather be shouted than said,
I'd rather be tin than lead,
I'd rather be behind than ahead,
I'd rather be X than Z,
I'd rather stride than tread.

Mary Noble

I'd rather be a bat than a ball,
I'd rather be fat than tall,
I'd rather be a room than a hall,
I'd rather shout than call,
I'd rather stand than fall,
I'd rather climb than crawl,
I'd rather be a shop than a Mall,
I'd rather carry than haul,
I'd rather be me than Saul,
I'd rather just you came than them all,
I'd rather be on stand-by than on call.

Taryn Youngstein

COLLECTIVE

NOUNS

Discussing collective nouns belongs, I feel, to the first few lessons with a class. It is another way of playing with words which can be enjoyable; it is also less demanding on slow workers whom you do not want to 'lose' because they find the sheer grind of writing too much. Later, when you have their interest completely, they will probably miraculously find they can write much faster, and so much more!

All the children do is make up their own collective nouns. Preparation for this naturally involves explaining what nouns are, and the different categories. It would be well to test the children's own knowledge of existing collective nouns and add to these others they may not know.

But then I always point out that these are so well known and overused that they are no longer fresh. It is now that you ask the children to make up new ones of their own – collections of anything. This involves their exploring the nature of the things they choose and thinking about the meaning of words very carefully if they are to find successful combinations. The best of these can then be illustrated in pictures, music, or drama. Here are some examples:

— ◆ —

a coil of pythons
a bask of cats
a muddle of grannies
a gossamer of spiders
a haystack of light
a diminution of ants

an eruption of wildebeeste
a lag of tortoises
a slouch of snails
a wheel of smoke
an echo of whispers
a Speaker's Corner of mouths

Following on from this, it can be good to make a list of all the

best new collective nouns and ask the children to choose one as
the title for a poem which they then write. By giving them a
choice you will probably find that there is something in the list
that will appeal to each child and there is also something special
about the choices having been written by them originally. It
encourages them to feel that their ideas are worthwhile, which
will help to give them confidence in their writing.

A Lock of Secrets

I hesitate to unlock secrets,
A long echo of whispers does it for me.
A dream of silence flares on my body
For I have disobeyed my secret.
A mask of darkness covers my view –
I strike it with light.

Charles De'Ath

A Team of Crickets

The crickets are
Icy, unpleasant,
Jumpy and small,
Green with anger and envy
Of the pretty caterpillar,
On the oak leaf,
That turns into the
Magnificent butterfly

Michele Collins

A Cloud of Gravel

Up in the air a cloud of gravel cried,
'My dream's come true – I can fly!'
It flew for miles and miles,
Landed on unfriendly grass
And was chased off.

Jason Sewards

A Dream of Silences

Silence,
Where is it?
Always being broken,
Never kept.
Silence is a dream
For us to look for,
To seek,
To keep.

Jane Alden

A Planet of Dust

A planet of dust
Not wanted among the kings of air.
Made to be blown away by the human breath,
Trapped by the skin of a local cat.

Tony Reed

SYNONYMS

AND NAMES

Since one of the things we are obviously trying to do is build up children's vocabulary and widen their experience and use of words, I have always found it useful to do some work on synonyms. One of the points I am constantly making to children is that, if possible, it is best to avoid using a particular word more than once, unless it is absolutely unavoidable or repetition is intended. To have to find other ways of saying the same thing is a good exercise and it trains the mind for later work. I have also found that it helps towards giving the children an enthusiasm for, and love of, words.

There is now a good thesaurus available for Junior and Middle schools called *The New Collins Thesaurus*[1], and I would recommend that there should be at least half a dozen in the classroom, if possible. However, in addition to that, it can be very useful if each child makes his or her own thesaurus. A class session, once or twice a week, is a good idea, when the children suggest a word for which as many synonyms, or near synonyms, are found as possible. The words are written in a list with the headword at the top. An index can be kept at the front and all the pages numbered. A good word with which to begin these books is 'to speak', as there are literally tens of words that could be included.

Another way of displaying this word-hunting is to draw diagrams with the main word written large in the centre. It can be useful to draw a series of circles or hexagons, like a honeycomb, and write the words into the spaces. They can be called charts, and different colours can be allotted to each part

---

[1]McLeod, W.T. (*ed.*) (1987), *The New Collins Thesaurus*, Collins

of speech: e.g. red for nouns, blue for adjectives.

This can also be done for antonyms where a line is drawn down the centre of the chart. The synonyms are written on one side of the line and the antonyms on the other side.

Happiness chart

A related exercise is that of making up names for people. I find it very tedious to read the names of brothers, sisters and classmates in the children's writing, in what are essentially explorations into fantasy. Although I can see that these familiar names probably give the children a secure base and, as it were, a lifeline back to reality, by the time they have reached nine or ten years of age they should be capable of entering these fantasy worlds with more unusual people! I ask the children to make up a list of names for different sorts of people.

— ◆ —

Colonel 'Shorty' Anstruther	Cynthia Masters
The Rev. Thomas Langland	Steve Parker
Lady Deborah Trinket-Smythe	Sid Fortesque
Penny Popplethwaite	Boris Bircham

If nothing else, this is fun to do and also to follow up by giving a short character sketch of each one. What's in a name? Well, we are all likely to have an instant mental picture of someone about whom we know nothing except the name. Names do carry some weight, and there is no doubt that people often seem to have names that suit them; or perhaps they grow into their names? However, this can be thought of as a game, although it may help children's writing generally.

NEW WORDS

FOR OLD

This is something to be done during the first few weeks of taking a class and is more for enjoyment than anything else. The main advantage is that it can help the children towards gaining a love of words, and of playing with words, which is essential if they are going to write well.

In the past, shepherds who were out with their flocks all day would evolve new personal counting systems for counting their sheep. It was probably one way of passing the time. Some of these kinds of systems can be found on the first twenty pages of the four books of *Junior Voices*[1] in the bottom right-hand and left-hand corners – for example, 'een 1', 'teen 2', 'tuther 3', 'futher 4', and 'fip 5'. Children can enjoy making up their own counting systems.

Also in *Junior Voices, the third book* there are some poems by Alastair Reid with the titles 'Squishy Words (to be said when wet)', 'Bug Words (to be said when grumpy)', and 'Sounds', which invent words for the sounds that things actually make. In *Junior Voices, the second book* we find 'Mean Song' by Eve Merriam which also makes up words, and of course we have 'Jabberwocky' by Lewis Carroll from *Through the Looking-Glass*[2].

All these can be read to the children for pleasure, but they may also lead them to want to make up their own words. They could write words to be said when happy, when singing in the bath, when stroking the cat, when you've just fallen in the mud, and so on. They might also write a longer poem on the lines of

[1]Geoffrey Summerfield (*ed.*) (1970), *Junior Voices*, Penguin
[2]Carroll, L. (1872), *Through the Looking-Glass and What Alice Found There*, Macmillan

'Jabberwocky' and go on to give an explanation of what their made-up words mean, as Humpty Dumpty does in Chapter 6 of *Through the Looking-Glass.*

A B C Books

This idea derives from those A B C books we were all probably given when young, which have a page for every letter of the alphabet. These might be 'A is for Apple so rosy and red', or 'C is for Cat with a long fluffy tail'. Each page would contain an illustration of the object and was aimed at teaching us to recognise letters and words.

However, making A B C books with older children can take on a very different aspect. When I did this with children aged nine and ten years, I explained what we were going to do, but said that our words and illustrations were going to be much more adult in their approach. We started with every child writing a sentence for any letters of the alphabet he or she wanted to use; the only condition was that one important word – a noun, adjective, verb or adverb – had to begin with the letter they had chosen. We then sorted through all the sentences and grouped them under themes. The themes that emerged were War, Life and Death, Mystery and Religion, Fears and Feelings, and Animals.

We chose one sentence for each letter under these headings, wrote them on a large sheet of paper and noted the gaps. The children wrote more sentences to fill these gaps. When the lists were complete each child chose which sentences he or she wanted to illustrate and these pictures were done in an abstract style. They tried to feel the essence of the meaning and to translate this into shape, colour and texture in their paintings. When everything was finished we made the pictures and sentences up into books.

The whole project took some time to complete and was greatly enjoyed. The paintings improved as time went on, and the children broke much new ground, as well as totally integrating their painting with their writing.

— ◆ —

A for an apple left to rot away.
B for the bitterness in every person's life.
N is a nephew murdered in a moonlit house.
P for the padlock that locks spirit in.
Q for the long queues waiting to die.
A is the army ambling through the lone fields.
E is extermination.
*I*nk is the blood of the pen.
Q quivers quietly in the corner.
T is the tangled barbed wire blocking fences.

COLOURS

Children are always being asked to write about colours from
the time they first enter the infant school. The writing
usually takes the form of 'What is Blue?' or 'What is Red?', and
the poems that result have a rather uniform quality. That is fine
for the younger children, but can become very tedious by the
time children are eight years and over. We have probably all
read the kind of poem that goes like this:

— ◆ —

Blue is the colour of the sea,
Blue is the summer sky,
Blue is my budgerigar,
Blue is a bluebell,
Blue is the little butterfly . . .

I decided to write about colours with a class of ten year olds, but
I wanted the results to be different. We began with a short
discussion of how colours are used in some sayings. For
example, red for anger, embarrassment, danger; green for envy,
go, inexperience; yellow for cowardice; white for fright. It was
decided that the only mention of the colour would be in the
title – the purpose being to prevent repetition, e.g. 'Blue is . . .,
blue is . . . ' The children were asked to write about things which
this colour made them think of, and not necessarily things
which *were* the colour. It was, therefore, a more abstract
approach, attempting to get at the essence of colour, its effect
and the feelings it aroused. After talking about this to the
children, I found they readily set to work and entered into the
spirit of it. After they had written the poems, they did some

abstract paintings based on the same idea.

The whole project was a success: it involved all the children in some deep thinking about words, shapes, thoughts and feelings, and made them aware of the other dimensions possible when dealing with a subject.

— ◆ —

Black

The old mine degenerating in the dead of night,
The exposed body lying helplessly on the ground,
An engulfing darkness in a maze of winding
    passages,
The dagger of evil stained with blood,
A cold and lingering silence.

Else Thompson

Black

The misleading dark mist grazing the moor,
The day drowned by the night's darkness,
The scattered dolorous graves in the graveyard,
An evil mind furiously thinking,
A terrorising thunder beating down rain,
The silent and still spirit.

Clare Dowell

Green

The icy day gloomy and still,
The deep full mind,
A handful of leaves in a forgotten place,
A seagull hopelessly flies into mist,
An eagle flying from a cloud, lost in a full deep
    shallow.

Jamie McGowan

Green

The sun shining through the leaves on the trees,
The eerie mist rising from the mountains,
A storm approaching from the south coast,
An endless night looming through a window,
An arrow leaping from the darkness.

Steve Webber

Turquoise

The mystic beauty of freedom,
The majestic silence of a deserted house,
The awesome splendour of a long built palace,
A precious gem glinting in a shaded corner,
The magical glow of love,
The howling of a lonely wolf.

Mischa Twitchin

Red

The forgotten hero lies on the battlefield,
The miners are trapped in subterranean passages
Crying for help,
A fire is lit and the flames are burning wood.

Nicholas Lee

Yellow

The opening way to happiness,
Warmth pertaining to wideness,
A revolving shadow,
An empty view,
A philanthropist,
The tardy wind carrying the leaves.

Diagoro Isobe

12

Acrostics

An acrostic is a poem in which the first letters of each line spell a word or sentence. For example:

— ◆ —

Lobster

L ate in the evening my claws are sharp and ready,
O n the sea in my shell I wait.
B efore my claws will open I will polish them till they shine.
S agging in the mist, a starfish is asleep
T hough I will wait till my enemy comes.
E vening stars brighten the green waters, but still I wait.
R etaining my courage, I see the crab slowly scampering over.

Steven Gregory

This introduces a limitation, small though it is, which requires the children to think just that much harder about the words they use. It often results in more interesting words and inversions which can contribute to the success of a poem. In the example above, how much more impact is made by such lines as:

'On the sea in my shell I wait',

or:

'Sagging in the mist, a starfish is asleep'.

Were Steven to have written 'I wait in my shell on the sea', the line would not have been so effective, although this might well have been what he would have written had there been no need to begin with the letter 'O'. Similarly, the word 'sagging' may never have suggested itself, but there is no doubt that it is successful, particularly as it is placed in a prominent position at the beginning of the line.

This is a popular exercise with the children and extremely valid, I feel. It presents an obstacle which it is possible to surmount, yet at the same time it effectively slows their writing up and demands extra thought. This can only be good because too often children write down the first thing that enters their heads and are then content to leave it. There are times, of course, when the spontaneous and immediate thoughts are most successful and this should not be forgotten; but, as a general rule, I have found that the deeper they can think about an idea, the better the results.

Some children will naturally learn to go back to a poem and 're-work' it, putting in revisions and improvements, but with most children we need actively to encourage this approach. One way of doing this is to provide other, different frameworks and technical limitations with which they can experiment. Many of these are dealt with in later chapters (see particularly Chapter 75, page 334).

— ◆ —

Catalogue

C atalogue –
A s you know,
T his has
A rticles listed in it.
L ooking for something?
O h, then look in this book.
G ood for you, there is everything here.
U ncertain? Trust us.
E verything O.K.?

Diagoro Isobe

Atoms

A lways within a finger's touch,
T errible murderers swallow us up,
O bnoxious beings prepare us for war and
M ushrooms grow where we are dropped.
S ee us tessellate under a slide.

Louis Lyne

Enormous

E nlarged to great extent,
N o end to bigger than big,
O r no start to smaller than small.
R adiantly, a huge heaven surrounding
M eant growing in fame and shrinking in age.
O utnumbered by no-one, nothing but itself,
U nited to all being creatures.
S oulless but living in voice.

Andrew Hall

Catkin

C rave of beauty and elegance
A bundantly growing to bring life,
T hat brings not evil but sweet smells,
K iss of life to earth.
I ts softness idly bending in the breeze,
N atural colours that gleam in the sunlight.

Stephen Bailey

(See also 'Caterpillar', page 192 and 'Moustache', page 122.)

13

INTRODUCING
ALLITERATION

I usually introduce the technique of alliteration in an early lesson with a class. The alliterative content is done to excess in this exercise, but this is in order to 'capture' the children's interest and let them feel that poetry is enjoyable. You can explain that, when children come to write poems in the future, alliteration is most effective if used sparingly.

The children are asked to write a sentence for each number up to ten, or further if they wish. Most of the words in a sentence will begin with the same sound, which takes its lead from the initial sound of the number, e.g. 'One wakeful walrus wondered if whiting could waltz, Two tremulous tomatoes tried to tickle a tench'.

The children should be encouraged to use a dictionary – you will need one for every child and, ideally, different formats and levels to give wider choice. The beauty of the sentences is their nonsense and their almost surreal element, and this means that children can be encouraged to use new words found in the dictionary without having to worry too much whether they have used them correctly. This will help to make them more adventurous in the future and give them a love of the sounds of words. If they use a word in the wrong part of speech it is very easy to show them gently the correct form (commenting meanwhile on the choice of such a good word!). It is also clear that this exercise can be used to help children grow more familiar with, and find their way around in, a dictionary – making it more like a game than a daunting task.

Give some examples beforehand, but not too many; there is good reason for going once through the exercise on the board with the whole class before asking the children to work individually. You will then have the opportunity to say that, although 'Six silly sausages sat on smelly socks' is funny, it would probably be improved by some more unusual words!

— ◆ —

One waggly walrus won a wet wager,
Two trustful twins tumbled into a typhoon,
Three thin thoroughbreds thumped a thick thief,
Four fiddly ferns ferociously ate a ferret,
Five fervent fleas sat famished in a farm,
Six shy shuttlecocks swam in shampoo,
Seven stupid strawberries sinned on a stripey
    stretcher,
Eight echoing earthquakes exterminated an eclipse,
Nine nosy nomads knitted knotted knickers,
Ten topless toffees told a tale.

Written by children aged 9 years

I Should

Like To . . .

The idea for this came from the poem 'To Paint the Portrait of a Bird' by Jacques Prévert (translated by Lawrence Ferlinghetti) which can be found in the anthology *Touchstones 3*[1]. Briefly, this poem says that you paint a cage with an open door and place the canvas against a tree. Then you must hide and wait for a bird to enter the cage. As soon as it does you paint the door closed and paint out all the bars. Then you must paint certain things to make the bird sing:

. . . the green foliage and the wind's freshness
the dust of the sun
and the noise of the insects in the summer heat.

It was this part of the poem that gave me the idea of asking the children to write about things they would like to do, which could not normally be done – for example, to hear things you could only normally see, touch or taste, and to see sounds, to taste smells or touch tastes (although this was not confined solely to the senses). They were asked to write for each 'wish' and to expand the description of it to make each picture more vivid.

I find this particularly useful as an exercise in the first few lessons with a class, since it acts as a key to open up their fantasy. When I read them the Prévert poem, at least two-thirds of the class always says it isn't possible. But once they are off their very rational plane and into this more fantastic world they soon begin to enjoy the idea. It opens up marvellous possibilities and paves the way for more interesting writing in the future. With all

[1]Benton, M. and Benton, P. (*eds.*) (1988), *Touchstones 3*, Hodder & Stoughton

the barriers down and the constraints of the real world
forgotten, the children are free to experiment with words and
ideas.

— ◆ —

I would like to paint the noise of a vulture on the eastern
    mountains on a summer's evening,
The buzz of the dragonflies on the marsh,
The sound of a humming bird's wings as they go up and
    down in a plant.
I should like to take home the rays of the moon on a
    frosty night,
The crinkle of the willows on the lake at the bottom of
    the world.
I should like to touch the magic of the witch in Hell.
I should like to hear dew on the grass on a cold winter's
    morning,
The painter's brush wipe on the canvas,
The glow in a tiger's eye on a very dark night,
The calling of a painting to an artist.
I should like to understand the ways of the gods of
    ancient Mexico,
The animals' thoughts of being locked up in a zoo in the
    Saturday noise,
The mystery of the dark,
And the paint in the tin, waiting to be mixed.

Roddy Mattinson

I should like to paint the snowflakes' hearts which are
    beating away to the second,
The disobedience of a flag that won't flutter in the
    breeze,
The heat of a candle in the middle of the night,
The happiness of a merry-go-round which has started
    spinning,
The coldness in an iceberg's fast running blood,
The hyena's hysterical laugh when it howls at night.

Daniel Phillips

I should like to paint the mating call of the bluetit,
The swan's death cry after a duel with a brother.
I should like to feel the happiness of a thrush when he is
     warmed by the sun,
The sound of a clumsy cockroach awakening in the
     morning dew,
I should like to take home the sound of the rushing weir.
I would like to see the whistling of the wind,
I would like to listen to the growing of the corn.

Louis Lyne

I should like to touch the song of the skylark wavering
     on the horizon
Or feel the stars in the night sky.
I would love to keep the moon shimmering in a jar.
I would like to hear the sound of the past
Or paint the liberty of life.
I would like to hear the frenzy of a mad lizard
And keep the future in a box.
I should like to see the scream of a monkey rebounding
     in the jungle.
I would like to hear the sunset going down below the
     hills
And see the donkey braying in the fields,
Also to hear the elderberry tree flowering in the Spring.
I would like to paint the second in which the honeybee
     dies.

Rebecca Luff

I Saw A Peacock

With A Fiery Tail

The origin of this exercise is an anonymous rhyme which is quite well known and can be found in, among other places, the excellent anthology *The Rattle Bag*[1] edited by Ted Hughes and Seamus Heaney. For the purposes of explaining how it works, I shall set out the whole piece here.

I saw a Peacock with a fiery tail,
I saw a blazing Comet drop down hail,
I saw a Cloud with ivy circled round,
I saw a sturdy Oak creep on the ground,
I saw a Pismire swallow up a whale,
I saw a raging Sea brim full of ale,
I saw a Venice Glass sixteen foot deep,
I saw a Well full of men's tears that weep,
I saw their Eyes all in a flame of fire,
I saw a House as big as the moon and higher,
I saw the Sun even in the midst of night,
I saw the Man that saw this wondrous sight.

I am sure that many people know this rhyme, but there may still be many who do not know how it is put together. If we read it the way it is written we are excited by the surreal images it throws up and the magical effect of the language. However, if we read it another way, something very interesting happens:

I saw a Peacock.
With a fiery tail I saw a blazing Comet.
Drop down hail I saw a Cloud.
With ivy circled round I saw a sturdy Oak tree.

Heaney, S. and Hughes, T. (1982), *The Rattle Bag*, Faber

And so on. Now the whole piece makes real sense, grammar apart. In fact, it was probably composed as follows: I saw a Comet with a fiery tail, I saw a Cloud drop down hail, etc.

What this simple but effective technique illustrates as far as a teaching point goes is how poetry can say more than one thing at a time. It is always difficult to explain satisfactorily what the difference is between poetry and prose, but one thing is certain: poetry uses language in a more highly-charged way. It is more economical and can often imply a number of different meanings within one phrase. (That, among other things; but I do not intend to try any further definitions. That way lie all sorts of problems.)

While not making too many claims for this rhyme, it is true that children respond to it and love having the second way of reading it pointed out to them. It is similar to those optical illusions, like the faces/vase, where it is maintained that it is impossible to see both at once, even though you know that both are there. The exercise this affords the mind I find extremely exciting.

Having explored this rhyme, the children inevitably want to write their own, and are eager to see what fantastic images they can create by chance. They write sentences that make sense in the real world and, by putting them down on the paper in a certain way, create often startling images that can send them off into the surreal fantasy area of their imagination. Whole wall displays can be made in the classroom with pictures and collages arising from the new images. What is always so amazing is that many of these surreal images seem to contain such truth. Some, of course, are just funny, but we should be able to laugh, too.

The children should begin by writing a line which makes sense, for example, 'I saw a rosebush branching out'. The first part of this is written on the second line of the page, and the second part is written on the second half of the line above:

                    branching out
I saw a rosebush

If the child wants to rhyme, care must be taken to choose words
which do not limit choice of rhymes or cause silly things to be
written. Then a second line is written and is slotted in. If the line
is, 'I saw a madman scream and shout', it will be entered like
this:

branching out

I saw a rosebush scream and shout
I saw a madman

The whole process continues until the piece is considered
finished. All that remains is to enter a suitable phrase at the very
beginning and to complete the final line (the examples show
various ways of doing this, which the children discovered
themselves): the pleasure is then to see what has been created.
The above examples were taken from the following rhyme: you
can now see how it continued.

— ◆ —

I saw a fire branching out,
I saw a rosebush scream and shout,
I saw a madman soar on high,
I saw a swallow start to lie,
I saw a nervous witness swim the deep,
I saw a shark fall asleep,
I saw a small child learn to fly,
I saw a baby bird cut the sky,
I saw the lightning by candlelight,
I saw a man who saw this without sight.

Rachel Meyers

I saw a leaf floating in the air,
I saw a mist riding a mare,
I saw a jockey gurgle and swirl,
I saw a whirlpool grow a curl,
I saw a poodle dance with laughter,
I saw a clown wear a garter,

I saw a prince burrow in the earth,
I saw a rabbit giggle with mirth,
I saw a young maiden grow a beard,
I saw a woodcutter who looked and peered,
I saw the eyes in the looking glass,
All as I was writing in the class.

Jessica Leff

An unrhymed one:

I saw a cow in a field,
I saw a daisy fly into the sky,
I saw a bird float from the tree,
I saw a leaf eat a crumb of bread,
I saw an ant trickle from your eye,
I saw a tear build a nest,
I saw a bird pick some grass,
I saw a man leap into the air,
I saw a flame linger on a house,
I saw a raindrop ride a horse,
I saw a woman jump on to a wall,
I saw a cat in the shape of the letter Y,
I saw a cloud being picked,
I saw an ear of corn fall down,
I saw a bush slide through the grass,
I saw a snake jump very high,
I saw a kangaroo swim under water,
I saw a frog fly to the barn,
I saw a baby owl.

Katy Clarke

And a variation:

I heard the laughter in the dead of night,
I heard a scream rustle together,
I heard the trees singing sweetly to me,
I heard a bird beginning to bud,
I heard the flowers wailing for love,
I heard a ghost's tearful stream,

I heard the gushing of an opening gate,
I heard the squeak of breaking glass,
I heard the crash of a working clock,
I heard the tick of the ocean waves,
I heard the buzz as the fly dropped dead.

Natasha Lawrence

I have lately discovered another example in literature of this technique which is set out below in case it proves useful to teachers.

I saw a fishpond all on fire
I saw a house bow to a squire
I saw a parson twelve feet high
I saw a cottage near the sky
I saw a balloon made of lead
I saw a coffin drop down dead
I saw two sparrows run a race
I saw two horses making lace
I saw a girl just like a cat
I saw a kitten wear a hat
I saw a man who saw these too
And said though strange they all were true.

Anon

KENNINGS

A kenning was an Old Norse technique used in writing or story-telling which was a new descriptive name for something, for example, 'seal's field' for 'the sea'. It was a way of making a colourful description of something without employing the actual name. It occurs in Anglo-Saxon writing and Old English, where names might be given to swords ('Skull-Splitter') or the sea ('Swan Road'). It draws on attributes of the subject to create a sort of compound noun which is highly descriptive of what the thing is or does. More modern-day equivalents would be those used by the North American Indians to describe the train ('the iron horse'), whisky ('fire water'), the Victorian bicycles the Boneshaker and the Penny-farthing, and, in the twentieth century, 'ice box' for 'fridge'.

A poem by Libby Houston, called 'Black Dot', first alerted me to this technique in writing; a poem by James Reeves called 'The Main-Deep' employs adjectives and verbs in a similar way.

One of the aims of teaching children to write must be to encourage them to notice things in greater detail, and to practise how to express what they see in order to communicate their ideas vividly. As an exercise in the early stages of writing, kennings offer a number of advantages. The title will make clear what the subject is, and from then on those words will not reappear. Since titles are the first thing a reader takes in, their rôle is very important, and this exercise helps to reinforce that premise. All the children need to do then is to concentrate their minds on the subject and produce phrases which will combine to build up a picture of it. The results can stand as poems in their own right, but the demands on the children have been structured so as not to seem too daunting. Here again we see the effect of a list and how it can work through a cumulative process. Rhyming can be used if wished.

Cat

A toe-nibbler
A dark-dreamer
A paw-padder
A floor-scratcher
A warm-sleeper
A night-creeper
A fur-cleaner
A flea-finder
A mouse-hunter
A house-minder
A secret-hoarder
A china-breaker
A back-street-wailer
A four-foot-lander.

Rachel Meyers

Dog

A pink-lump
A small-blob
A fat-flopper
A fast-runner
A carpet-sweeper
A road-walker
A non-talker
A tail-turner
A paw-print-maker
A greedy-eater.

Shamba Barnett

Cat

A cunning-purrer
A cautious-crawler
A mouse-pouncer
A danger-seeker
A fur-ball
A quick-lapper
A playful-bouncer
A careless-stroller
A good-briber
A hissing-sneerer.

Shazeia Qureshi

Dog

A red-dot
An ear-hearer
A blind-mind
A furry-friend
An open-eye
A heavy-sleeper
An easy-waker
A soft-growler
A loud-barker
A burglar-alarm
A ball-catcher
A sneaky-sniffer
A tail-wagger
A cat-chaser
A fast-eater
A warming-lover
A soft-sneaker
A Boneo-raver.

Alex Norman

Storm

An angry-skygod
A lightning-thrower
An electricity-charge
A tree-destroyer
A howling-wind
A roaring-sky
A sky-splitter
An earth-quaker
A sky-army
A booming-record
A giant-bomb
A crackling-fire
A crumbling-mountain
A sky-tidal-wave
An erupting-volcano.

Guy Higginson

Mouth

A food-gobbler
A wide-opener
A constant-eater
A yawn-helper
A noise-bringer
A finger-sucker
A lip-smacker
A teeth-clicker
A lip-licker
A loud-shouter
A loving-kisser
A sharp-whistler.

Anadil Hossain

ALLITERATION

AND ASSONANCE

Always a popular technique with children, central as it is to the rhymes known as tongue twisters, alliteration can cause problems for the teacher who is introducing it year after year to classes. One simply becomes weary of reading the same sort of lines which result from exercises. In an earlier chapter (see page 70), I detailed how one might teach alliteration through a counting pattern, and it is true that children enjoy doing this. However, as a teacher, one is always looking for new ways of achieving the same end in order to maintain one's own enthusiasm, without which the children are less likely to learn.

I was delighted, therefore, to come across a rhyme by Colin West called 'The Darkest and Dingiest Dungeon'. The opening lines are as follows:

Down in the darkest and dingiest dungeon,
Far from the tiniest twinkle of stars,
Far from the whiff of a wonderful luncheon . . .

and it ends:

I sit here alone with myself in the cellar,
I do so like getting away from it all.

Each line in between begins with the words 'Far from . . . ' and includes alliteration, assonance (repetition of similar vowel sounds) and rhyme (both end rhyme and internal rhyme). This gave me the idea of encouraging children to write pieces which follow a simple similar pattern and which give greater scope for writing something more interesting, both for them and for me to read. It is a good idea to write up a few lines which can act as starting points, but children may, obviously, make up their own. The sort of lines might be:

1 Sat at the top of the tallest tree
  Watching . . .
2 Down at the bottom of the deep blue sea
  Down by . . .
3 Soaring upwards in a summer sky
  Over/above the . . .

In each line that follows, the child tries to employ alliteration where possible, but without forcing it; each line can highlight different sounds. Rhyming is optional and should be avoided at first if it proves too difficult. Some attempt at keeping to a reasonably regular rhythm should also be made. The exercise teaches children to be aware of the possibilities of alliteration (the repeated initial sounds which add texture and music to a poem) without overdoing the technique. Later, in other writing, they will remember this and use it sparingly to good effect.

— ◆ —

Sat at the top of the tallest tree,
Watching the badgers bustling busily,
Watching the magpies eagerly steal,
Watching the squirrels scrambling dangerously,
Watching the family over their meal,
Watching the hunter load his gun,
Watching the rabbits in the midday sun.

Neill Crawford

Way up high in a misty mountain,
Above the shouts and shrieks of the streets,
Above the lumbering and laughter of the days,
Above the echoes and bellows and beats,
Above the boats that float to the bay,
Above the buildings seen from afar,
Above the sky and the tallest tree,

Above anything you can ever see,
Above the golden, glittering sand,
I like this place, it's just for me.

Ghassan Radi

Stuck in the lift between two floors,
Looking at the blasted black and white buttons,
Looking only at the two grey doors,
Looking at the carpet all brown and rotten,
Looking at the tropical tree in the corner,
Looking at the cushioned stool for the porter,
Looking at the peculiar photograph,
Looking at the clock – it's three hours and a quarter,
Being here alone with my terror
Is really driving me up the wall.

Jessica Leff

And sometimes odd things come out of such an exercise:

Stuck on a screeching skyscraper,
Stranded in a crawling plant,
Abandoned on a dirty, dangerous, deserted island,
Stuck in a soggy, sloppy, swamp,
Stuffed in a box of circles – no end,
Sucked into another anonymous world.

Dena Knight

18

STARING

We have all, no doubt, experienced the act of staring at something for a long time – flames, water, clouds – and know the kind of meandering thoughts this provokes as well as the succession of pictures conjured up by the shapes and movement, given form in our imagination. As children, we would often play the game of seeing pictures in the open fire. A poem by Ted Walker, 'Clouds', which can be found in his book *The Solitaries* (Jonathan Cape), deals with this kind of experience.

Staring can be used with great success as an exercise in writing for the children. The idea is to stare at something for a long time and to jot down all the pictures you begin to see. The sort of things which lend themselves to this are a blank area of wall, a single brick, a puddle, a piece of bark, a square of earth or grass or playground, the palm of a hand, a post or railings, a gate, looking through a marble to the light, a cloud, a dark corner, and so the list can go on. If you stare long enough, your imagination begins to take over and a succession of thoughts and pictures emerge which should be written down immediately. These impressions form notes which can be worked on to produce poems. It is a simple exercise, easy to organise, but can lead to fascinating results, particularly when children are used to writing and can draw the threads together so that they say even more than a straight description. This gives practice in finding other ways to describe something, which leads naturally into the use of metaphor, an important technique in the writing of poetry. However, in the early stages with a class the purpose of opening up the imaginative processes of the mind makes this an exercise of great value.

— ◆ —

Railings

The sea rippling on a cool day,
Kings and queens standing in a row,
Pieces of string, some tied loose, some tight,
And a head of hair.
Rows of hills reflected in water,
Faces staring at each other
And a row of spears,
Nine pieces of paper, each with a tear,
A line of washing hanging to dry.

Helen Alexander

Seeing

I see thickets where deer run and hide,
I see the ocean with its snatching tide,
I see the field where hero Harold died,
I see my death bride.

I see Cranmer flame in pain,
I see the ark awash in biblical rain,
I see the chalk stallion's silver mane,
I follow thought's long and winding lane.

Nicholas Tomkins

Stone

Great Britain,
A group of magpies
Screaming for ancient coins.
Dirty beach,
An old stone ruin.
An owl sees his future.

Joanna Cooper

The Image in the Brick

In the darkness of the brick
I see a steep rocky cliff with one dull grey colour.
I also see ghostly objects like stiff witches,
Outlines of blurry skulls with no bones
And gorillas with no eyes.
I can see rocky objects,
Meteorites falling from the sky
Making volcanoes which dry up
To make a mountain with a steep hill,
Almost a cliff, but without rock.

Pawel Gorajewski

19

GIFTS

When a child is born it is customary for relatives and friends to bring presents for the newborn baby, and when it is christened the godparents usually give a gift. When Jesus was born, the Bible tells us the three Wise Men brought gifts of gold, frankincense and myrrh, while (according to legend) the shepherds gave a lamb. In fairy stories there are similar tales, notably in the Sleeping Beauty, of gifts being wished upon a child. In the one case it is three wise men and in others it is three wise women (or witches, as they were sometimes known in past times). I believe it was also the custom among North American Indians to grant the new baby certain attributes and fortunes along with its special name.

All this led into an idea for poems which the children might write. And the idea is simply to write poems, possibly conceived as lullabies, which offer gifts which the children would like to give to a newborn child, whether they are within the bounds of possibility or not. This idea can be used as a new angle for Christmas poems or can be written for an imaginary baby. The poem can also be written for a particular baby – perhaps a new brother or sister – or can be given an historical setting which would enable the writer to bring in details of fact or legend, as has been done with the 'Viking Cradle Song' in these examples.

— ◆ —

Lullaby for Christ

I have brought you a fox so you will have knowledge,
I have brought you a wolf so you will have courage,
I have brought you a hare so you will be swift
But your heart will be weak and sometimes fail you.
Now I bring you myrrh, I bring you gold,
I bring you wise men with stories to be told
I have brought you frankincense with a sweet smell,
I have brought you followers who wish you well.
You will have no temper, you will have no wrath,
And you will die an heroic death.

Ben Owen

Viking Cradle Song

Hush, child, hush,
No need to cry,
For you will be the strongest of them all.
Stronger than Thor and his mighty hammer,
And do good and bad,
But you will have no love to give.

Hush, child, hush,
For Ymir the Ice Giant
Has asked for your hand in marriage.
There you shall dwell in twelve years' time.
But beware, Ymir will steal your love
And let the dwarfs change it into hate for Asgard.

Hush, child, hush,
For you will become goddess of all women.
Live to be healthy, grow to love,
Live till Ragnar's day.
See the world from Odin's cliff of powers.

Hush, child, hush,
For Jormungand
Has offered to let you round the world
Upon his back,
If you can steal the Brisingamen
And let him have a glimpse of it.

Hush, child, hush,
For one of its beads
Is a torch of the world
And of Ragnar's day.
Steal back the torch
And Odin will give you
A drop of the Mead of Inspiration.

Melissa Cooke

Lullaby

I bring you sea so that you can create
Fish and underwater mammals.
You will go on a voyage
And see new lands and natives.

You have a fault in your right arm
And will cast away the death from it.
You will be eternal, eternal,
Eternal, eternal, eternal.

Your life has begun but has far to go.
The baby will be gentle and prudent.
I've brought you a world so you may live in it.
You shall be eternal, eternal,
Eternal, eternal, eternal.

The world is big, make use of it,
The ocean is wide, sail in it
You shall become a poet,
I give you paper, scar it.
You shall be eternal, eternal,
Eternal, eternal, eternal.

Karen Bounds

Different Doubles

Girl Your face will resemble half
      Of the first flower in Spring.
      You shall be as clever as an owl is not,
      You will be clumsy as an owl is not,
      You will be impatient as the moon is
      While waiting to rise.

Boy Your face will resemble the other half
      Of the first flower in Spring.
      You shall be as fast as a cat being chased by a dog.
      You will be forgetful as a man taking honey from bees,
      And as slow at thinking as you will be fast.

Pippa Monjardino

A Belly

Like A Bream

There is a traditional rhyme which uses similes in a creative way which I have found very useful for encouraging children to think about the language they employ when describing something. The literary concept of a simile is quite easy to understand; it is best described as a phrase that tells you that something is similar to something else. Using the word 'like', you give your description an added depth and uncover fascinating parallels for yourself, and your readers. However, most of the similes we use in everyday life are now very overused and do not make for interesting writing. The excitement that children can experience in creating their own similes is one of the stepping stones essential to good writing. They will naturally lead on to metaphor (so important in poetry), and the excitement is an all-important ingredient in helping children to attain the feeling of having achieved something worthwhile and the satisfaction that comes with that.

I have found that writing about animals lends itself to this exercise and that use of alliteration tends to creep in, too. All these techniques contribute to a denser, more interesting poem; they help to train the mind to be alert to ways of looking and translating this into language which is richer and, consequently, more effective.

The traditional rhyme goes as follows:

— ◆ —

How a Good Greyhound is Shaped

He needs
A head like a snake, a neck like a drake,
A back like a beam, a belly like a bream,
A foot like a cat, and a tail like a rat.

Tiger

He needs
A body like a big, bright, blooming, yellow, furry
  balloon,
Paws like pouncing proud baby pompoms,
Claws like sharp cutting craft knives,
Stripes like black snakes slithering down his side.
His gleaming sharp white teeth snatch and slash at his
  prey.
Ears prick up and pinpoint particular sounds.
His muscular, magnificent moving tail swishes to and
  fro,
His golden eyes glow in the setting sun
And his massive majestic head observes everything in
  the forest.

Satesh Dadlani

Dragon

He needs
A body like a baggy brown bag of balls,
Eyes like enormous exploding eggshells,
A tail like a thistle's thatched tendril,
Claws that tap like Cleopatra's clicking needles,
Jaws that jabber like a Japanese jay
And feet that flap like frogs' flippers.

Edith Rogers-England

Troll

Has
A nose like a narrow nauseous nodule,
A body like a big bulky blob,
A beard like a noxious noisome nest,
Knees like knobbly knots
Hands like hairy hooks
And arms like abominable arches.

Mary Noble

How to Make a Vulture

He needs
Wings like wrangled wire winding through one
    another,
A beak like a bone banana, bent and split,
Talons that tabulate terror, teasing his prey
And a body of a bush, blossomed but bedraggled.

Taryn Youngstein

Taking this subject and extending the use of alliteration, children can write more adventurous poems. It is advisable to try out a simpler alliterative exercise first before going on to this one, and then the results can be quite exciting. The children will be familiar with the idea and be freer to concentrate on finding the right description instead of being bogged down in mastering the technique.

— ◆ —

My Dog

My dog has fiery, fluffy, frisky hair full of fleas!
His eyes expand extremely when we go exploring in
    the evening.
He's a breath-breather;
He breathes all over beautiful bowls of fruit, like
    bananas.
Sometimes his tail is terribly tatty,
Tangled with thistles, thrushes' feathers, tulips and
    other types of stuff.
His best game is playing with the pigeons
And trying to catch them with his pink padded paws.

Vicky Swallow

Gerbil

She has fragile furry fingers that fiddle with her food,
And wild wiry whiskers that whisk in the wind.
She has pink perky eyes that peer carefully through
    her cage,
Her tiny teeth are tough and her tail twitches timidly.
She secretly stores her supper of seeds
In her cosy comfy hidden hole.
She's a busy burrower
Building her bed out of bits and bobs.

Lucy Head

My Dog

My dog's eyes can be filled with expression – ecstasy or
    envy.
Her fur is fleecy and fair and brown-flecked.
She believes her bark beguiles
But it bellows from her belly below.
Narrow nostrils has her nose
And nobody knows what a nauseating noise she
    makes at night.
Pacing paws my dog has, and padded and pale,
Patting pekineses and periwinkles
Her paws persist in perturbing and petrifying them.

Louisa Duggan

My Horse

My horse's hooves hammer the heathery hollow hard,
He canters crazily and cantankerously
Across the cold and coarse countryside.
I sit on Sam's suede saddle
And slither down onto the silver sand.

Vanessa Hedley

Cat

She bends back her ears in ecstasy
And as she walks
Her whiskers wobble and waver in the wind.
She clasps her claws into her climbing tree
And thinks she'll catch a chick.
Her skin is soft and silky like a shiny seal
And she has a tender little pink tongue
That wants to taste all tempting food.
When she walks, her tail tags along behind and twitches.
Her gently padded paws leave pretty patterns in the sand.

Lucinda Wright (BYW)

Last Will

---

and Testament

It is a fact that children frequently write about death, whether of animals or people, and this can often disturb some adults. A preoccupation with death would, naturally, give one cause to worry if it were overriding but, generally, this is not the case. I believe that those adults who say that children should be writing about 'beautiful' and 'wonderful' things only are merely displaying their own inability to consider the fact of death and usually their ignorance of poetry. It is often these people, it seems to me, who tend to encourage children to read and write the harmless, often pointless, doggerel which passes for poetry in some anthologies and contains nothing of the craft, intelligence and exciting use of language we should be expecting from the children's work. One of the aspects of serious poetry which I look for and admire is its ability to disturb readers from everyday complacency and set them thinking about something in a way they never have before.

Children are quite fascinated with the subject of death and as yet have little or no experience of the absolute horrors which can come with age. They are upset if a relative or pet dies, of course, and it can be a marvellous release to be able to write about it. This applies to adults as well, although they do not use this release enough. It is good to let children ask their questions and talk about death – it is a healthy curiosity.

The idea of writing a last will and testament is an attempt to bring in an almost positive side to this subject, and to make the children think of the joys of life which they might wish to leave to someone. This will is not meant to be a list of possessions in the material sense – that side of things can be rather morbid. It is, instead, to be a catalogue of things bequeathed which you could not normally leave to anyone. It will contain qualities of humanity, feelings and emotions, health and happiness – all the things you would want to wish for someone if you had the ability and chance. There is also scope for leaving things for the improvement of, say, someone you perhaps dislike – the corrective kind of will. The children will learn something about themselves doing this exercise – what things do they consider important and of value? – and will be looking at life and relationships in a way that should probe beneath the superficial layers, as long as they are honest with themselves.

Note: Before embarking upon this piece of writing, you should of course check that no child in the class has recently experienced the death of a relative or close friend. While it is true that some people experience a great release in writing about a recent bereavement, for most this represents a trauma that should be handled with sensitivity, by others.

— ◆ —

Death Will

I have scrutinised my friends to write my death wishes.
My brother will receive my energy
Which I do not wish to keep.
With it I bestow my scorched reputation,
With this I have sighed too much.
To my sister I render my slumberous imagination
Which is of little use with its many a flaw.
To my father, my greatest love, I leave my life
As a memory that I hope will live with him.
I leave my joys and emotions
For him to find pleasure
As I did.

John Nathan

Last Wish

To you I grant a heart
For it is you who truly needs one.
I leave to you understanding
For though you seem to know it all
You are totally devoid of knowledge.
I take away from you the power to worship
For you seem not to want it.
I give you humility,
Practise having it in your possession.

Hedy-anne Goodman

Last Thoughts

My last ten minutes are given to you
In writing this will.
The last day of battle
And the French are ten thousand strong.
I have not long to live.
To my wife I give
All the flowers in a hundred acres
And my blessings go with all of them.
To our only son
I leave a choir of nightingales
Conducted at your command.
But to the enemy I am fighting
I leave the darkness of a hundred generations
And the Devil's curse.
Now I must leave for the pounding of hooves
Are drumming in my ears
And the roar of the cannon
And the shouts of the soldiers
Are ringing through my head.

Ben Owen

Last Thoughts

I grant a rib cage to the otter
Who has felt lead many a time.
The rib cage is as strong as a heart.
A bullet would not harm his confidence and trust.
I give a fish wisdom
For the fish has felt the hook
In his mouth many a time.
I hope it will not feel the pain again.

Zaki Standing

PLACES AND
DETAILS

This exercise is yet another way of concentrating the mind on details in order to present a vivid picture of a place to the reader. This method makes it a little easier for children to cope with and can lead to some good results.

The words 'Town', 'Country' and 'Seashore' are written on the board at the top: these will head three columns. The children are then asked to suggest as many things as they can think of which can be found in these places. All the words are written in a column down the board under the appropriate heading. The sort of things which they might suggest are contained in the lists below.

Town	*Country*	*Seashore*
bricks	hedges	rocks
roads	ditches	cliffs
street lamps	fences	sand
cars	animals	shells
shops	trees	seaweed
pillar boxes	grass	rockpools
telephone kiosks	streams	crabs
dust	barns	deckchairs
chimneys	farmhouses	donkeys
windows	drystone walls	gulls
street signs	lanes	boats
gardens	woods	sandcastles
kerbs	ponds	driftwood
pavements	birds	waves

These lists can be as long as you like, or as long as your board! The headings are very wide but can be more specific if you wish. Other possible titles could be City Street, Parade of Shops, Market, Farm, Mountains, River, Village, Harbour, Underground Station. You could also do the same thing with seasons or months of the year. A good poem for showing the detail and feeling of a month is 'November' by Ted Hughes[1]. You can also ask the children to make their own lists in their books rather than as a class.

The children are then asked to write poems using the words from the list so that they write one or two lines *only* on each word. They must concentrate on a one- or two-line description of each thing and the whole poem will provide a detailed description of a particular place. The individual lines should be as interesting and vivid as possible; the value of this approach is that the children can pause to think after every one or two lines. The effort required for sustaining a long poem is broken down into manageable units. This also shows children one method of working, which is this layer upon layer approach. It is good practice for them to become used to making notes in this way before writing any poem. In their other writing they can always be encouraged to jot down quickly all thoughts and ideas on a subject and afterwards to select and order those which they wish to work on and improve for the final poem.

— ◆ —

Suburbia

The roar of jets and trains rattles over old tracks,
Cars come to a halt at a zebra.
An old woman shuffles with her shopping
Crossing her prayers with kerbstones.
Outside her flat, a briefing with a neighbour,
Past her own screams she grudges babies,
Her shabby shawl limp on her shoulders,
Retired from her job she pumps on her pension.
Her lifeless card lies among lonely photographs

---

[1]Hughes, T. (1960), *Lupercal*, Faber

Her husband still alive in his uniform,
Daily she visits his memory,
While through her open window car fumes cloud.
Unfinished knitting on an armchair.

Ben Owen

The Beach

The beach is empty except for a sleeping few
Under cover, lying on lilos with punctures.
The low-water seaweed strangling the little fish,
The sand heavy with water from a weekend rainfall.
The ice-cream van with the yellow stripes
Is parked outside the town home
With its windows shut.
Empty deckchairs sunk in the ground.

Nicholas Midgley (YWW)

The Town

The smothered building on a page,
A castle with too many pictures behind it.
The factories still have their spirit.
Children scream while the milkman is not heard,
The trees will never reach their destination.
The milk clutters against the crate
To make our sound of life.
The dustmen will always belong
Like chess pieces on the move.

Debbie Stephens

Winter Seashore

Brighton beach wet, cold, damp,
Pier distorted in the sea,
The wind howling through a ghost train tunnel,
A witch stares a plastic stare.
Deck chairs form little pools

Where a tramp sleeps huddled against the cold.
The rain penetrates a sandcastle which has been
 defeated.
A lonely fishing boat chugs a tune over the silky sea,
A summer beach a postcard picture.

Jason Weir

Town

As feet wear away thought and time
The highrise flats watch
From high up on their cement thrones.
Street lamps line up
Like long regiments of soldiers
Their stems rooted to the ground.
The few trees that stand in huddled bunches
Slowly choking, their withered branches hang low.
The old alley cat playing in the dust,
A thick dusty bundle of fur and a slight purr.

Matthew Wevill

(See also 'Seashore', Chapter 41, page 170, and 'Seashore'
Chapter 74, page 32.)

The Country

Tall trees guarding fields
Like soldiers on their watch towers.
Grass stalks stand in suspense,
A pigeon on a garden fence
Gently cooing as if reciting poetry.
A goat gnawing away
Through the remains of the past.
A robin hovering.

Matthew Wevill

Portland

Needles prick into the bloodshot eyes of the sky,
As the Race combs its white hair.
The rock bathes in the font of the sea,
Cleansing its skin,
Whilst its expression is held taut in malice.
Cries sing together from the prison on the hill.
Their hymn whispers in the long yellow grass,
And echoes in the open air chapel of the quarries.

Miles Greene (YWW)

The Cloud

The mountain reached up to touch the sky
With its white hand.
The cloud looked down upon the tired climbers
With the food on their backs
And their fame in their heads
And the flag up above them.

The ocean threw a wave at the sky,
The cloud watched the boat waddle through the water
With the sail in its chest
And the air in the sail
And the water slapping water.

The city threw smoke at the cloud.
The cloud watched the worker
With a grey-blue anorak
And his small packed lunch
And nothing else.

Nicholas Midgley (YWW)

FROM EVERY

ANGLE

One of the things we are teaching children through poetry is how to use their senses. It is too easy, and many children do it, to write about something in a superficial manner. Anyone can say that 'the flowers are pretty colours', or that a stone is 'an interesting shape'. These sort of observations are not special, they do not make anything 'come alive' or startle us by their originality. Television feeds us with constant pictures and sounds, occasionally drawing our attention to significant or interesting points, but hardly ever asking us to look properly for ourselves or describe our experience in words. As children grow older they begin to lose the infant's fascination with new sights, and it is necessary to make them look harder, use their minds and find fresh ways of describing what they see. So often it is details that make poems. Universal truths are more poignantly expressed by the small experience described in detail. The concrete images that symbolise the wider aspect of life are the things that we notice and remember.

Therefore, the old idea of presenting children with objects, or sending them out to look at a particular thing, has a very definite place in the teaching of poetry. Like any other exercise, of course, it should be used with discretion and not 'done to death'. In fact, almost all the exercises in this book are aimed at encouraging the children to think more deeply about their subject. This one merely highlights the necessity for using detailed concrete images.

The children must work hard to produce something which is good. It will take time and this should be allowed for. If you can read some good examples of the kind of thing you are after, and make it clear that it is new and original descriptions you expect, most children will respond and will experience that greater feeling of achievement that comes with producing something that is not just 'dashed off'. As teachers, we often expect too little and the children react accordingly. We all need to be pushed, enthused and encouraged before we necessarily work to our best ability. In time the children will want to do this for themselves, for their own satisfaction, but to begin with outside stimulation is needed.

The Stone

White as chalk
It glistens at me
Like glass when cut.
Its surface smooth,
In places rough
Where it has been chipped
And cut from a white sea-stone.
I feel it is alive.
After all the cold mantelpieces
And dusty shelves
It has been laid on
And all the careless hands
It has been dropped from
It is surely dead.
But no, it still glistens,
And its depths glow white
Like cats' eyes.
Yet if it is alive
How can it stay the same so long,
Chipped once, and only once
And no marks to show how old it is?
While I grow
I change my image
And will later die,
This stone will never die
And other hands will hold it as I do.

Diccon Alexander (YWW)

Paperweight

As I looked at it, I took it all in; the conical top, the imprisoned
purple flower with the light shining
through, the green colour flecked with brown that surrounded the
flower and the tiny air bubbles trapped, all trapped inside the thick
smooth glass. I picked it up, it was heavy, cold and hard. It was quite
large and took up all my hand. I turned it slowly around. The petals
were distorted and the green-brown surroundings seemed to bob like
tiny waves one minute, then turn menacingly to protect the flower.

Facing it to the window I saw thousands of tiny windows reflected
onto the glass. I pulled away lest the windows too would get trapped
inside the heavy-looking air. Startled by the thought I held it close to
my face. It smelt warm and reminded me of pressing my nose
against a window in the pouring rain. Looking again I saw my own
face reflected. Shuddering I replaced it in its spot on the mantelpiece
and looked out of the window at the sun bouncing off the crazy
paving.

Megan Trudell (YWW)

Meadows

The bull walked on the ready spread lawn,
He looked at his reflection in a small pool.
The wind blew the water and his face splintered.

Sheep stood grazing in the rising of the sun,
Hidden in trees lay a fox, his teeth burning,
Nearby cows watched the grass grow.

The cat watched the drenched fieldmice
Dart from shadow to light.
Fish slipped through weeds
Breathing bubbles greenly into the sky.

Melissa Cooke

A Thought in Lulworth Church

Midsummer
and the sky burns mellow in the light.
Golden and sweet roll the beaches,
glossy and warm.
Is a tear enough to quench the throat of time?
But the wind still hums through the dry chalk hills.
Such gossip blows round the old white fields.
Is a cry enough to deafen the ears of time?
I look through the leadlined windows
to see the wind singing in long white gowns
and the short sea-beaten bushes standing still
like pews in the dull summer breeze.

Miles Greene (YWW)

Daffodil

Yellow bells attached to green bell ropes,
A trumpet of pollinated notes.
Their starry shaped bonnets with curved edges
Hide their yellow faces.

Anna Cheifetz

RIDDLES

There are many examples of riddles to be found in the anthologies available to schools (notably in the books of *Junior Voices*[1] and *Voices*[2]). Many of them are translations from Anglo-Saxon. Most children enjoy riddles; they love guessing games.

Riddles generally seem to fall into two categories. There are the sort that spell the answer, a letter a line. For example:

My first is in *b*ook but not in cover,
My second in *si*ster but not in brother,
My third is in *r*ain but not in sun,
My fourth is in brea*d* but not in bun.

There are quite often one or two lines at the end of these which give a clue to the whole word.

The second sort are veiled and interesting descriptions of the subject which provide enough information and clues without giving the answer away too easily. Rhyme is often used, but near rhymes can be just as effective (e.g. 'cover' and 'brother'). The lines of a riddle also have a 'magical' quality about them: something of the element of chants and spells and of the impossible being possible. It is present in the old song 'I will give my love an apple', and can also be seen in the following riddle:

[1]Geoffrey Summerfield (*ed.*) (1970) *Junior Voices*, Penguin
[2]Geoffrey Summerfield (*ed.*) (1968) *Voices*, Penguin

— ◆ —

In marble walls as white as milk,
Lined with a skin as soft as silk,
Within a fountain crystal-clear,
A golden apple doth appear.
No doors there are to this stronghold,
Yet thieves break in and steal the gold.

Traditional English
(Egg)

One of the benefits of asking children to write riddles is that, since they are not allowed to mention the subject, they are forced to think harder about it. They must choose their words carefully so as not to make it too easy to guess, and they must search out the hidden aspects of the subject, thus looking at it probably more closely than they ever have before. Being able to find other ways of expressing what might be a commonplace object will be of great value later on in other poems. In the example above, the 'yolk' of the egg is called 'a golden apple' and the 'shell' is the 'stronghold'. These are imaginative descriptions of the kind that we hope will give the children practice for their future writing. And there are the beautiful contradictions which often add to the power of riddles, and other poems too. For example:

No doors there are to this stronghold,
Yet thieves break in and steal the gold.

and

I will give my love a palace wherein she may be
And she may unlock it without e'er a key.

— ◆ —

Often talked of, never seen,
Ever coming, never been,
Daily looked for, never here,
Still approaching ever near.
Thousands for my presence wait,
But by the decree of fate,
Though expected to appear,
They will never see me here.

Andrew Hall
(The Future)

I am a stone but not a stone,
I occur in flocks and am never alone.
A nebula of falling lights
Which dive at earth like tiny kites.
I sometimes pain but rarely kill,
I pound and thump like a minute drill.
Occasionally floods I cause,
I plummet down with tremendous force.
The traces of my presence are seldom clear,
I merely change my shape and disappear.

Adam Lyne
(Hailstones)

I'm isolated to the rest of the world.
Some say I'm mean,
Some say it's natural,
Although I'm never seen.
I steal day and night,
I'm usually unknown,
Sometimes I'm fast, sometimes slow,
And I always come alone.
I'm all over the world
And in space,
I'm mass and single.
I happen in one place.

Steve Webber
(Death)

My metal coat is hard,
My body substance a white smooth cream,
My head you must screw on tight.
Morn and noon and night,
Each day I'm losing weight.
They rob me for their bristles
To fulfill my pasted fate.

Jason Turner
(Toothpaste)

ANIMALS

Children always like animals, whether they be domestic pets or the more exotic wild creatures of the world. They will frequently write about them as well as thoroughly enjoying the books they read which have animal characters. Books such as *Tarka the Otter*[1], *Watership Down*[2], *The Mouse and his Child*[3], will always have a devoted following. This can be a subject which presents pitfalls, however. Either they write stories and poems anthropomorphising the animals in often a banal way, or the poems are superficial in their observation of animals and their behaviour. Wild animals too often 'pounce on their prey' without any clear picture being given of what the 'prey' might be. 'Prey' is a word that seems to appeal so much to children that, if you are not careful, it occurs time and time again. It has become one of my *bêtes noires*, as it were, and belongs to the woolly abstract language that does poetry such a disservice. 'Dripping jaws', 'blood' and 'death' also tend to occur with monotony in the 'prey' poems; we have all read too many of them for one lifetime.

Nevertheless, animals are a subject that will always fascinate children and, if we are going to encourage better writing, we must make sure that the same detailed approach is followed with this subject as with any other. We should not allow our sentimentality towards animals to affect our judgement of the poems.

One of the best ways to assist the children is to arrange for

---

[1]Williamson, H. (1965), *Tarka the Otter*, Bodley Head
[2]Adams, R. (1972), *Watership Down*, Rex Collings
[3]Hoban, R. (1969), *The Mouse and his Child*, Faber and Faber

them actually to study a real live animal, either in the countryside, the classroom or the zoo, so that they can describe it in proper detail. Alternatively, or additionally, they can find a picture to have in front of them while they work. They can be encouraged to read up about the animal in order to be able to use interesting facts which will help the authenticity of their writing. All these details will ensure that the poems are more successful than those written entirely from imagination. It means they must use their senses more and find ways of describing the animals which are more vivid, perhaps involving the use of metaphor and simile. A storyline can be interwoven in the poem, but the whole thing will start with the concrete image.

There are many good examples of famous animal poems which can be read to the children to help encourage them to be more specific in their observation. Notable amongst these are some poems by Ted Hughes, e.g. 'Pike', 'The Jaguar', 'A March Calf', 'Swifts', and there are countless other examples by different poets to be found in most anthologies. It is also very worthwhile to look through individual volumes of poetry to find poems which are not generally anthologised. There are some marvellous discoveries to be made which are all too often overlooked. Anthologies, of course, are most useful in schools, but unfortunately one frequently gains the impression that the editors have only read other anthologies and the same poems occur time and time again.

— ◆ —

The Bullock

Your neck like an old empty sack,
Hooves like polished wood,
Your fur stuck together by mud.
Every time you chew
Your whole bottom lip moves back and forth.
You fill the air with your repeated breath,
You come forward inquisitive,
You stare at me.

Pippa Monjardino

The Welsh Mountain Pony

The small head of the Welsh pony
Drops to pluck the coarse heather on the mountain side,
Like a miniature Arab he prances and sidles.
He flicks his pure white tail to and fro,
Whilst the flies irritate his hindquarters.
His hooves are like pebbles on a beach
Tattooing a steady pace.
His mane is like watered silk
As it flows in the wind.
His legs, small but fast-moving,
Beat out a canter into the horizon.

Rebecca Luff

The Cobra

His marks are honeycomb
His eyes are like flying saucers,
His ribs stretch like elastic bands.
The curled teeth shining and ready for a victim.
His back patterns are stars in the moonlight.

Sharon Purves

Sheep

Standing erect against aged wind
Grazing on familiar grass,
Raises its head as if woken from sleep.
Two pointed ears stick out of that meek head,
Only fields are known to him.
Never venturing far, stopped by a brambled boundary,
The feel of life's countdown slowing its stride.

John Nathan

House Fly

I am sworn at and unpraised. My eyes are like deep chocolate pools. I love to wallow in sugar for that makes me live longer. My wings are transparent and my chest is grey but the rest of me is a type of gloss and soot black. I swerve and dive and complete many irregular triangles.

Laurence Hopkinson

The Vulture

A bald old man with old fashioned ruffs, his suit looks like an old black flag fluttering in the wind. He is like a scarecrow, a raggedy tramp, he looks out of place in his many habitats. His feet are smooth yet bumpy. You can't see his fingers until he flies, then he has many. On the ground he looks like a solemn undertaker.

David Travers

Unicorn

A colour so difficult to describe. Perhaps the colour of the foam in the sea – so white, but yet so dark. A single horn of a twisting tapering design set neatly in the middle of the forehead. Belonging to this horn are magical powers such as it can cure any disease or wound. The deep brown eyes give off the image of the forest in which the unicorn lives. They live alone in a forest that never grows old, with pools so clear they can see themselves, for knowing they are the most beautiful they are a little vain. The hooves are cloven and give the unicorn such a graceful movement that no other animal has except deer in shy imitation and goats in dancing mockery. Unicorns are immortal and no place is ever more enchanted than where one has been born.

Andy Henry

26

'Cat' and

'Mous'

The title 'Cat and Mous' is really only an attempt to give a unity to something which has none. A sequence of 'Cat and Mous' poems will have nothing in common, but the title provides a jokey cohesion which can tempt the children.

The children are asked to suggest as many words as they can which contain either 'cat' or 'mous'. This is best done as a class lesson with the words written on the blackboard. Two lists will emerge containing words such as the following:

catapult	enormous
cataract	venomous
catseyes	moustache
catamaran	famous
category	mouse
catalogue	anonymous
catacombs	mousse

When the children run out of words you may be able to provide more, or they can look in dictionaries. This process alone is good for extending vocabulary and helping with spelling. There are many other groups of words that can be dealt with in the same way – for example, 'ages', 'able', 'ant'.

When the list is complete (or as complete as you wish), the children are then given the choice of any word about which to write a poem. This offers a wide range of subjects and every child should find at least one that appeals. To help them form a framework, it is useful to remind the children of techniques they have learnt – e.g., acrostics, riddles, rhyme schemes, patterns.

—◆—

Catkins

A lazy remnant of early Spring,
When it was hot (but not too much),
And foliage on the trees made shadows on the ground
Which looked like a half-finished chess board.
With pure blue lying skies,
That pretended that last night's storm had not been
    there,
And still the willow weeps.
And people see nature
Through a rosy haze of laziness,
Where catkins take first place spinning in the breeze.
The home of dizzy beetles and greenfly.
And still the willow weeps.

Sarah Simpson

Famous

Moths fly to the lamp in ever decreasing circles,
Hypnotised, fascinated,
But when they fly too near they get scorched and
    burnt.
That is fame.

People flock like moths around fame's lamp,
Hating but loving its glare.
The one who survives being burnt attains fame.

You emerge made of tinsel, dressed in glitter,
With blinding rays and a gaudy mask sprayed with
    gold.
The filmy paper notes people pay you get burnt up in
    the lamp.
But the rain of old age puts out the lamp of fame
And the moths find another star to flock round.

Search in the tinsel to find your real self –
You'll only find ashes and dust.
That is fame.

Sarah Simpson

Moustache

Most men have them,
Others shave them off, or they grow them.
Useful to twiddle round when thoughtful,
Shaped to the style you want –
Tenderly sticking up,
Awfully showing off,
Covering a wart on a top lip,
Hoping everyone will admire you.
Every man should have one – a moustache.

Jansen Semmens

Anonymous

A name being nameless.
Surprising if you think
That man has nearly named everything
Except this.

Is it because it's weak and frail,
Or too strong and tough?
Perhaps it never had a chance
To show itself.

Jason Turner

(See also 'Caterpillar', page 192; and 'Catalogue', 'Enormous', and 'Catkin', page 69.)

27

PATTERNS

Many poems that one reads are written to a pattern. It may be a simple repetition of a line which acts like a chorus to hold the poem together, or it may be more than that. A pattern, in the sense I mean, is like a framework which helps the poem almost to write itself. A poet who has often used this idea to very good effect is Pete Morgan, in such poems as 'Ring Song' and 'The Meatwork Saga' which can be found in his book *The Grey Mare Being the Better Steed*[1]. It can also be seen particularly in 'Who Killed the Leaves' by Ted Hughes in his book *Season Songs*[2]. This last is derived from the old rhyme 'Who Killed Cock Robin?'

The idea is to find a pattern out of which the poem can grow. Sometimes old nursery rhymes can provide this or a pattern can be made up. It is interesting to look through poetry books to find poems which belong to this kind. The following examples should give a clear indication of some of the possibilities.

— ◆ —

Window

There once was a very small window,
hidden away in a corner of a room.

One day a small boy looked through the window
and saw a bright red fire engine.

An actress looked through the window
and saw her name in lights.

---

[1]Morgan, P. (1973), *The Grey Mare Being the Better Steed*, Secker and Warburg
[2]Hughes, T. (1976), *Season Songs*, Faber and Faber

A farmer looked through the window
and saw a field of harvested wheat.

A housewife looked through the window
and saw a spotless kitchen.

A ghost looked through the window
and saw life.

A writer looked through the window
and saw a blank paper.

A press-man looked through the window
and saw his story on the front page.

A carpenter looked through the window
and saw a bed, varnished and ready to sell.

A gardener looked through the window
and saw a mowed lawn.

Then God looked through the window
and the window broke.

Steve Webber

Who Killed Who?

Who was the one who ate the apple?
I, said the worm.
Who was the one who ate the worm?
I, said the bird.
Who was the one who killed the bird?
I, said the boy, with my slingshot.
Who was the one who beat the boy?
I, said the headmaster.
Who killed the headmaster?
I, said the boy
With my 007 cap gun!

Anthony Freidin

I Say (ing), I Say (ing)

O Lordy, O Lordy,
I feel such woe,
I let the cat out
And it scratched me so.

O Lordy, O Lordy,
Why must it be me?
I spilt the beans
And now there's no tea.

O Lordy, O Lordy,
I'm so upset,
I dropped the milk bottle
And now my foot's wet.

O Lordy, O Lordy,
I am so sad,
I helped make the broth
And now it tastes bad.

O Lordy, O Lordy,
It pains me such,
I counted my chickens
And now there's too much.

O Lordy, O Lordy,
It isn't fair,
My arse is so good
The sun burnt me there.

O Lordy, O Lordy,
I think I'll retire,
I looked for the smoke
But got caught in the fire.

O Lordy, O Lordy,
I think I will die,
I tried to fool him –
He threw wool in my eye.

Donal Crawford

The Shadow of Death

I stood under the rainbow
And my shadow became the seven colours.
I stood by the boiling furnace
And my shadow turned red.
I stood in the greenhouse
And my shadow became green.
I stood under the noon sun
And it was short.
I stood under the dusk
And my shadow was long.
I stood under the moon
And my shadow became grey.
I died and there was no shadow,
Only death's.

Matthew Festenstein

28

SKIPPING RHYMES

AND CHANTS

Playground games come and go during the school year; sometimes it is marbles, or conkers, sometimes jacks or hopscotch, but there are generally some children skipping, even these days. Some of the old rhymes are still used in various versions and sometimes new ones will appear. As these are used by children at play, they can also provide a good theme for creative writing.

One ingredient of skipping rhymes is the magical, almost riddle-like, quality which includes symbols and superstitions. Magic numbers – 3, 13, 7, 9 – abound, as do precious metals and stones – silver, gold, pearls, rubies and diamonds. Colours are often used and sometimes exotic places, as well as natural things like snow, trees, seasons. Birds which have a place in superstition, such as the robin, crow, raven, magpie and swan, also appear. All these occur in riddles and folk songs and are probably familiar to children.

Some discussion of the above ideas should act as a good preparation for writing, and a look at the Opies' book, *The Lore and Language of Schoolchildren*, will provide more examples. The children themselves can supply rhymes that they use and you may be able to look at these in some detail.

A poem by Alan Brownjohn called 'Skipping Rhyme' (which can be found in his *Collected Poems*[1]) takes many of the ideas I have mentioned, but adds another dimension. The first verse uses a pattern of words which is completely reversed in the last verse.

---

[1]Brownjohn, A. (1988), *Collected Poems*, Hutchinson

First verse   Paín of the leáf, ońe twó –
                 Woŕd of the stóne, threé foúr –
                 Foót óf the daŕk, pít óf the hańd
                 Heárt óf the clóud, fíve, síx and
                 OÚT!

Last verse   Ońe, twó, leáf of the páin
                 Threé, foúr, stóne of the wórd
                 Fíve, síx, daŕk of the fóot, hańd of the pít
                 Cloúd of the heárt, ańd
                 OÚT!

This is a good example of how to make words work for you and is more difficult to achieve than might appear. It is almost making each line into an anagram of itself, thus changing the meaning totally. The kind of words used is important and the exercise can lead children towards a better understanding of how words are put together for an idea as well as giving them a fascination with manipulating them.

— ◆ —

Skip Towards Death

Kill the seeds of life.
Eat them, eat them.
Destroy the brain of reason.
Confuse it, confuse it.
But let the hollow of death live.
Feed it.

Let the Devil mould it,
Then pass it on to man,
For man has got unlimited hate,
He will spread it if he can.

The seeds of life will kill,
They will eat you, eat you.
The reason of the brain
Will destroy you, confuse you.
But the hollow of life will bring death.
So starve it.

Donal Crawford

Zodiac Skipping Rhyme

Pisces caught two fish,
Aquarius caught none,
Gemini hit baby brother
And cooked the cakes for mum.

Seven gives me good luck,
Three gives me bad,
Five people in the rope,
First one's had.

Sagittarius hit a white goat,
Capricorn fell down dead,
Virgo went out hunting
And brought back Leo's head.

Three gives me good luck,
But seven gives me bad,
Five people in the rope,
First one's had.

Mary caught Cancer,
Cancer nipped the bull,
Taurus swallowed Scorpio
And Aries fooled them all.

Petra Coveney

Rhyme

When you throw a penny in the middle of a stone
Down comes a jelly bone.
No-one knows what I mean,
A penny in the stone
That's what I've seen.

Four is an unlucky number –
There are four ways out.
Don't even know which is the proper door.

Nine is a strange number –
When you throw the dice
You will lose the dime.

Thirteen is an incredible strange number –
You will be unlucky
When you walk through the forest.

Fifty is such a big number –
But I don't call it
Too much.

When you throw a penny in the middle of a stone
Down comes a jelly bone.
No-one knows what I mean,
A penny in the stone
That's what I've seen.

Lai Ling Leung

Skipping Rhyme

The corn grows,
Skip to it.
Its yellow lamps dazzle,
Pass it,
Don't tread it.
Let the crow peck the golden lamps.
Golden lamps, dirty, plain,
The scarecrow tired, forlorn,
The crows pull his straw out,
Then laugh.
The corn droops like a haggard woman,
Tread on it.
Out.

Jane Alden

Superstition

The waters were uneven,
The black and red ship 300 miles from land,
Death not far behind.
A sailor with a glass of sherry
Dipped in his finger to taste.
The one and only passenger
Rubbed his finger round the top of the glass.

Jane Alden

29

'THIRTEEN WAYS OF LOOKING

AT A BLACKBIRD'

To those who already know Wallace Stevens' 'Thirteen Ways of Looking at a Blackbird' (from his *Collected Poems*[1]) it will be obvious where the idea for this exercise originated. How many ways are there of looking at something? I suppose the answer to that question is there are as many as you can find.

The object, then, is that the children choose a subject and try to look at it from many different angles. I suggest six or more is the best to start with, although it is as well to discourage the too ambitious from attempting ninety-nine ways! On the other hand, that could be interesting.

Obviously this should stretch their imaginations and make them work for their poems. As with many of the other ideas in this book, this should encourage, indeed force, the children to examine their chosen subjects in far greater depth, which will be good practice for all their writing. The resulting flexibility of mind, and the ability to see things from different angles, cannot but help their approach to other things besides poetry.

— ◆ —

Six Ways of Looking at the Wind

The wind in the open
Tosses and hurls the leaves about the trees.

The wind in the mountains howls like hyenas
And wisps around the mountain tops.

---

[1]Stevens, W. (1984), *Collected Poems*, Faber and Faber

The wind in the trees,
Whirls around the birds' ears and blows in.
It winds itself in and out of their legs.

When the sun and the wind meet
They make shadows like people dancing, moving swiftly.
The rain comes and kills them.

The flag droops on the flagpole.
Suddenly the wind draws up its breath
The flag flies around gaily and shows the Union Jack.

The saltant wind drives up the steep walls
And goes in through open windows.
The windows bang shut and crack into a hundred pieces.

Steven Gregory

COMMUNAL

POEMS

The communal poem, as its title suggests, is one to which a number of people have contributed a line or a verse. This is a good method of involving a group of children and can be achieved in a number of ways.

Begin by choosing a subject for the poem and putting it at the top of a piece of paper. The paper is then passed round from child to child, each one in turn adding a line. All the lines will be related to the subject and may follow logically on from those preceding, or they may begin a new idea on the theme. The children find this fun and can all feel they have contributed a part of the final poem. The children can do this themselves as a group. The difference in styles can add to the texture, and one child's idea can often lead others on to exciting developments.

If this is done with a whole class, three or four different poems can be going round at the same time, or the class can be divided into groups to write separate ones. It can of course be done during a writing session as an extra while other things are being written. The children merely pause from their work to add their lines when the paper is passed to them.

— ◆ —

Light and Dark

Two separate forces that blend together,
The terror and joy of life.
The living of light and the death of dark.
Light jumps and dark crouches.
Light burns in the fire and dark lives in the ashes.
Light breaks and dark grows.
Light is a golden sound without sound,

Light moves silently and quickly, dark moves slowly and
    loudly.
A blanket of light, a blanket of dark,
Fight the other, one always wins in time.
A shadow is dark against the light,
Light is dark without the gusto.
The light brings hope and the dark brings sorrow,
Hand in hand they waltz the day away.
Light and dark blend to a shadow.

Written by children aged 10 years

Time

Slowly it passes by.
Some notice it, some do not.
Like a huge wheel rotating
It comes, leaves and is forgotten.
Everlasting,
Ever slowly,
There's never not a time.
Time kicks the hours away.
It goes fast when you're happy
And slowly when you're not,
Comes, goes, unnoticed.
Something never to be conquered,
Time the brother of infinity.
Dead or alive, time is still there.
It didn't start – it just is.
Through the sandglass time passes
Going backwards not forwards.
It goes slow but fast,
It flourishes past.
Time will never end
But lives its ticks away
And ticks away its life.

Written by children aged 10 years

Another variation on this is to have a large sheet of paper on the wall with a title at the top and a pen handy on a string. Any child at any time during the day/week can add a line to it. It is exciting to see it grow, the lines being added as, and when, the children feel like doing so. You could call this a kind of doodle or graffito poem.

A further very successful way of making a communal poem is to suggest a theme and give the first one or two lines, as in the example below. Some discussion may be necessary beforehand for this kind of poem. A list of possible subjects for each verse can be written on the board. The children then choose from this list and cross off the items as they are chosen. This will ensure that there is a variety of different verses for the final poem.

The children write short poems (about six or eight lines long); they can write more than one poem on different items. The best are collected together and arranged in an appropriate order to make a long poem. The children can do this themselves as a group. This poem will have a unity given to it by the repetition of the first line or lines and will, of course, relate to the overall title.

— ◆ —

Lumb Song

All of my attics used to sing:
Down the stairs, down the stairs
And down to the dark rooms
To see the rotting wools.
And the dusty smells of the old tattered mattresses.
Old statues and paintings show
Signs of pleasant work.

All of my windows used to sing:
Look through us, look through us,
Look, so our views are seen
And we do not get dusty.
Wash us so we are clean and fresh,
We do not care if you look in or out –
Only look, look.
If you do not look we will crack and mist.

All of my floorboards used to sing:
Walk upon me, walk upon me,
And I will creak with pleasure –
But just walk upon me, walk upon me.
Although I am old and dirty I still remain
And I will not collapse
Until my nails begin to bend,
So walk upon me, walk upon me.

All of my books used to sing:
Please read me,
Please read me –
Read me till my pages go ragged,
Read me till my story
Grows old.

All of my fireplaces used to shout:
Leave us alone, leave us alone.
We dislike being filled with rocks and dirt.
We do not like fire,
It burns our black friends, the chimneys.
We will burn the hand that puts the match to us.
Please leave us alone.

All of my cellars used to sing:
Come into me, come into me,
Collect my coal from my dim corners.
Come down my steep steps
And explore the dark rooms.
See the big spiders in their webs.
See the secret forgotten corners
Where the daring fairies play.

All of my windows used to sing:
Come look through us.
Come wipe the dusty old years away
And see through our glinting body.
Stare
At the open landscape.

All of my balconies used to sing:
Look out yonder to my valleys,

Look out yonder to my streams.
There you'll see the chickens feeding
And the trees rustling in the wind.
Water gliding
Slippery-slidey,
Stones and rocks,
Reeds and waterfalls.
My boney mountains,
My sweet valleys,
My crisp-cut cliffs
And my running streams.

All of my mountains used to say:
Study my rock:
Bring the geologist to research me,
My wildlife, my trees.
Bring the professor to protect me,
My jagged nooks.
Let the climber climb me and be proud to.
Bring life
For me to rejoice in.

Sharon Purves, Fiona Weir, Nicki Nathan, Nikola Powell, Donal Crawford,
Nicholas Brooks, Petra Coveney, Christina Young

(See also 'Worlds', page 159.)

Up On The

Downs

'Up On The Downs' is the title of a poem by Wes Magee and, apart from enjoying it for itself, I have found it very useful as a teaching tool and a stimulus for children's writing. The poem is written in three stanzas, each one an entity in itself and written to a pattern. It is this pattern which is particularly interesting and, in order to explain the process, I am reprinting the first stanza here.

— ◆ —

Up On The Downs

Up on the downs,
Up on the downs,
A skylark flutters
And the fox barks shrill,
Brown rabbit scutters
And the hawk hangs still,
Up on the downs,
Up on the downs,
With butterflies
   jigging
    like
      costumed clowns.

If we analyse the form of this poem, we find all sorts of techniques being used, and yet it has a simple appeal to which children readily respond. The children actually enjoy working out how the poem has been made and, if sufficient time is spent on doing this (without making it seem a chore – more like being a detective), when they come to write you will be surprised how much they are able to incorporate.

These are the techniques they might mention:

1 It has a strong rhythm (basically two heavy stresses per line).
2 There are repeated lines (1, 2, 7 and 8).
3 Rhyme is present (3 with 5; 4 with 6; 1, 2, 7, 8 with 10 – i.e. the final line).
4 The last line (10) contains a simile.
5 There is alliteration (hawk hangs; costumed clowns).
6 There is an example of consonance – close repetition of consonant sounds before, or after, different vowels (foX barKS).

The children do not need to know the proper terms in order to identify what is going on. They can hear and see the effects, especially if you help a little by emphasising certain characteristics when you read the poem out loud. This, in itself, is a good lesson in learning to train the ear.

What follows, as a writing exercise, is based on the techniques used in the poem, and it is up to each child to choose how many he or she wants to try to include in the work. The basic pattern of 10 lines (the last split over three), with 1, 2, 7 and 8 repeated, is for everyone to follow. After that it is up to the individual. This gives scope for pupils of all abilities to write something at their own level. Funnily enough, because the rhythm and music of the original can be felt, even if not intellectually understood, most children will have no difficulty in managing to include most, if not all, of the techniques. Only when you analyse the techniques do they seem complex. We all do many things naturally which, if we stopped to think about them, would probably seem far too complicated to attempt.

The following pieces arose from this stimulus, but teachers can use any appropriate poem as a model on which to base writing. You can even make up a short stanza (6–10 lines), including examples of language techniques you want the children to learn and practise. You could have a theme and collect all the stanzas written by the children on the same pattern together into a long communal poem.

For this exercise, various first lines were suggested and children were also encouraged to write their own. Here are some of the results, written by 9 and 10 year olds:

— ◆ —

Deep in a cave,
Deep in a cave,
A stalactite drips
And a stalagmite holds,
A rocky wall slips
And the air is cold,
Deep in a cave,
Deep in a cave,
While the bat
wings silent
like
a black bow tie.

Awake one night,
Awake one night,
I heard a dog bark,
A car's horn beep
In the moonlit park.
I tried to sleep.
Awake one night,
Awake one night,
The curtains
flapped
like
a ghost in flight.

Down by the stream,
Down by the stream,
Where the grass snake slithers
And the flowers shine,
A long branch withers
To a bony vine,
Down by the stream,

Down by the stream,
And the sun
still shines
like
thick white cream.

Out in space,
Out in space,
All is dark
And the earth looks small,
No sign or mark
Of anything at all,
Out in space,
Out in space,
You can
disappear
without
a trace.

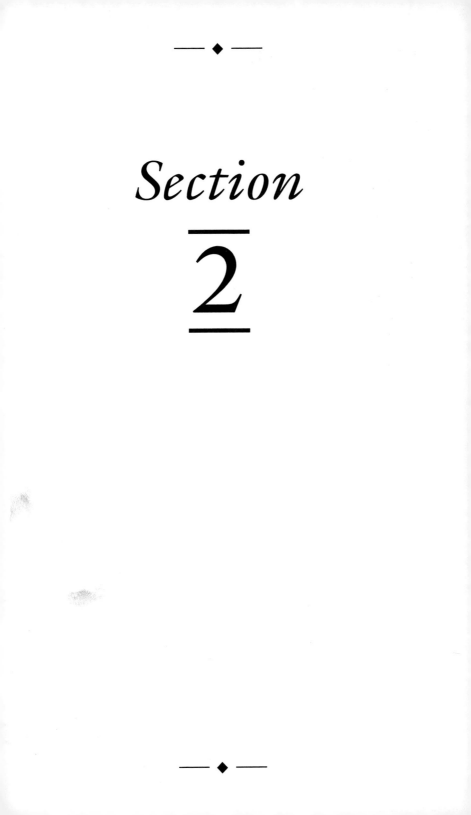

Section

2

32

Haiku

Haiku is a Japanese form which consists of three lines of 17 syllables. The first line has five syllables, the second seven and the third five. These haiku are small poems which somehow manage to say much more than would seem possible in so few words.

They are quite easy for children to write and are best described as small 'snapshots' which capture a moment and feeling and, if possible, can comment in a wider sense about life or the spirit of the subject. Because they are so short, all children can attempt them and feel successful (which is very important). The poems have an almost childlike simplicity, although to write a very good one is harder than it may appear. They can be illustrated and make a good display on the wall or in a book. Using school instruments, some children may also wish to compose short pieces of music to illustrate their poems. These pieces can be played as an accompaniment to a reading of the haiku (a useful idea for assemblies for those teachers who are obliged to arrange such things!).

To explain a syllable, equate it with a 'beat' in music and sound out some of the children's names – it is easiest to use the fingers of one hand to tap out the 'beats'. Although children will wish to have the correct number of syllables in each line – five, seven, five – I do not feel this to be absolutely necessary. The main object is to write short lines where every word counts. Children should be told to write about one thing only at a time, to concentrate their thoughts on their chosen idea and to describe it in such a way as to make it interesting and vivid to the reader.

— ◆ —

The goat eats this,	(4)
The goat eats that,	(4)
Brandishing his beard.	(5)

Michael Corti

A kingdom of birds,	(5)
The voice of wings fluttering,	(7)
A tune gathering.	(5)

Andrew Hall

The cup fills.	(3)
It lies on its side.	(5)
And bathes in lukewarm water.	(7)

Adam Lyne

Tramp

Sam is lying here	(5)
A silhouette of yellow dust.	(8)
This will be his home.	(5)

Louis Lyne

There are many examples of translations from the Japanese to be found in the *Voices*[1] and *Touchstones*[2] anthologies, and in *The Penguin Book of Japanese Verse*[3] edited by Anthony Thwaite and Geoffrey Bownas.

One of the great lessons to be drawn from writing haiku is that choosing words carefully, to express as much as possible, should be carried over into all writing. Here also is an opportunity to point out the importance of titles. I believe that, where possible, a title should add something to a poem and, with haiku, the extra syllables you can gain by giving a title can be very useful.

[1]Geoffrey Summerfield (*ed.*) (1968), *Voices*, Penguin
[2]Benton, M. and Benton, P. (*eds.*) (1987), *Touchstones*, Hodder & Stoughton
[3]Bownas, G. and Thwaite, A. (*eds.*) (1964), *The Penguin Book of Japanese Verse*, Penguin

33

TANKA

Tanka is another Japanese form of poem and is almost like an extension of the haiku. It has five lines of 31 syllables used in the following way: five, seven, five, seven and seven. Like haiku and cinquains (see Chapter 34) it limits the writer within the strict confines of the form and can serve the same useful purpose of making the children choose their words carefully to express 'much-in-little' as the Muskrat would say in *The Mouse and his Child*[1]!

With tanka it is probably more necessary to adhere to the form than it is with haiku, where I feel the children can be a little freer. An explanation of how to count syllables and perhaps one or two class efforts, or your own, would be enough to give them the idea, especially if they have already written some haiku, which I think would be advisable.

Tree

Swaying in the wind
I catch people's attention.
I begin to wave,
They never wave back to me.
I think nobody likes me.

Dominic Dowell

---

[1]Hoban, R. (1969), *The Mouse and his Child*, Rex Collings

Singing

I'm singing my song,
The words slipping through my lips
Meet their waiting ears,
Then fall into memory
To be whistled out again.

Matthew Festenstein

Across I travel,
Desolate and cold it is.
My shadow follows.
Just whistling to pass the time –
It helps when you're so lonely.

Christian Tattersfield

34

CINQUAINS

A cinquain is a short poem whose form was invented by an American poet with the memorable name of Adelaide Crapsey. It is a kind of English haiku or tanka and somehow fits our English rhythms better. The form of a cinquain is five lines of 22 syllables: two, four, six, eight and two. If the children are already familiar with counting syllables it will be very easy to introduce this new form to them; if not, see Chapter 32 on haiku. The short last line with only two syllables needs to make some impact. As with haiku and tanka, the limitations of the form force the children to use words carefully and to convey the meaning clearly. The lines can run on and it is often better if they do. The rhythm should be predominantly iambic (as in 'What *is* this *life* if *full* of *care*'), but this is not essential, and may only confuse the children if you insist on it.

Mr Death at the Door

Butler,
Open up for
It is Mr Death come
To see how well I am doing.
How kind!

Rebecca Bazeley

The Dreamer

Dreamer,
What do you see
In that pot of dreams you
Hold? I see nothing you can't see
But you.

Rebecca Bazeley

Barbershop Quartet

I saw
Four alley cats
Sitting in tin dustbins
And banging the lids together
Loudly.

Callum Crawford

The Trees

I saw
Two old oak trees
Playing with a ball. One
Threw it in the other's branches
And laughed.

Jane Alden

News Flash

News Flash:
An elephant
Was seen walking over
The queen at Buckingham Palace.
She died.

Anthony Wakefield

Short Form

Extensions

As an obvious extension to the work on the three short syllabic forms (haiku, tanka and cinquains), longer poems can be written using one of the forms as the stanza (or verse) pattern. Once children have practised, and become familiar with, each form, they can choose one to provide a framework for a more sustained poem. Renga is one such framework based on the haiku, although it has the added complication of requiring links between each stanza. However, there are other, more straightforward, forms/ways of helping children to write at some length with confidence, working from the secure base of a known and mastered form. Using these forms dispenses with the need to make decisions about layout on the page – often a very real problem that is not always appreciated by teachers – and frees children to concentrate on the content of their poems. It also enables them to enjoy the feeling of achievement when they 'pull off' a longer poem than is perhaps usual for them at this stage of their development.

The following are three examples of what can be done, one for each of the short syllabic forms featured in the previous chapters. Notice that an overall theme or subject which is itself a pattern can often help children to organise their thoughts. Patterns such as the rainbow, the four seasons, days of the week, months of the year, and numbers 1–7, are frequently useful in offering a framework to start children thinking.

— ◆ —

Haiku Rainbow

A red glow sunset
Stretches across the horizon,
Fading from our sight.

An orange car light
Flashes as it turns the corner,
Getting splashed by mud.

The yellow desert,
Tiring to walk through, is as
Golden as the sun.

A cool green meadow
Has cows under an oak tree,
And poppies dotted about.

The bluest of skies
Is above me, clear and fresh
With a gleaming sun.

An indigo skirt
Hangs lightly around my legs
As I run through trees.

Under a birch tree
Stands a bunch of violets
Swaying in the breeze.

Carolyn Deller (PH)

Grandma (Tanka)

She sat quietly:
Grandma was knitting for us,
Red woollen jumpers
To wear to a party feast
With our new special trousers.

Seventy-two years
Grandma has lived happily
Enjoying her life,
Except when Grandpa was ill
With a serious fever.

Now Grandpa has died,
She dreams every night of him.
But during the day
She thinks of her grandchildren.
Grandma is part of our life.

Y5/6 group (BYW)

The Sea (Cinquains)

The sea
Has waves that flow
In glist'ning ripples on
The sandy beach and break upon
The rocks.

Pebbles
Run in and out
With every wave that comes.
Seaweed swishes and clings on to
Your feet.

The shells
Lie where the sea
Begins, and when the tide
Goes out they sink into the soft
Wet sand.

Y5/6 group (BYW)

NAGA-UTA

The naga-uta is another Japanese form based on syllables. This form, however, is much longer than haiku or tanka and is more suited to a lyric poem. There is no set number of lines and the poem can be as long as you like. Each line contains a particular number of syllables – either five or seven – and these alternate throughout until the end when you finish on two seven-syllable lines. Teachers familiar with haiku and tanka will recognise the syllable pattern: haiku – five, seven, five and tanka – five, seven, five, seven, seven. The nagu-uta, then, is a logical step on from the other two forms, and children who have had practice in them will enjoy the chance to write at greater length in a pattern they already know.

— ◆ —

Shadow

I wish I could be
Set free from my shadow and
Be able to do
The things that please me to do.
Black weird replica
Of myself, imitating
My every move, I
See you silhouetted on
The wall, the ground, and
The grass. It is myself that
Is seen, leering in
Monstrous positions, sometimes
Long, then sometimes short.
But now it is dark and my

Shadow is gone for
One more night; only until
Light comes for another day,
Only to follow
And twist my body into
Weird grotesque forms yet again.

Rosie Roche

RENGA

This is a Japanese form of poem based on haiku – a seventeen-syllable poem in three short lines containing five, seven and five syllables respectively. Renga, as I understand it, is a series of linked haiku. The second haiku takes as its subject something touched on in the first. The third deals with something mentioned in the second, and so on, creating a sort of chain of thoughts linking one haiku with the next. The final haiku (we make it the seventh) has to try to draw together in its three lines all the themes of the previous six. This is the hard part, needless to say.

I have tried writing renga in two ways, one more successful than the other. Firstly, it lends itself to a communal effort where each person writes a first haiku and then passes the paper on to the next person. The second haiku is then written and the papers passed on. This is repeated until the seventh has been completed. Seven people will have had a hand in writing these renga, which can be extremely interesting. It does, however, make writing the seventh one very difficult. I cannot honestly say I have had much success with this approach with children.

The second way seems to be better, where each child writes his or her own complete renga. Whether or not you consider the following suggestion to be a cheat, it is actually easier sometimes to write the seventh haiku first and work backwards. I do not see anything wrong in this approach, but purists may differ. As an exercise I feel it is very valuable but should not be attempted before the children are familiar with, and practised in writing, haiku. (A fuller explanation of haiku can be found in Chapter 32, page 145.) Any subject should be suitable, but it is perhaps easier to choose an overall theme (e.g. time, cats, food, the seasons) to run through the poem. Each haiku can then concentrate on specific examples which interlock, one verse with the next.

— ◆ —

Renga

Perpetually ticks
Catching the moments of time,
The clock's hands move on.

The car moving on
Towards its destination
Of a place unknown.

Shrouded in darkness
Warriors knock at the door.
When will they come out?

The door made of oak
Has seen many visitors,
Some arrived at night.

In a veil of
Darkness a murder is done,
Mystery all round.

The man is prostrate
Stabbed to the heart, memories
Have caught up with him.

Messenger of fate,
The memories have murdered,
The clock is the cause.

Robert Northcott (YWW)

38

COUNTING

SYLLABLES

Before introducing children to the idea of writing poems to certain syllable counts it is advisable for them to have attempted haiku, tanka and cinquains, probably in that order. They will then be more familiar with writing to a syllabic pattern and will be ready to experiment with their own systems.

In advising them of the possibility of setting themselves a form based on syllables you are really giving them the idea of a self-imposed discipline, encouraging them to experiment with their own forms. The ten-syllable line is an obvious one to suggest to the children, but thereafter I feel they should be left to find their own line lengths, the rhythms and patterns that suit them individually.

With the ten-syllable line I am not talking specifically of iambic pentameter whose particular rhythm is quite difficult for children to grasp at first and should not be imposed. However, it is possible to ask for poems of ten-syllable lines and many children will find this rewarding. They will even write some iambic pentameters, as the rhythm is natural to many. At this point I should say that none of these forms ought to be considered as lessons in themselves; they are merely tools and frames for fashioning creative ideas. The ideas come first!

The following example is a communal poem written by ten-year-old children, each having started with the same first line (my own) as a way in and a link between verses. Each line has ten syllables.

— ◆ —

Worlds

I have long walked in worlds unknown to you
Where landscapes start and finish in the same
Instant. Where seas flow over cracking ground,
Where whirlpools swallow and store knowledge which
Is attacked by parched thoughts and where logic
Can barely defend its own sanity.

I have long walked in worlds unknown to you
Where red floods cascade down tunnels of blue.
This is my globe, this is my paradise,
Yes mine, and it belongs to no-one else.

I have long walked in worlds unknown to you.
Birds fly through broken sunbeams in the mist,
Flowers are born with legs and arms to live.
A sky boat that moves with a breath of wind,
A person swims through the sea on a bird.

I have long walked in worlds unknown to you
Where the moon sweeps across the sky at night,
Where the sun rockets through the clouds at noon,
The world no-one has ever stepped upon
Apart from me. I rather disliked worlds.

I have long walked in worlds unknown to you
Where the rain does not fall to break the day,
Where the rays of sun burn up the days,
Where life will not die for sadness or good,
Because life is both – they live together.

I have long walked in worlds unknown to you
Where no creature has set foot before me,
Where moonlight is day and sunlight is night
And the stars are teeth in a gaping mouth.
Where the mountain river sings like a bird.
But I am old, these worlds have long been dead.

I have long walked in worlds unknown to you
Where the cock crows at the pitch of the black
And where the exit of peace now lies dead.
The day never comes and where men lived,

It is no longer a world but a mass.
The towers that stood fell into decay.
The money that was saved was the world's death.

I have long walked in worlds unknown to you
Where song has died and colour's fallen out
Away to a place where blue means nothing.
I have been in the happy worlds of peace,
But the worlds of peace died so very soon.
From that peace came war, the one of darkness,
The king of the black world beneath our mind –
He always conquers in these lands of mind.

I have long walked in worlds unknown to you
Where the sun is covered with sheets of black.
It took a hundred years until I came
Past the Atlantic through the seven seas.
I may be old but this world serves me right,
This earth is dark and grey and so remains.
There are no beams of light just disaster.
You shall not age because there is no pace.

Orson Nava, Callum Crawford, Richard Packer, Julie Howson, Michael Hales,
Rebecca Bazeley, David Bailey, Matthew Festenstein, Darrol Kenworthy

(See also Chapter 45, page 181.)

Here are a few examples of other poems which contain lines of
nine, eight, or seven syllables. I have noticed that these three
numbers seem to be particularly popular for line lengths and
provide certain rhythmic patterns which children seem to use
naturally. It may be noticed that some of the eight-syllable lines
fall naturally into the iambic meter. For example:

- – I saw a hundred flaming guards
- – I saw the sky alight with fire
- – I saw a lioness give birth
- – Where shadows are a man's best friend
- – The stage returned its life once more

I wonder whether this links up with song rhythms, particularly
folk songs, written in 4/4 time?

— ◆ —

What Casca Saw

I saw a hundred ghastly women	(9)
Piled on one another.	(6)
I saw a hundred flaming guards	(8)
Marching towards the Capitol.	(8)
I saw the sky alight with fire	(8)
Spitting and crackling in its hearth.	(8)
I saw a lioness give birth	(8)
To twenty cubs or more.	(6)
I saw it raining blood this night,	(8)
Could it belong to Caesar?	(7)

Rebecca Bazeley

Anonymous

A warning to all the red waters	(9)
That have been bleached by the sun,	(7)
Black horizons on still waters.	(8)
I am a victim of this time	(8)
Where shadows are a man's best friend,	(8)
Where your home is your graveyard	(7)
As it is mine.	(4)
This is the way I now speak	(7)
On a stone slab above me.	(7)

Miles Greene

The Return

The dawn rose as the shadow returned,	(9)
The bare area came in sight.	(8)
The stage returned its life once more,	(8)
The masked area became unmasked	(9)
As the shadow had returned its share.	(9)

Catriona Ferguson

39

EPITAPHS

There are many examples of epitaphs in a number of poetry anthologies (notably *The Faber Book of Epigrams and Epitaphs*[1] edited by Geoffrey Grigson), and many of them are amusing. They either comment on the person's life, the character, the profession or the manner of death, and often incorporate a play on words.

Here lies one who for medicine would not give
A little gold, and so his life he lost:
I fancy now he'd wish again to live
Could he but guess how much his funeral cost

Anon.

Fleet Street Epitaph

Go tell our master, all you passers by,
That here, obedient to his laws, we lie.

On King Charles the Second

Here lies our Sovereign Lord the King,
Whose word no man relies on;
Who never said a foolish thing,
Nor ever did a wise one.

John Wilmot, Earl of Rochester

---

[1]Grigson, G. (*ed.*) (1974) *The Faber Book of Epigrams and Epitaphs*, Faber and Faber

A good exercise is for the children to write epitaphs for a type of person or a well-known character (fictional characters can be included). As many examples as possible should be read to the class before they begin, to illustrate the nature of epitaphs. Discussion of the various ways they might use to begin their poems might also be helpful. For example, 'Here lies . . . ', 'Beneath this ground/stone/earth . . . ', 'Beneath your feet . . . '

One of the problems that arises here is that of rhyme: most epitaphs rhyme. If you have not encouraged rhyme, it may be necessary to discuss its use with the children in order to prevent the really silly things that they can present you with. It may be that you will wish to delay this idea until rhymes, internal rhymes, and near rhymes have been dealt with and the children have more experience in using them. (See Chapter 47, page 189).

Grave Words

Here he lies in sleep –
He does not snore.

Alex Gollner

To a Chess Champion

Here lies a chess player,
He's played his last game,
For he who you walk upon
Has been checkmated again.

Matthew Festenstein

To a Dustman

Here he lies this poor chap,
Been cleaning since a kid.
He was really quite all right
Until he flipped his lid.

Matthew Festenstein

CLERIHEWS

I have not included the humorous verse form, the limerick, in this book, since I believe it is probably well known enough, if only through Edward Lear's examples. Personally, I do not enjoy Lear's limericks very much, my preference being for limericks with a punchline at the end that is different from the opening line. I also believe that, with a few honourable exceptions, the best limericks are unrepeatable in polite society. It stands to reason, therefore, that I do not feel that children are capable of getting the most out of this form in the classroom (in the playground, maybe). However, many teachers' sole contribution to poetry consists of asking their classes to write limericks. Perhaps they can be tempted away from this practice by another, less well known, humorous form – the clerihew.

Clerihews are named after their inventor – Edmund Clerihew Bentley. W H Auden enjoyed the form and wrote a book of them, called *Academic Graffiti*[1].

Clerihews are short – just four lines long – and rhyme as two couplets, i.e. a, a, b, b. They are biographical quatrains, normally about a famous person whose name usually occurs in the first line. Lines vary in length, and this provides much of the vehicle for injecting the humour. The content offers a potted biography of the subject, often containing a witty or moral reflection on an element of the person's fame or notoriety. Clerihews are fun to write, but they are a little more difficult than might at first appear – certainly for children. Some research may be necessary into the background of a subject; at any rate, factual knowledge is required in order to compose a clerihew. I feel that they

---

[1]Auden, W.H. (1967), *Academic Graffiti*, Faber

provide a better training ground for children's future writing
than limericks, at this stage.

Edmund Clerihew Bentley
Evidently
Was a poet –
And don't we know it.

Noushin Sorayyapour (**BYW**)

William Shakespeare
Began on a career
Of writing plays,
Which seldom ever pays.

BYW group

Robert Maxwell died
And was washed up on the tide,
Which then turned
At least as far as the Mirror pensioners were concerned.

BYW group

William Tell
Was a brilliant shot which was just as well.
As an extra boon
He got a snazzy theme tune.

I am writing some bootiful clerihews
About that kiev-eating, turkey-basting Bernard Matthews.
For that village-idiot expression he's got
He should be shot.

Calum Roche (**BYW**)

IAMBICS

When children do an exercise aimed at introducing or improving a technique of writing poetry, inevitably, in many cases, much of the spontaneity is lost. But if they wish to improve their handling of words and to add depth to their poetry, it is essential that they should learn the craft of writing. Far from being a limitation in a bad sense, the use of various techniques can, in time, provide a release to the creative processes of the mind and produce better work. When the children are accustomed to differing forms they will find that what they want to say will somehow select its own form when they come to writing it down.

However, as with any other discipline, it is necessary to practise the techniques in order to understand their possibilities (and limitations) and to become thoroughly versed in how to use them. Therefore, although it may seem a little forced to introduce a technique for its own sake, it will lead to better things. It is like playing scales or learning tables – a certain degree of satisfaction is obtained from being able to do it and a great deal of useful knowledge is assimilated without which the children will never progress.

One of the ingredients of poetry is rhythm, and there are many different types of accepted rhythms quite apart from one's own personal rhythm, which everybody has. (Finding it is another thing!) One of the forms which interests me and which I find slightly more adaptable and easier on the ear, is writing in iambics.

The rhythm of iambics can be illustrated as follows:

Whĕn Í | dŏ cóunt | thĕ clóck | thăt télls | thĕ tíme

Thĕy flée | frŏm me | thăt some | time dĭd | me séek

These two lines are in iambic pentameters, which means they have *five* feet, as shown by the dividing lines (rather like bars in music). Each foot contains two syllables, the first weak (unstressed) and the second strong (stressed). The rhythm is best felt by reading the lines aloud. This is the rhythm used for sonnets. Iambic comes from the Greek ιαμβικοζ meaning 'limping'.

T̆was bríll | ĭg ánd | thĕ slí | thy tóves

Hăd wé | bŭt wórld | ĕnough | ănd time

These lines have only four feet but are written in iambic rhythm. They are iambic tetrameters. You can find many examples of poems written in iambics which can be used as illustrations when introducing this form to children. You will notice often that small deviations occur in the rhythm of a predominantly iambic poem, and this is good to point out to children. It shows, as with any technique, that when you have mastered it, you can legitimately afford to 'play around' with it to a certain extent. Sometimes it is necessary to vary the rhythm just a little to avoid a monotony of pace or to achieve a dramatic effect. If it feels and sounds right, it should be acceptable.

Since iambic rhythm corresponds fairly naturally with English speech patterns, this exercise is not too difficult. When used well, iambic rhythm can be reasonably unobtrusive and easier to write in than some of the more 'plonking' rhythms that people still sometimes associate with 'real poetry'.

One way of helping the children feel the rhythm is to spend a short time when everyone tries to speak only in iambics. This can be fun, and after a very short while it soon becomes difficult to speak in any other way. This will help to ensure that the children are 'steeped' in the rhythm and understand how to use it.

Another point worthy of mention is to encourage the children to run the lines on, i.e. not make each line an entity of meaning in itself. This will vary the feeling of the rhythm and help to

relieve the pattern. An example of what is meant here can be
seen in the first poem below.

I held him in my hand, his body limp
And shaking, a cat watching all my moves.

The first line runs on naturally into the second. Punctuation can
also be used for this effect.

The Dead Bird

I held him in my hand, his body limp
And shaking, a cat watching all my moves.
I buried him, dead in his garden grave
Where rain had fallen on his stone cold corpse
Like tears of crystal from an unknown friend.
I placed him in the grave and covered him
With soil – a lolly stick to mark the place.

Lucy Tizard (YWW)

The Strange Man

His will had said
To burn the bed,
To burn the chest
And all the rest.

The people said 'We disagree,
You must send it to charity.'
But the lawyer's word is good enough
And so they had to burn the stuff.

I watched the fire burning,
And the fire slowly turning,
For the creature of the air
Had claws to scratch and tear.

It reached out to devour me,
As if to show its mockery
The fire gave a bubbling roar,
Then it was black, and was no more.

Nicholas Midgley

Untitled

But I am always walking in the rain
To wash away all sighs and hopes of joy
And stamp out all the time I spent with you.
The sorrows cloud around me as I think,
Thinking of days when we prevented tears
But now the crying pain pours down on me
And slowly shrinks my heart to the size of yours.

Hedy-anne Goodman (YWW)

If I Should Die Before I Wake

If I should die before I wake
I leave my will to all of you.
My money and my profit take
But do not take more than you're due.

If I should die before I wake,
Take my home and take my land;
Share everything as I would wish
As it is written by my hand.

If I should die before I wake
I shall be free from all of you,
I do not care what you do now
For all my mortal days are through.

Nadya Kassam (YWW)

Death

If only sleep would come and with it peace
My mind would rest and bring me thankful dreams,
Yet all I do is twist and turn, I burn
With fever. Friends are gathered by my bed
Like vultures crouching here to watch me die,
Their claws are grasping, eyes alight with greed.
The room around me seems to spin with fear.
The door admits a blackness, shadowed death,
For is not shadow merely death's own slave
To clasp me close, to take me to the grave?

Megan Trudell (YWW)

Seashore

She crouched amongst the mounting hoards
Of seaweed, wood and cut rope cords,
Of white eyed fish washed on the beach
And bobbing buoys beyond her reach.
Her chubby hand lifted to feel
The battered boat's rough bite of steel
And felt around the water cool
Depressions made by the rock pools.
And feeling past the water's face
Her hand felt crabs in hard shell case,
And as she let her hand hang free
Her gaze flew out across the sea.

Tilly Ballantine (**YWW**)

PANTOUMS

The pantoum is a Malay verse form introduced into English by the poet Austin Dobson. It is a series of quatrains (four-line stanzas), usually rhyming a, b, a, b. Each quatrain is interlinked with the previous one, as the second and fourth lines of one are repeated as the first and third lines of the next. In the final stanza, the first and third lines of the very first quatrain become the second and fourth lines, but in reverse order: thus the poem begins and ends with the same lines. It is constantly amazing how often the predetermined last stanza comes neatly together and works well. If this sounds complicated, a look at the examples below should make everything clear, and the form is quite within the capabilities of Y6 children and above. Younger children can also produce something on this pattern if they work in groups or as a class with their teacher.

It is an extremely satisfying form to work in, particularly because half the work is done for you, as it were. For example, in a pantoum of five quatrains (twenty lines), you only need to write ten lines: with all the interlinking repetitions, this will provide the required twenty lines. Rhyming can be difficult, at least at first, so it is advisable to forget about it initially. If children become proficient at handling the rest of the form they can try rhyming pantoums later. One interesting exercise, arising from the repetition, is to try to use the repeated lines in different ways. This is most often achieved by varying the punctuation, as can be seen in some of the examples. This can provide very practical evidence of the importance of punctuation, and its role in the creative process.

Unrhymed Pantoums

— ◆ —

The Storm

The lightning struck at the tree
And the tree fought back in rage,
But the threat of the fire was too strong,
The oak leaves shrivelled to ash.

And the tree fought back in rage,
It trembled and cried with pain.
The oak leaves shrivelled to ash,
The trunk was split apart.

It trembled and cried with pain,
Its roots shook under the ground,
The trunk was split apart
And splinters blew away.

Its roots shook under the ground,
They shivered in the cold
And splinters blew away
Into the electric air.

They shivered in the cold
But the threat of the fire was too strong.
Into the electric air
The lightning struck at the tree.

Y5/6 group (BYW)

The Poppy Meadow

Out in the field where poppies grow
A butterfly settles on a lavender bush.
The night air is warm and damp
As the insect flutters its wings.

A butterfly settles on a lavender bush
And the sparrow perches, ready to roost.
As the insect flutters its wings
The sparrow squawks a melancholy cry.

And the sparrow perches, ready to roost
While the nightingale sings and shadows grow long.
The sparrow squawks a melancholy cry,
Then all is silent for a while.

While the nightingale sings and the shadows grow long
There is the sound of footsteps.
Then all is silent for a while
Till the moon penetrates through the cloud.

There is the sound of footsteps.
The night air is warm and damp
Till the moon penetrates through the cloud
Out in the field where poppies grow.

Rebecca Ireland (PH)

Rhymed Pantoum

The trees were marching on the town
To take revenge for woods long gone.
They came to claim their rightful crown;
Though some were dead, they still pressed on

To take revenge for woods long gone.
Heartened by the drumming beat
Though some were dead, they still pressed on.
Their battle cries turned up the heat,

Heartened by the drumming beat.
Their sharpened roots caused untold pain.
Their battle cries turned up the heat
And fearing fire, their only bane,

Their sharpened roots caused untold pain.
Deadly bullets did no harm
And fearing fire, their only bane,
They skirted areas of alarm.

Deadly bullets did no harm,
They came to claim their rightful crown,
They skirted areas of alarm –
The trees were marching on the town.

Y7 group (BYW)

RONDELETS

A rondelet is a traditional poetic form and means a 'little rondel'. Like all the other rondel forms, e.g. rondeau, roundel, etc., it contains repeated lines or refrains, much as a rondo in music has a recurring tune. This structure is short and manageable for top primary children (and older) and can provide an enjoyable challenge. Like all established forms, it provides a framework for ideas and makes the writer work to express them, thereby ensuring that each word has been properly considered before being written down. The final poem has then been crafted, an experience which will bear fruit in the future. Too often children can be easily satisfied by the first thoughts that come into their heads. Having to grapple with the demands of a strict form can give them the vital practice and teach them to be self-critical over their choice of language.

Inevitably, doing such an exercise takes somewhat longer than a straightforward freeflow type of writing. But poetry should be different from prose, and one obvious way it differs is that it manages to say things in a more succinct way. Rather than trying to understand the theory of this, I am convinced that we learn by doing. That is why I introduce different poetic forms at intervals because they train the mind to operate in this way. It can be quite remarkable, considering the exigences of some forms, how fluently and easily some results read, though the writer may have agonised over individual words and lines to fit them to the form. Even if the final poem does not completely work, the time spent on it is far from wasted (this goes for every writing session). All practice is worthwhile and keeps the mind in trim, and sooner or later everything will come together in a successful piece. Nobody could expect to run a mile in under four minutes without training, and the same goes for writing (and any other discipline too).

THE FORM

The rondelet has seven lines, with lines 1, 3 and 7 being exactly the same. This is always encouraging to a writer, because there are fewer lines to write! Only two rhymes are used: children should be warned to choose these carefully so that they allow themselves plenty of scope. For example, there are more words that rhyme with 'see' than with 'up'. The rhyme scheme is as follows: A-b-A-a-b-b-A. The capital A means that the rhyme is exactly the same word – these are the repeated lines. The examples below will make all clear. The rhythm should be iambic – (ˇ ´ ˇ ´ , the 'limping' rhythm, as in dĭ-dúm, dĭ-dúm) and lines 1, 3 and 7 have two feet, while lines 2, 4, 5 and 6 have four. (See also Chapter 41 on iambic rhythm.)

The first example below is a communal effort done as a class on the board: I have marked the feet to show the rhythm. I suggest that, depending on the age of the children, it might first of all be a good idea to work on an example together so that everyone has a good grounding in the form before beginning an individual piece.

Wĕ're bý thē séa,
Thē waves arĕ bréakĭng oń thē rŭcks,
Wĕ're bý thē séa.
Thē gúlls swŏop dowń expĕćtańtly
Tŏ snátch thē fĭsh arŏúnd thē dŏcks,
Thē báthĕrs ráid thĕir pícnĭc bóx.
Wĕ're bý thē séa.

I caught a wave
While I was swimming in the sea,
I caught a wave,
It slipped away – I could not save
The water's ripple. Cautiously
I stalked a crab. It stared at me –
I caught a wave.

— ◆ —

Guy Fawkes' Night Bonfire

The smoke rose high.
It caught the wind and spiralled round,
The smoke rose high.
The fire leaped up to the sky
And in the flames the guy was drowned,
His head with burning twigs was crowned.
The smoke rose high.

Mary Noble

Snow

The soft snow fell,
It made the whole world dazzling white.
The soft snow fell,
Freezing the water in the well
Transformed the whole world in a night,
When morning came and all was bright.
The soft snow fell.

Edith Rogers-England

Rain

The black cloud burst,
The sound of thunder faintly heard,
The black cloud burst.
The patter of rain coming first
The image of the birds was blurred,
The leaves upon the ground were stirred.
The black cloud burst.

Luke Townsend

Bird

There she flies
Across the open muddy glade,
There she flies,
Hears echoes of her lonely cries.
With bits of leaves and twigs she played
And in her nest an egg was laid.
There she flies.

Taryn Youngstein

OTTAVA RIMA

Ottava rima is another short form – eight lines – which is written to a set rhyme scheme (a, b, a, b, a, b, c, c) in iambic pentameter (five feet), each one an iamb (one unstressed syllable followed by a stressed syllable). (See Chapter 41 for further explanation of iambic rhythm.) The ottava rima was invented in Italy in the fourteenth century and was used by Boccaccio. It is better known in English as the form employed by Byron in his long poem 'Don Juan'. Byron developed the satirical possibilites of the form, and we now tend to think of ottava rima as an opportunity to mock institutions and people.

A short form like this is an ideal way of letting children explore what they can do with rhyme and rhythm combined. However, ottava rima should not be attempted until children are well practised in other short forms, and also in using rhyme and iambic rhythm separately. Of the examples that follow, the first two are in the tradition of the more light-hearted approach with a hidden 'bite', while the third is altogether more serious. As with most poems written in iambic pentameter, there are occasional deviations from the strict ten syllables.

— ◆ —

We're Getting There

The five-fifteen from Glasgow is delayed,
The passengers on board are not informed.
The train guards aren't what you would call well-paid
And we are told the system's been reformed!
Those who have no tickets aren't afraid
And every small mistake's been pre-performed,
But now the Citizen's Charter is in place
It's better than a slap in the face.

David Stallibrass (BYW)

The ritual summer water fight is near –
A world of espionage, counter attacks,
When battle-hardened troops persevere
In chucking water down each other's backs.
Until the killjoy teachers interfere,
We soak each other through like maniacs,
Except the one who hides behind the wall
And doesn't see the point of it at all.

BYW group

Rape, Murder, Arson

I hear many news headlines read –
Families weep tears of anguish,
Their daughters either raped or dead,
Somebody they care for, they cherish.
I hear many news headlines read –
The firemen cannot extinguish
The burnt-out, treasured, private place;
The arsonist won't show his face.

Noushin Sorayyapour (BYW)

SONNETS

If anyone had suggested to me a few years ago that I might have eleven-year-old children writing sonnets I should have laughed at the idea. However, after teaching the same group of children for two years, I found they had progressed so far, and their enthusiasm was so great, that I decided to try them on sonnets as an experiment.

I felt the lesson required a more lengthy build-up than usual so I wrote out two of the more accessible Shakespearean sonnets on the board – 'When I do count the clock that tells the time' and 'My mistress' eyes are nothing like the sun'. We looked at them one at a time.

I read the sonnet and explained any difficulties of meaning, but principally asked the children to explain what it was about. When this was done, I asked them what they noticed about the form. Since by now they knew quite a lot about poetry, they were quickly able to spot the rhyme scheme and the ten-syllable lines. I then explained the rhythm of each line by marking the feet in the usual way – ˘ / ˘ / ˘ / ˘ / ˘ / – and by tapping the rhythm while speaking the lines. We enjoyed a short period of time trying to speak to each other solely in iambic pentameters, which made something of a game out of fixing the rhythm in their minds. They had to be steeped in the rhythm in order to be able to escape its constraints and concentrate on what they wanted to say when it came to writing.

I then told them of some different sonnet rhyme schemes. They were able to choose which type of sonnet they would write, and I gave them a free choice of subject. This particular group were never short of ideas for their writing, so I did not always prepare a subject. With many groups it may be necessary to talk around a particular idea.

Here are three examples of completed sonnets by these top primary children: all of them used the Shakespearean form. I would say that it was a valid exercise, although some of the spontaneity is missing at times; but it was a difficult task! All the children enjoyed doing it although, by the very nature of the work involved, not all managed to complete their sonnets.

They may never write another sonnet in their lives, but I feel this lesson was worth doing. It opened up a further influence on their work and it certainly made them think hard about words, especially rhymes which, at their reasonably advanced state of development in poetry, they were not content to use to the detriment of their poems. A large amount of re-working was constantly going on to try to make the lines right rhythmically; the rhymes worked, and above all the poems said what they wanted to say.

The Four Men

The man approached the place of the four men.
You come to take my sleep? said the sleeper,
I do not want your sleep, so sleep again.
You come to take my food? said the eater,
I do not want your food, I have enough.
Do you come for my thoughts? said the thinker,
I do not want your thoughts, your thoughts may bluff.
Do you come for my drink? said the drinker,
I have no thirst so drink all that you can.
I am the joker and I come to fool,
I shall keep joking as when life began.
I'll take your heart and stuff it till it's full,
I'll take your brains and carve them with my knife,
And what I come for, I shall steal – your life.

Darrol Kenworthy

Sonnet

Hundreds of people shouting to the world,
Too many speeches to let people breathe,
Too many hopes in vicious flags unfurled.
Eventually for blood they all will seethe
And war and bombs will start to smother us.
And on Death's pillow which will be uplifted
You'll see without regalia or fuss,
How we the nations civilised have drifted
To dust and hell upon this arid plain.
But from this desert new races will grow
And godliness and peace will live again,
Live men not dead machines will reap and sow.
Then they shall learn to love one another
And so to curse the man who hates his brother.

Matthew Festenstein

Sonnet I

The tramp has walked these many weary miles
And now lies down to rest in a hayloft
On bales of hay that lie stacked into piles
Put by the road. The hay feels very soft.
Through London and the country he has been,
Sleeping in the alleys and the street
And in old houses he by chance had seen,
But every kind of weather he would greet.
His ragged coat shows many signs of wear,
His once white trousers show up mud and grit,
Around his head hang strands of lank, black hair,
A cigarette is in his mouth unlit.
As night came down the next day looks like rain,
But in the morning he moves on again.

Timothy Cousins

(See also 'True Love', Chapter 70.)

METAPHORS

AND SIMILES

The difference between a simile and a metaphor is that a simile says a thing is *like* something else, and a metaphor says it *is* something else. Both demand that the user takes the creative step of putting together two very disparate ideas.

Similes are easier to deal with first as the children will probably be familiar with such sayings as – 'as like as two peas in a pod', 'as black as coal' or 'as cold as ice'. Discussion of some of these can serve two useful functions. Firstly, the children will become aware of the use of language to compare two things, and, secondly, it can be pointed out that many of these sayings are rather limited, not to say overused now. The way is then open for children to make their own comparisons on a more imaginative level. Some of them may have done this already in their writing and it is useful to quote from their own work. They should be told the word 'simile' as they always enjoy knowing the correct term, and it can lend weight, in their eyes, to the work they are doing. It may be a good idea to have a specific subject or object about which they can think in some detail.

When the idea of using similes is first introduced, you often find that the children overdo them, but this does not matter. They will learn to use this technique in moderation in later work.

— ◆ —

Birds

Around me, beside me, inside my head,
Yellow beaked, black beaked, pin tipped eyes,
On that sea-bleached horizon in the sky,
Coming like deadly bees swarming from their hive.

Miles Greene

The Fingerprint

As it starts in the centre,
As it grows from in to out,
As a stone into the water
The shape becomes its size
Like a tree with its lines.

Stephen Buechner

Pond

Nothing stirred,
Only the reflections shivering in the wind
And the slime oozing its way to the edges.
A drooping branch hung
Like a dead man from a gibbet.
At the bottom
Long fallen leaves lay still
Like a forgotten cemetery.

Dominic Dowell

Fish

Fish,
Darting through the current,
Like arrows to a dartboard
Jabbing at the waves.

Jenny Tuffrey

Metaphors are a logical extension of the simile. It takes a rather
bigger mental leap to say a thing *is* something else, but in the
end I find metaphors more exciting. Children are quite capable
of making this leap, and a good way of helping them is to play
the Furniture Game set out in Chapter 2. It might also help to
take specific objects and see if the children can make them into
metaphors for other things. A fine example of this is the
following poem by an eleven-year-old boy:

Summer

Summer is a cigarette,
Inhaled until it has nothing left to give,
And the charred remains are left
To make a smoky pillar of autumn.

Mark Nathan

This is an extended metaphor where the idea is continued in the same terms throughout the poem.

Tramp

Sam is lying here
A silhouette of yellow dust.
This will be his home.

Louis Lyne

Candlelight

A flutter of light came from the flame of a candle.
I watched as the candle was lit,
The way it hurt.
And as I remembered each second of its dying light
A tear rolled down its melting body.
The light of the candle stuck in my head
Like drying wax.

Catriona Ferguson

The Cobra

His marks are honeycomb,
His eyes are like flying saucers,
His ribs stretch like elastic bands.
The curled teeth shining and ready for a victim.
His back patterns are stars in the moonlight.

Sharon Purves

Hyena

I howl around the mountains with my yellow chest
   glowing,
My black blobs a sign of beauty,
My eyes the oil ocean forever swirling.

Nikola Powell

People use metaphors all the time in daily life without even
realising that they are doing so, and probably without being able
to give the technical term for their use of language. 'Dead
metaphors' abound. These are expressions like 'the foot of the
stairs', 'the mouth of a river' and 'the arm of a chair'. They are
called 'dead' because they have become so much part of
everyday speech that they have lost their original vitality. When
we write we need to try to find new metaphors.

Young children can sometimes be heard using metaphors
when they call other people names! 'You're a pig!' or 'You cow!',
although the sort of language not to be encouraged, are both
used in a metaphorical sense. (Such expressions are not terribly
fair on the animals, but then there are many other expressions
which take the names of animals in vain, e.g. 'snake in the
grass', 'bitch', 'You dirty rat!') Politicians are always employing
metaphors in their speeches, notably those with sea or cricket
connections. The 'ship of state' might be described as
'rudderless', 'drifting in stormy waters', 'weathering the storm',
'entering calmer waters' or 'sailing full steam ahead'. People
might be said to be playing the game 'with a straight bat',
'fielding' difficult questions, 'delivering bouncers' or as 'having
had a good innings'.

When we do this, and when we write extended metaphors, we
are using the language of one thing to describe another to make
our point in a vivid and memorable way. Children as young as
nine and ten are able to appreciate how this works and to
attempt their own extended metaphors. The following is the way
I have always introduced such an exercise.

I usually take a pair of scissors and list the words that come to
mind in connection with them, e.g. they are pointed, made of

cold steel, you can score paper with them, they have two pieces that rub together, they cut through things. Once we have the list, we then think of something completely different which the scissors could stand for. In this case, I opt for a quarrel. The next stage of planning involves making a second list of words relevant to such a quarrel, e.g. it might be between two people, there is anger, people shout and often make hurtful remarks. Then, I begin my extended metaphor with the words, 'A quarrel is a pair of scissors', and 'back up' this statement by describing what happens, using words and ideas from my two lists. The kind of poem that might emerge is as follows:

A quarrel is a pair of scissors
Scoring points that go too deep,
And with steel in their cold hearts
Two people cut each other to shreds.

Before children begin their own poems, I usually also show them the four-line poem, 'Summer', by Mark Nathan, printed earlier in this chapter, as another example of what can be done. The initial statements ('Summer is a cigarette' and 'A quarrel is a pair of scissors') could never stand on their own – they would not make sense. The exercise is to find your metaphor and then to justify it by the language you use.

Note the effectiveness of the penultimate line in this further example:

A cat is a fire
Limbering up ready to spring forth.
Its eyes are spitting sparks
Into the fiery air
As the purring heat shimmers
In the surrounding atmosphere.

Simon Davison

(See also 'Window', Chapter 60; and 'Approaching a Bend', Chapter 68.)

RHYMING

Some people still think that a poem is not a poem unless it rhymes. Because children are brought up on nursery rhymes, they tend to use rhyme when first asked to write poems – and they generally use it very badly. Many of the anthologies that used to be available in schools contained poems that were little more than rhymes of the most facile kind. There are now many anthologies and volumes of poetry that treat children with more respect and try to extend their understanding, and in which rhyme is shown to be more sophisticated than cats sitting on mats or chasing rats!

I make no apology for deliberately banning the use of rhyme when teaching a group of children for the first time – unless the rhymes occur naturally. Much later I reintroduce it when the children have become more aware of how to use words to their best advantage.

Explaining 'near rhymes' is often a useful way of starting the children off again. Near rhymes, or half-rhymes, are what the name suggests, where two words are similar enough in sound although they do not rhyme exactly. For example, a full rhyme would be 'sand' with 'hand', but a near rhyme might be 'sand' with 'blend', 'heat' with 'leek', or 'summer' with 'dimmer'. It can be the vowel sounds, or the consonants which make up the main part of the words, which are the same. There are some rules pertaining to hard or soft sounds, but at this level I do not feel it is necessary to stress them. Since one of the main problems with rhyming is that children spoil the flow and sense of their poems by using ridiculous words for the sake of rhymes, the introduction of near rhymes can give much greater freedom and wider choice.

The Sun Murder

Mr Mistleshot's shot the *sun*.
He is to be *hung*
For every reason under the moon.
The weather will be as follows:
It'll pour for sure
And it certainly won't feign
To rain,
Whether you like it or not
It won't be hot
Because Mr Mistleshot's shot the sun.

Rebecca Bazeley

Clouds

Wet *colour*,
Has one *brother*,
Both make seeds grow to flowers,
And make the seed wait less hours
To *uncover*.

Allon Rimon

Extract from The Four Men

The man approached the place of the four *men*.
You come to take my sleep? said the *sleeper*,
I do not want your sleep, so sleep *again*.
You come to take my food? said the *eater*.

Darrol Kenworthy

The use of full rhymes can be gently encouraged after this; it
may be that children will use both full and near rhymes, as can
be seen in some of the examples above. Quite often a sparing
use of rhyme in a poem which otherwise does not rhyme can be
very effective. The rhymes act as emphasis and can also impart a
musical and rhythmic sense to a poem. Children should be

made aware that forcing a rhyme is bad, and indeed
unnecessary, but using rhymes occasionally can add another
dimension.

— ◆ —

Schoolkeeper

The man who walked the tarmac ground
From here to the wire fence,
He knows his work will *die*
Just by the look in a child's *eye.*
Hands clenched under weather-beaten donkey jacket,
His eyes turn to the next door along
And fall to where
The broom and waxwork cup of *tea*
Are posted amongst the *greenery.*

Miles Greene

June

A light colour of crimson blossom *falls,*
The trees part with their leaves and begin *life,*
The birds crowned with their high tuned *calls.*
The windows reflected like a sour *knife,*
The ground rested with its surface melting.

Catriona Ferguson

Grandad

A quiet man,
A thinking man,
Always down in his *shed*
Working on a broken clock
Or fixing a car *instead.*
A quiet man,
A thinking man,
But now he's *dead.*

Rebecca Bazeley

A third use of rhyme is the internal rhyme which occurs where words are rhymed (full or near) but not at the ends of lines. These act as echoes within a poem and add to the texture and flow.

Caterpillar

Crawls like a miniature ocean,
Arriving at an unknown destination,
Tenderly feels around a *leaf*,
Every contact is *brief*, as if entering a naked flame.
Repeatedly moves its short legs,
Purposefully arches then straightens,
Ignorant of the prodding *hand*
Leans, and falls to *land* upon a leaf below.
Lazy, yet possessing a delightful beauty
Adrift in a world of dizziness –
Red stripes like bloodstained gashes on its back.

Mark Nathan

Tom Cat

In the middle of the night you hear a growl,
You know the tom cat is on the prowl.
Its fire eyes remind you of the devil.
Its *paws* are soft as velvet,
Its ice-like *claws*,
Its ears like horns.

Darius Saunders

When children are used to experimenting with rhyme it can be interesting for them to be encouraged to make up their own rhyme schemes using the traditional way of describing them, e.g. a, b, a, b, c, d, c, d . . . Once when a group of children wrote a riddle as a class they also determined what the rhyme scheme would be. They chose a, b, c, d, d, c, b, a; and enjoyed following their scheme, making use of near rhymes.

— ◆ —

Communal Riddle

I once lay with the sand
But fire gave me life.
My body is cold, I have no heart.
I am hard yet hollow, you must treat me gently,
I am empty but full; once full now empty.
I shatter and destroy, but intend no hurt,
I blur and distort the human eye,
You can break the heart I never had.

(A bottle)

DIFFERENT KINDS OF RHYME

Full rhyme
e.g. 'cat' and 'mat'; 'under', 'asunder' and 'thunder'.

Half rhyme (or near rhyme)
e.g. 'robin' and 'cabin'; 'single', 'angle' and 'jungle'; 'cut', 'set', 'bit' and 'dot'.

Eye rhyme (or spelling rhyme)
e.g. 'glove' and 'move'; 'though', 'through' and 'bough'.

Alliteration
Repeated initial sounds before stressed syllables, e.g. 'at *l*ong *l*ast she *l*eft the *l*and be*l*ow and *r*ose to *r*ing the *r*osy clouds a*r*ound'.

Assonance
Repeated vowel sounds in a series of words (minimum two words). These may also give half rhymes, e.g. 'when s*u*mm*e*r c*o*m*e*s the h*u*m of b*u*mble bees is heard, and br*i*ghter l*i*ght sl*i*ces through the gr*ee*n l*ea*v*e*s of the tr*ee*s'.

Repetition
Of words or lines, done intentionally to create a refrain or particular effect.

Endstop rhyme

Full or half rhymes coming at the ends of lines, e.g.:

There was a furry little *cat*
Called Wilhelmina Pudde*phat,*
Who loved to curl up on the *mat*
And dream she was an aristo*crat.*

Internal rhyme

Full or half rhyme occurring within lines, e.g.:

Over the land was a blanket of *snow*
Aglow in the sun which hung *low* in the sky.

Section

3

48

Mary Had A

Tiny Sheep

Some time ago, I came across an idea for playing with language which immediately appealed to me. I cannot claim to have invented the idea, but I could see its potential for helping children to become more proficient at handling language in a 'safe' exercise, i.e. one that does not place too many demands at once, which can deter people from having a go. As with many other exercises I tend to use, it is also great fun. However, a word of warning! It is not as easy as it might first appear.

The idea is to rewrite well-known nursery rhymes (or popular songs) without using certain letters of the alphabet. What results can be extremely amusing, although if you set out to try to be funny the piece is less likely to succeed than if you take the exercise seriously.

It is best to set down the original version first and then to rewrite it omitting one letter at a time. I have found that about three or four versions are enough to create the effect. It is essential that you only change what you have to in order to satisfy your self-imposed limit. In order to do this you must fully understand what the original is saying, which is why it is good to use nursery rhymes, which create few problems in understanding.

This is an exercise in finding synonyms, or finding another way to say the same thing. It can demand enormous concentration and when doing this with younger children (10/11 year olds) I have often found that they can work better in twos. The more able will possibly manage on their own.

What this does for the development of children's language is twofold. Firstly, they learn to come to grips with meaning.

Sometimes, long discussions develop on the meaning of individual words in the quest for another way to express them. This is a very necessary process in learning to write and use language. When forced to do an exercise like this (also paraphrasing), children are often made aware for the first time that the whole is made up of many parts – that even small words like 'a' and 'the' are important. When they come to write their own thoughts on other occasions this should encourage them not to write just anything down, but to search for exactly the right word to express what they want to say.

Secondly, the exercise gives them experience of the technique of rewriting, which they should be encouraged to do with their own work. It is important that children are made aware of the necessity of working drafts in order to polish their writing. This is often a difficult area for some. Reworking your own writing is hard, particularly when you are not used to doing so. Also, if children are working to a pattern or form (especially one which employs rhyme or set rhythms), very often what they want to say will not fit the required form. It is usually best for them to write down what they want to say and then to find another way of saying the same thing which will fit the form. Practice on this nursery rhyme exercise will help children to train their minds to be able to accomplish this task. Only by practice will they gain the facility to do this. Of course, it will also increase their vocabulary and confidence generally.

It is virtually impossible to do this exercise and retain the rhyme scheme of the original and I do not recommend trying. In fact, because lines often become elongated in order to achieve the meaning, the result can be more amusing without the rhyme. The first example here is my own attempt and the others were written by 11 year olds.

— ◆ —

Mary Had a Little Lamb

Its fleece was white as snow,
And everywhere that Mary went
The lamb was sure to go.
It followed her to school one day
Which was against the rule,
It made the children laugh and play
To see a lamb at school.

(without 'T')

Mary had a small lamb
Which had a fleece colourless as snow,
And everywhere Mary wandered
Her lamb would surely go.
Following her schoolwards one day
Which was considered illegal,
Convulsed every child, who laughed and played
When seeing a lamb in school.

(without 'A')

This girl owned this little sheep,
Its fleece the colour of snow,
Everywhere she went
The sheep went too.
It followed her to school one time
Which broke one of the rules,
It resulted in the children being helpless with giggles,
    they were sportive too,
To see this sheep there.

(without 'L')

Mary had a tiny sheep,
Its coat was white as snow,
And everywhere that Mary went
The sheep was sure to go.
It shadowed her to an education institution one day
Which was against a decree,
It made the boys and the opposite sex guffaw and cavort
To see a sheep there.

The Grand Old Duke of York

He had ten thousand men,
He marched them up to the top of the hill
And he marched them down again.
And when they were up they were up,
And then they were down they were down,
And when they were only half way up
They were neither up nor down.

(without 'E')

A grand old aristocrat of York,
Had an army of six plus four thousand.
That grand old aristocrat took his army to a top of a hill
And brought it back down again.
And if it was up it was up,
And if it was down it was down,
And if it was only half way up
It wasn't up or down.

(without 'O')

The grand ancient Duke, named after a place in England,
Had a hundred times a hundred men.
He marched them up where the hill peak is
And he marched them back again.
And when they were up they were up,
And when they were back again they were back again,
And when they were simply half way up
They weren't up, neither were they back again.

(without 'D')

The noble sovereign prince of York, ruling a small
    state,
(He wasn't young),
Was the employer of an extremely large group of men.
He got them marching to the top of the hill
Then to the bottom again.
When they were up they were up,
When they were at the bottom they were at the bottom,
Also, when they were only half way up
They were neither up nor at the bottom.

Lisa Rose and Sophie Martensson

Doctor Foster Went to Gloucester

In a shower of rain,
He stepped in a puddle
Right up to his middle
And never went there again.

(without 'A')

Doctor Foster went to Gloucester
In the thunderstorm,
He stepped in this puddle
Right up to his middle
Then the doctor didn't ever go to Gloucester in the
    future.

(without 'E')

A doctor took a trip to a big town
In a rain storm.
This doctor put his foot in a rain pool –
It got his tummy soaking –
And that put him off going to that town again.

(without 'O')

The physician, let's call him Smith, visited a city
In the rain.
He stepped in a puddle,
It came as far as his middle,
And he never went there again.

Joana Monjardino

49

PARAPHRASE

POEMS

I first came across this idea from the poet Vernon Scannell, to whom the credit should be given. The idea is to take a famous poem, but one which you hope the children do not already know, and write a prose paraphrase of it. You should avoid using key words but aim to have all the information in the correct order. The completed paraphrase is then read out to the children, written up on the board, or handed out on photocopied sheets. If it is read out, it may be necessary to read it at least twice while the children take notes. They are then asked to write a poem using all the information they have been given, and preferably in the same order. When they have finished, they read their poems out to the group and the culmination of the reading is to hear the original poem.

There are many interesting sides to this exercise for teacher and children alike. Firstly, making a paraphrase of a poem can be quite difficult. One of the essential qualities of a poem is its economy of language. A paraphrase almost always turns out much longer than the original. This is a useful teaching point to show one of the differences between prose and poetry and to emphasise how the language of poetry is more highly charged.

Secondly, poetry in this highly-charged manner uses words which can have more than one meaning. To communicate this in prose can tie you in knots, whereas in the poem you instinctively assimilate all meanings at the same time. Poems can also appear to say one thing and really mean another. I tried to paraphrase Stevie Smith's 'Not Waving But Drowning' and found it almost impossible without making the prose very clumsy.

Not being allowed to use key words from a poem forces you to search around for other ways of saying the same thing and very often this causes problems because there are no obvious alternatives. I find this very stimulating as an exercise and, of course, it makes you look at a poem much harder than you may have done before. You realise many nuances which previously may have escaped you and you can grow to appreciate the poem even more or look at an 'old faithful' in a new light. I suppose it could also put you off a poem too – but at least you would know what you were rejecting!

These are all aspects which I feel can benefit the teacher. For the children, it is fun to hear the original and compare it with their own poems on the same subject. It is also a way of introducing them to good poems which ensures that they understand them and listen to them, and, probably, remember them. A good discussion can follow such a lesson, looking in detail at the original and appreciating the way the poet wrote about the subject in the light of their own poems.

An extension to this can be done by dividing the class into two or more groups. Each group can take a poem and paraphrase it in prose, with the help of the teacher if necessary. The groups can then exchange paraphrases and write poems of their own based on the paraphrase they have received. Neither group should know the original of the other, and they can hear the results at the end. This teaches children to look at poems in detail, but with another purpose in view, which is an added incentive, and links the reading of poetry (and what can be gained from that) with their own writing. This exercise is particularly useful as a way of introducing poems for study at GCSE and A level.

For adults, and perhaps for children too when they have had some experience of this, a kind of quiz game can be played which can be quite amusing. You take it in turns to paraphrase famous lines of poetry and the others must quote the original. This is not as esoteric as it may sound – most people know quite a few lines of poetry when it comes to it! You can introduce variations such as paraphrasing in dialects or particular accents. A travesty? No, just fun!

There follows an attempt at a paraphrase of 'Adlestrop' by

Edward Thomas, followed by children's poems, and, lastly, the original.

No, I'll never forget that small railway station.
It stuck in my mind because I was on an express train which should not have stopped there at all, but it did, one hot day after lunch, at the beginning of summer.

I remember hearing the sound of steam escaping from the valve and somebody coughed or something. But there was just an empty platform. Nobody got on to the train, or off it, there was absolutely no-one about. I just recall noticing the name of the station.

That was the only thing I saw except for a few trees, some grass and a couple of different sorts of wild flowers. There were also some small stooks of hay standing about drying in the sun. Everything was as still as the tiny clouds high up in the sky.

Well, we only stopped for about sixty seconds but somewhere, not far away, just then I heard a particular bird singing and I felt as though I could almost hear all the other birds there must have been in that county and the next, singing away as well, with him, off into the distance.

— ◆ —

Poems

(a) Steaming through thirsty June countryside
     My eyelids heavy, I doze.
     A rush of steam, a moment's panic,
     Have I missed my stop?
     I lean out of the window.
     A small dilapidated station,
     A ringing silence.
     Brambles guard an old bench with its peeling paint,
     Hay spread out to dry, only attracting insects.
     I wait for the bang of a door, the guard's whistle,
     But only the uneasy silence.
     And then a bird's song, strong and confident,
     It fills the air and overtakes the silence.
     All this packed into sixty seconds, deep in my memory.
                                              Anna Cheifetz (YWW)

(b) It was the trans-continental express.
   We stopped for a minute at the deserted station,
   The engine let out steam and a mystery man coughed,
   It was the cue for a strange bird to start singing.
   The sound echoed amongst the dancing daisy patches
       and heather,
   Even the firs, and the pines, along with the hay and
       grass,
   Revolved to the bird's singing.
   We were all lazy from our lunches
   And the picturesque setting of the small high clouds
       was typical.
   I shall never forget Ploines,
   Though I couldn't find it on the map.

                                        Robert Northcott (YWW)

The Station

(c) It was a hot June day,
   The express train drew to a stop.
   I lazily looked out of the window,
   Were we there already?
   No, it was a peaceful country station
   Where the train shouldn't have stopped.
   The crimson poppies nodded in the sun
   Making a patriotic combination
   With the cornflowers and the cow parsley.
   The prickly hawthorns stood crooked
   At either end of the short station.
   Nobody got on,
   No-one got off.
   The people in the front and back carriages
   Didn't have a chance
   Because the platform didn't stretch that far.
   Then slowly, steadily, building up steam,
   We left the station,
   That little country station,
   That I'll never forget.

                                        Laura Bacharach (YWW)

And now for the original.

Adlestrop

Yes, I remember Adlestrop –
The name, because one afternoon
Of heat the express-train drew up there
Unwontedly. It was late June.

The steam hissed. Someone cleared his throat.
No-one left and no-one came
On the bare platform. What I saw
Was Adlestrop – only the name.

And willows, willow-herb, and grass
And meadowsweet and haycocks dry,
No whit less still and lonely fair
Than the high cloudlets in the sky.

And for that minute a blackbird sang
Close by, and round him, mistier,
Farther and farther, all the birds
Of Oxfordshire and Gloucestershire.

Edward Thomas

GRAVESTONES

Although the theme may seem morbid, it is a fact that children often write about death. This exercise manages to capture children's imaginations as well as to encourage them to learn something from history which they may not have interested themselves in before.

The idea originates from the *Spoon River Anthology*[1] by Edgar Lee Masters which contains poems written from the viewpoint of deceased inhabitants of Spoon River. Some of these are reproduced in *Story, the third book*[2], or can be read in the original.

Children *can* make up names and dates of imaginary persons, but another idea is to visit an old churchyard and collect real names. (An interesting diversion here is to look out for epitaphs which are often found on older gravestones or on tablets inside a church.) The children then write poems about the life and death of these people, as if the people themselves were speaking. Details of the period can be included to make the poems more authentic; particularly a study of the social conditions will help to add colour. Some class discussion may be useful for this, especially if it 'ties in' with a particular history project being studied at the time. It may indeed lead into a class project.

In many smaller villages, whole generations of families are buried in the churchyard and the same surnames recur. This may lead to a sequence of poems about one family. It can be very effective if the poems are written out on paper cut to the

---

[1]Masters, E.L. (*ed.*) (1915), *Spoon River Anthology*, Collier-Macmillan
[2]David Jackson and Dennis Pepper (*eds.*) (1973), *Story, the third book*, Penguin

shape of a gravestone and even coloured to look like stone –
mosses, lichen and all.

It is probably unnecessary to advise caution, but teachers
should be aware of any recent deaths in a child's family. It may
not be appropriate for some children, although I know of at
least one child who found a great release in writing about a
grandfather who had recently died. It is also possible that a visit
to a previously unknown graveyard would be better than to one
which is local and may be full of associations for some children.

— ◆ —

STAN HARTLEY
1701–1761

My son I brought from London,
Bill was his name,
But soon I joined him in his grave.
A retreating death I had,
A war against the Scottish rebellion.
I died, forced back at Heptonstall.
They came up from behind.

Daniel Rubin

BILL HARTLEY
1747–1758

A Cockney man I was.
Bill Hartley my name.
At 4 I came to live at Heptonstall,
But not for long.
I soon became sieved
Because I was struck with Hepton Church by lightning,
And buried where I died.

Daniel Rubin

STELLA HARTLEY
1779–1804

Where were my savers
When danger was near?
They never helped anyone.

I don't need friends where I lie
Beneath the rock where I fell.

That strange wind force
I suffer from now
By myself in my earth-bound cell.

Petra Coveney

CHALK

OUTLINE

This idea was first suggested to me by the poet Kit Wright, who used it very successfully with a group of top primary children on an Arvon course (see Chapter 80, page 360, for a description of the Arvon Foundation). It uses the element of surprise and therefore needs to be set up carefully in advance of a lesson.

A place must be chosen with a large enough floorspace (or outdoors) to enable someone, preferably an adult, to lie down in an unnatural pose, as if he or she had fallen. I have done this myself and asked a colleague to chalk round the outline of my body on the floor. On one occasion this was done in a small room not much used in school, and first thing in the morning before the children arrived. I then took them to see it, having told them there had been a break-in and that the person who had left the chalk outline on the floor had been taken by the police. Some crime had perhaps been committed? However, the children do not have to think on these lines at all. The outline of the person is merely a different stimulus for writing and they should be encouraged to approach their poems in any way they choose.

It perhaps offers more scope if the outline is drawn on the classroom floor under a carpet, if you have one. At the appropriate time you can roll back the carpet to show what you had found, to your surprise, that morning. The children should try to forget they are in a classroom and just stare at the chalk figure. They should ask themselves how it might have arrived on the floor, who it was, what story lies behind it? With the right sort of discussion, which leads them away from the present into the imagination, the resulting poems can be quite astounding.

An extension of this could be to present the children with pictures of the many fascinating chalk figures which can be seen around the countryside, or better still, if possible, take them to see one or two. Those who live in the West Country are lucky in this respect, as that is where most of these figures can be seen. Some of the most famous are the Uffington, Osmington, Westbury and Pewsey Horses, the Cerne Abbas Giant, the Wilmington Man and the Whipsnade Lion.

The Strange Native

At number 27 Harfude Street
A native lived.
He came from South America.
He had taken a hobby up.
Discarding his native dance
He danced the way of Africa.
The swerving movement left no time for air.
He had a record of Ipi Tombi.

Christina Young

No Way of Knowing

It lay there, mangled and twisted, like a snake digesting. As soon as the story was told, that Peter Shortly had slipped into the river and had been churned into pulp and flesh, sparkling like flamboyant blood, the fireplaces were being used, and his family knew before he got to the third house. His wife, mother and two sons came out crying.

Now he lies there without knowing what his future will be. He hopes a good one but it may be as bad as a frog's life, or it may be a golden king for the children of Bob Wood.

Roddy Mattinson

(*Note:* The above piece draws on local superstition in the area around Lumb Bank, Yorkshire, where there is supposed to be a ghost in Bob Wood. The 'fireplaces' refers to the custom in

Heptonstall of banging on the fireplaces down a row of houses
to pass messages quickly if something was happening. This
would bring people to their doors. This information was given to
the children by folk singer, Bob Pegg, who was resident oral
traditionist at the Arvon Foundation for a few years.)

— ◆ —

The Strange Case of Inspector Welsh

'Inspector Welsh' was going
from the kitchen to the dining room
when a cricket ball flew through the window
and hit him right on the temple
which killed him immediately.
His body was taken away
and a chalk outline drawn.

All this happened
and the sausages sat through it all,
eye-witnesses that didn't say anything.

Susan O'Dell

The Chalk Horse

On a giant green blackboard
Is a horse
Drawn by a million teachers
With white dusty chalk.
A thousand pupils have come to admire it,
To stand on the gritty figure
Or to admire from afar
Their teachers' handiwork.
Historians attach legends and battles to it,
Great kings defeated,
Human sacrifices burnt on it,
Iron Age tribes performing ancient rituals,
Bonfires were lit on it,
Dragons were fought, people were killed . . .

Laura Bacharach (YWW)

The Dragon's Flight

I stop out of breath and rest,
Then continuing I trudge up the hillsides,
One after the other.
The sun comes out, over the wild deserted hills.
It is a dragon that is resting on the hillside,
It is a dragon,
I can feel it
Winging through the sky on the back of the clouds.
The sight before me dazzles my eyes,
It is there, the dragon,
White, huge, beautiful.
The dragon moves,
Its hot breath stirs my hair.
It starts to tramp across the hill
Its white chalked body following obediently.
The head looks up to the rushing clouds.
Its legs poise, white wings unfurl,
Gently its body lifts off the hill.

Nadya Kassam (YWW)

52

REINCARNATION

This is always a fascinating subject, whether you believe it is possible or not. Its introduction here is merely as an imaginative exercise. The word exists, and its meaning can be explained and the concept presented as a hypothesis which need not be taken too seriously if you do not wish it.

Some class discussion about reincarnation as a possible reality can be interesting and enlightening, but the final object is to write a poem. Each child can look at the task from a variety of angles. Either *he or she* is to be born again, or a relative, friend, famous person, fictional character, or an imaginary person. The idea is to describe what the person would return as, possibly *choose* to be reborn as, were the opportunity to arise. Anything should be eligible, both animate and inanimate, real and abstract. The poems can be serious or humorous. The most surprising poems can result from a lively discussion, as the first example below shows. It seemed to appear from nowhere after a session when one child asserted that her mother would come back as a telephone because she talked non-stop, and a whole group of children were convinced that a girl's uncle was a chicken they could see in a field.

Re-incarnation

When he came back he came in a carriage of numbers.
The carriage was made of every number.
Every number except the number 4,
It was inside.
Yet this 4 was different.
Different from every other 4,

Every other number.
It is alive. In every possible way it is 4th.
It is 4th at cleverness, 4th at stupidity.
It is 4th at riding, 4th at walking.
Everything it touches assumes the form of a 4.
Nobody knows him, but everyone now looks similar.

Donal Crawford

Reborn

The song of my heart no longer is within me,
My hands no longer hold my life,
My story is to be told but that is behind me,
But this part of me starts with an empty page
Which is yet to be written.
Somebody spare me, whoever is there.

Miles Greene

53

THE MAKING

OF . . .

This idea had its starting point in a poem called 'The Making of the Drum' by Edward Brathwaite which can be found in *Other Worlds*[1] (The English Project, Stage One). This led to thinking about the making of other objects. A craftsman, a maker, essentially needs three things: an idea of what to make; the materials with which to make it; and the tools for the job. When making something in words the same rules can be applied – the materials will be mainly nouns and adjectives, and the tools will be verbs.

Once you have an idea, perhaps something you could not normally make, one way to begin is to compile a list of phrases (nouns and adjectives) to be used as the materials (often including things you could not really use), for example, 'the undertow of the treacherous tide' or 'the crackle of static'. Each phrase is chosen to illustrate a quality of the object. The verbs are the tools that mould and shape, so a list of interesting ones can be made, for example, 'lever', 'tilt' or 'skim'. All that now remains is to use the tools to shape the materials, to put the ideas together using the verbs and create the original artefact.

The Making of the Tiger

One chip and another
As the line of his back
Begins to take shape,
The smooth curve
The gentle slope.

---

[1] Paul Davies (1988), *Other Worlds*, Penguin

Another chip, and one more,
An ear begins to form,
The small hollow
With every detail
Comes to life.
The face and the staring eye
Seem to be alone,
Not with the body
The staring eye,
Not with the body
The motionless face,
The harsh silence.
The smooth stomach line
The graceful sloping curve
That glides to form the perfect shape.
A leg and a foot form in oak
As claws are cut
Like blades from a penknife.
The shape of the leg
The bend of the knee
Perfect to every precise detail.
As sandpaper smooths its body
And he breathes his breath into the form,
The great carver's work is done.

Nadya Kassam (YWW)

The Making of a Grave

The rock is levered out of its home,
Scrambling woodlice roll into balls,
In the van it longs for freedom.

A silent scream echoes through the room
As the chisel stabs.
The distant chomping of a spade can be heard
Where the man with the measurer stands.

Charles De'Ath

The Making of a City

The making of a city,
A huge city,
In the middle of a large space of land.
They knew it would take time,
They must not hurry or it would be ruined,
They must not take time
Or it would never be finished,
They must do it steadily, very steadily.
The bricks must be made out of huge pieces of rock,
The tools cut out of metals and wood.
Holes must be dug to make this city.
It will take years of hard work.
They must build fences pleased with their
    surroundings,
Dustbins annoyed with their uses,
Lampposts filled with joy at being able to see
    everything.
There will be parks of happiness,
Bricks filled with death,
Windows open to the sunshine,
Pavements filled with pain,
Trees that have the feeling of freedom
And branches happy with hope.

Lydia Masseron

The Making of a Redwood Tree

Come fire and burn open the cone,
Come wind and blow the seeds in all directions.
Come ash and make a bed for the newborn seeds.
Come rain, come sun, give water and heat,
Come time and wait for the seedling to appear,
Come buds and decorate with leaves.
Come birds and populate the tree,
Come birds and build a nest,
Come, eggs, hatch
For I feel dead without you.

Ben Owen

The Making of a Picture

To make a picture go into a wood.
Find a stream without a current
And cut a slice of water which will be paper.

To make a picture you must have tools.
Dig down and find a treasure chest,
Maybe it will have a paintbrush.

To make a picture you must have paint.
Sketch a ladder up to the skies
And cut some yellow off the sun,
Green from the treetops and blue from the sky.

To paint the picture collect a tree,
Some grass and a cat, iron them flat,
Stick them on and paint them over
In all the colours of a century.

John Nathan

OMENS

Superstitions thrive on people's susceptible imaginations and, whether we are inclined to believe them or not, we all probably experience a twinge of foreboding if we spill the salt or look at a new moon through glass. Many of the superstitions have their origins in history or common sense, e.g. crossed knives usually did mean a quarrel when swords were still in use, and walking under a ladder may result in a tin of paint falling on your head. But many of them seem to have no basis in reality and can be flouted with no apparent consequent misfortune or good luck.

However, they do present a rich store of ideas which can be exploited by the writer and can help to build up a powerful atmosphere in a poem. The idea of sitting down to a meal with an extra place laid, for the visitor who might come, has always fascinated me, and the breaking of a mirror with its legendary seven years' bad luck can provide an immediate response from that part of our imagination that delves deep into fantasy. A useful poem that relies to some extent on superstition is 'Flannan Isle' by Wilfred Wilson Gibson.

Children are interested in this subject and enjoy writing about it. A whole class can spend a lesson just talking about various superstitions and old wives' tales which they know and discussing the value of them. Do they seem to make good sense and what might be their origins? Do they link up in any way with other beliefs? For example, throwing salt over your *left* shoulder with the *right* hand is supposedly good triumphing over evil, the salt thrown in the Devil's eyes. This can be associated with the story of Christ being tempted in the wilderness by the Devil traditionally looking over his shoulder, and gives substance to our use of the Latin word *sinister* (meaning 'left').

The children can then be asked to take a superstition and use it as the starting point for a poem. Alternatively, they can be encouraged, after a discussion, to create their own superstitions and enlarge on them in their writing. This is 'tapping' their interest in the magical or inexplicable element of belief which co-exists with rational thinking and can be worked into 'real' situations to give them more point and 'edge'.

Black Holly

Black evil pricks my earthly skin,
A sample for the underworld.
The days argue with each other
As I wait for my escort.
I lie on the cross of uncertainty
My life too short but death made it long.
I cherish each intake of earthly breath.
Black holly will be laid on my grave.

Hedy-anne Goodman

The Swans

The river runs red with the blood of many men.
The white trio with stuck out necks
Abandon the water to fly their death flight.
The trees are bare, the heavens dark,
There is no sound from the once singing lark.

Nicholas Tomkins

A Life Story

The first year
A slightly longer blade of grass –
Death under a knife.

The second year
The garden tree snapped –
I shall collapse.

The third year
A crack in the earth.
No coffin for my long sleep.

The fourth year
A crazy paving path.
A shattered gravestone for no-one to remember me.

The fifth year
The old man died.
My heart shall weaken.

The sixth year
I see a black-chested robin,
He came from the Devil's crucifixion.

The seventh year
A black cat crossed my path.
I wished for the curse to break.

Zak Hall

A Week of Strange Cats

On Monday a mischievous white cat followed me home
To be stroked and tickled.

On Tuesday I saw two kittens scrounging in a dustbin
And fighting over a dead fish.

On Wednesday three wild cats ate food out of my hand
Then vanished when it was gone.

On Thursday a tom cat killed four butterflies
And left them on the lawn.

On Friday five friendly cats spat at me
And arched their backs until their ribs ached.

On Saturday I heard six shy cats
Singing songs of sorrow.

On Sunday my cat died,
(Of scarlet fever).

Lydia Masseron

ODD ODES

Odes are lyrical poems generally employing exalted language to praise or celebrate their subjects. Famous odes include Keats's 'Ode to a Nightingale' ('My heart aches, and a drowsy numbness pains/My sense, as though of hemlock I had drunk, . . . '), 'On a Grecian Urn' ('Thou still unravish'd bride of quietness, . . . '), 'To Autumn' ('Season of mists and mellow fruitfulness,/Close bosom-friend of the maturing sun; . . . ') and Shelley's 'To a Skylark' ('Hail to thee, blithe Spirit!/Bird thou never wert, . . . '), among others. These are lofty, serious poems, lauding their subjects often in the language of hyperbole. Many of us remember learning these when we were at school, and they still have much to offer children today.

However, writing in this vein is not really applicable to modern poetry and children are unlikely to take kindly to the suggestion that they try. This does not, however, mean that they cannot write odes. There may be some people who will dislike the idea of playing this form for laughs, but there is no doubt that it is a good exercise that always captures the children's imagination and interest.

The idea, then, is to write odes about incongruous subjects, addressing them directly (in the second person) and praising them to the skies in language that would generally be considered inappropriately fulsome. Choosing the subject takes some care, but most everyday objects would be suitable. Some planning in the form of notes is helpful: children should make lists of all the ways the objects can be/are used, and everything they can think of to describe them.

When it comes to writing the ode, a thesaurus should be on hand to ensure that a range of the best words is used. For example, there are many different ways of saying that you 'like' something, e.g. I 'love', 'delight in', 'admire', 'rejoice in', 'revel in', 'cannot live without' . . . Also, different words for 'praise' can enhance the final effect of the ode, e.g. 'magnify', 'glorify', 'laud', 'trumpet', 'celebrate'. . .

It will be evident from the examples below that the writers became very familiar with what a thesaurus has to offer, and made good use of it. One obvious improvement is noticeable in the use of the word 'ambrosial' instead of 'sweet' in 'Ode to a Jelly Tot'. Certainly it is always advisable not to use any important words more than once in a poem (unless intentionally); it smacks of laziness and can spoil an otherwise good idea. There is always another way of saying something, and the sooner children realise how wonderfully useful a thesaurus can be, the better. It was in trying to find other ways of saying 'eat' that Kathryn hit upon the idea of adding texture to her poem through the use of alliteration. Clearly this technique has 'lifted' the final poem and helped it be successful. You will also notice that there are several instances of internal rhyme as well as alliteration in the examples. I might just add that the children find this whole exercise great fun to do and that they plunder the thesaurus voraciously, once they understand what it can do for them.

Ode to a Jelly Tot

Hail, O Jelly Tot!
Most wonderful of all.
When you are near
I have no fear
As you are the answer to everything.
Your elegant figure is so divine
And your sugary coating
Fills my mouth with ambrosial flavours.
Without your presence
My stomach would be empty.
Most marvellous jelly tot –
Never shall I touch another toffee,

Never shall I chew another fudge,
Never shall I chomp another chocolate,
Never shall I gulp another gobstopper,
Never shall I absorb another aniseed ball,
Never shall I gobble another piece of gum,
Never shall I crunch another candy stick,
And never shall I munch another Mars bar.
Never shall I swallow another inferior sweet –
Without you my life wouldn't be complete.

Kathryn Smale (PH)

Ode to a Towel

O wondrous towel! O perfect and exquisite towel!
You are everything to me.
Your rough towelling texture sends shivers down my spine;
Your off-beat red/blue Paisley motif I adore.
I praise your mint-flavoured toothpaste stains,
I tremble with ecstasy at your Marks and Spencer label.
You are everything to me, and more.
I love to lie on you beneath the golden sun on sandy beaches,
I worship you as I wrap you around my head to ward off noxious
    fumes,
I cherish you as I huddle inside you on cold wintry nights,
I relish you as I use you as a mini raft to sail down rivers,
I savour you as I wet you for hand-to-hand combat,
And, if you're still clean enough,
I treasure you as I dry myself off with you.
You are a prized possession indeed, a perfect medium –
Larger than a flannel and conveniently smaller than a duvet,
You travel everywhere with me
Like a guardian angel from Benetton's heaven.
You are divine, you are beautiful,
You are a towel.
My towel.

Kieran Grant (PH)

Ode to a Stone

Oh stone, I adore you in every way.
I admire the way you trip me up
As I walk down the path;
I appreciate the way
You never make sudden moves or butt in.
You are my prize possession,
I value you greatly,
I worship the superb scratch across your back.

Oh chip off the old block!
I am truly grateful
That you have loved me for so many years.
Behold the marvellous mudstain across your side.
I'm sure if I used you I could kill two birds;
If I lost you
I would leave no stone unturned until I found you.
I envy your ability
To sleep through terrible storms at night.
Oh stone, you give me sheer delight.

Alex Burdett (PH)

Ode to my Bike

Oh my brilliant bike! You are so splendid.
Covered in mud, you take me all around my garden.
My excellent bike, I am ecstatic about you.
You have eighteen gears, I need them all,
And you are built for me, my Zappy Zeus.
You are my king.
I jump, slide, skid, and grind
And slither to a halt on you.
You are my mountain bike.
Your handle bars are straight,
With the brakes and gear-shift levers
Placed at easy-to-reach positions,
My Marvellous Minotaur.
Your wheels are 26 inch
And the tyres are so knobbly and wide

It's impossible to slip.
My Excellent Eagle,
My Miraculous Mercury,
Your gears are so quick and smooth
And there is no effort required to work them.
My Brilliant Bike,
My Super Smokey Bear.

Toby Jeffries (St.A)

POSTCARDS

I have always been against the sort of poetry workcards that were around in the sixties/early seventies and which used to consist of a picture accompanied by questions supposed to stimulate children to 'do creative writing'. The pictures were usually photographs which fell into different categories, i.e. the beautiful landscape, the everyday object in close-up, the characterful face, and the socially significant scene. I do not deride the sincerity of those who devised these cards, but in practice they just did not work. The questions, of necessity, were simple, and many teachers thought that by giving the children one of the cards they had satisfied their consciences over the need to 'do poetry'. There was generally no discussion, nothing caught fire in the imagination, and often all that was produced was a glorified answer to the 'questionnaire' format.

However, I do think there is a place for pictures as stimuli for writing. I have made a collection of postcards over the years – the sort that normally you find you cannot buy in the museum shop (they never seem to have pictures of the things you want!). I pick them up whenever and wherever I see something I like. And I have found them very useful on occasions to use with children.

There are different ways of using them. When children have not done very much writing, I sometimes hand them out (on the 'pick a card, any card, don't tell me what it is' principle) and ask the children to see if they can write something arising from what they see in the picture. But mostly I find them useful when the children are more experienced and just want to write without any discussion. At this stage, they are capable of being their own critics and finding a way to approach their poems on their own.

I also find the cards useful for when a child wants to write but is stuck for a subject. If you do not overuse this method you can build up the idea that the cards are a special treat. If a child finishes a task or exercise and wishes to continue writing, the reward can be to come out and choose a card. Sometimes they do this 'blind' and sometimes they spend a little time choosing one which attracts them and gives them a lead into a poem. In other words, because this approach is not used very often it becomes a desirable challenge, particularly if they take potluck in choosing one. It also means that as far as you, the teacher, are concerned, the subjects of their pieces are different and this can be a boon when sitting down to mark.

The object is to look hard and long at the picture; in fact, to use as many of the senses as possible in the imagination. I also encourage children to research facts about the subjects, as these can help to give them a peg to hang the poem on and make the piece more interesting. They may, though, just use the picture to spark off a memory of their own or to elicit some other idea which would seem totally unconnected but which has arisen as a result of seeing the card.

I know of poets who do a similar thing with interesting objects and I recommend this method too. Having a bag containing these objects and letting the children have a 'lucky dip' can be fun. Unlike the picture, which needs imagination to use the senses, these tactile objects offer easier access, especially for children who prefer to write about what they can actually see and are not so happy having to imagine it all. Naturally, an object can also serve as a jog to the memory and then it will no longer be needed. This idea is just another addition to the teacher's bag of tricks but it is essential to vary the exercises all the time so that the children do not become bored, and also to give every child a chance to find something that appeals to him or her. Along the way the children will be learning the tools of the trade and eventually there will be no need for any 'tricks', for they will become masters of the language and set their own goals.

The Postcard

An old forgotten mountain,
Only a black and white postcard
To prove its existence.
Blank;
No-one sent it to anybody,
Not because it's too beautiful
But in case he lost a friend.

Jonty Leff

The Sculpture

It is like a man
Giving away a man
To a man.
It is almost like God
Giving away someone He loves or hates.
A man is being brought into the world
A stranger,
Not from birth, from manhood.
He is looking around gasping at what he sees.
But the hand has no arm, therefore no body,
It is just a hand.
A giving hand or a taking hand?
Yes, a taking hand.

Gemma Bullent

A Coin of the Past

This coin of the past
Is still and disdainful
Away in its own world,
Stamped with its own recognition.
A horse is suspended in mid-air,
A landscape is enclosed in the network of the coin.
In my mind the man was shouting to me.
When I looked later
All that was left on the coin
Were a few scattered bones.

Daniel Cheifetz

Spotted Dogs

You stand motionless
With your tails overlapping.
You grin like clowns
With your fangs hanging loosely about your mouths.
Your ears are like leaves with veins everywhere.
You are proud as you stand with your chests blown
    out.
Your whiskers are pale, a light creamy colour,
Your eyes are just slits glaring at any interference.

Amy Lankester-Owen

The Gargoyle Blues

I woke up in the morning light
And felt I was in Hell,
I feel that I am down in the dumps
And my face don't ring a bell.
I am the majestic gargoyle
I look down from on high,
All I do is sit on my throne
Perched up in the sky.

The gargoyle stands,
The gargoyle stares,
He looks down to earth
With his mesmerised glares.

My hair is locked
As I lean on my hand,
I pierce my onlookers
As they sit on my land.
I am the majestic gargoyle,
I look down from on high,
All I do is sit on my throne
Perched up in the sky.

Nicholas Purchen

SHADOWS

An important aspect of light and reflection is shadow. These dark, featureless forms can be clear-cut and fairly recognisable in direct strong light, but in oblique or pale light they can take on grotesque or eerie shapes which can be a great stimulus for writing. Fear of the unknown plays a part here. Words like 'looming', 'shadowy', 'melting into the shadows' and 'spy' all come to mind. Shadows that grow huge, threatening to engulf you, and the shadow that goes everywhere with you, from which you will never be free, are both familiar thoughts or nightmares, ones which can easily provide inspiration for writing.

Silhouettes, on the other hand, seem rather more benign. Puppets and shadow stories told with shapes made by the hands against a light and thrown up on a wall can also provide good subjects.

As preliminary work before writing, I recommend one or more of the following. (They also help to make interesting wall displays for the classroom.) If it is a dry day with plenty of sunshine (in the UK?), send the children into the playground in twos or threes with a large piece of paper and some chalk, charcoal, or pastels. The paper must be about the same length and width as the average child. The paper is laid out, weighed down if necessary, and one child stands at one end with the sun behind him or her. The child twists himself or herself round into an interesting shape which is projected on to the paper. The others draw quickly round the shape while the child stands still. These shadows can then be filled in in any way the children like, for example, as magazine collage, painted, printed, in fabric, with natural material like wood or leaves, and so on. They make fine large, bold, wall displays and children can write directly from them.

It is also very simple to make silhouette heads of children by sitting them in front of a wall, on which has been pinned a sheet of paper, and setting up a slide or film projector opposite. If this is done directly on to black paper the resulting shapes can be displayed, and for days afterwards people try to guess who is who. Simple, but effective.

Experiments with light in a darkened room, using prisms and mirrors, shining torches under chins and from different angles on to faces and objects, produce effects which range from the sinister to the ridiculously funny. All this, while yielding other educational benefits, can be just what is needed to stimulate the children to write.

— ◆ —

Shadow

A shadow is a spy,
It follows you everywhere
Closely watching every step you make,
Dressed in black so as not to be seen.
It stands idle if you try to look at it.

Shazeia Qureshi

Six Ways of Taking Your Shadow by Surprise

The first way to achieve this would be
To strangle, poison or stab yourself.
The shadow is so astonished
He cannot follow you like a faithful dog any more.
Also the blood adds colour.

The next way is
To move strangely and to change your walk.
Walk in a different way than you usually do,
Your shadow will be surprised
And will find this very difficult.

Another way is
To gain or lose a lot of weight,
Your shadow will find it hard to adapt to this.

A fourth way is
To change your character drastically
Because it shows in the way you move.

The next way to take your shadow by surprise is
To turn round quickly and leap on it.

The last way is
To kill someone.
Then you are forcing your shadow into those moves.

Natasha Lawrence

Shadow

You follow like a slave awaiting orders
But never do anything except pursue.
The light is your maker, you are the dark.
You have no form of your own,
You are just a type of darkness,
A ghost tagging on behind.
You are irremovable
Except when you choose to be unnoticed
Blending in with your resemblers.
You are eerie, gloomy-looking,
Silhouetting the ground wherever there's light.

Melissa Papadakis

Shadow

Oh, shadow, where are your eyes?
Your ears, your nose?
You can't see
But I still feel you glaring at me.
You can't hear me
But I sense you can.
You can't smell me
But you still follow me wherever I go.
Oh, shadow, where are your eyes?

Your ears, your nose?
You live in a time of your own,
You follow me wherever I tread,
You are my companion for ever.   *Jamie Beesley*

Shadows

The classroom is filled with vague shadows
All rushing about.
My shadow sits there like a blot of ink,
It has no face or fingers.
I begin to write
Wondering if my shadow has a pen in its hand.
If I cry, does my shadow cry?
Does my shadow eat when I eat,
Or does it eat at all?
Can it think, does it have feelings?
Can it grieve, or can it rejoice?
Does it feel the rain or the sun?
Does it ever want revenge?
But the question I most want answered is –
Do shadows die?   *Maya Ortiz de Montellano*

Underneath an Oak Tree

As I sit underneath an oak tree
Watching pompous pigeons
Fighting over bits of blossom
A cool breeze glides lightly round me
Making the tree leaves quiver
As if a chill had gone up its trunk.
The tree's shadow dances in the sunlight
Making bright blobs over my book
And a strong wind blows
Pulling back the branches of the tree
To reveal hot sun on my back.   *Jessica Ludgrove*

(See also 'Shadow', Chapter 36.)

MEMORIES

Memories are ever fruitful sources of subjects for writing, not the least because we write from first-hand experience about something we know. This is more likely to ensure that an authentic and original 'voice' comes through, which is a goal of all writers. The first problem, however, is to find keys to unlock these memories; when put on the spot, people's minds often go blank. I have found various ways of achieving this, a few of which are set out here.

It is always a good idea for teachers to collect a bank of interesting pictures – postcards are the obvious choice, but cuttings from magazines and newspapers also offer plenty of scope. Working in twos or threes, children are each given a picture and then talk together about what they have. The idea is to see if the pictures recall incidents from their memories. Anything in the pictures may do this, even small details. The pictures serve as spurs to jog the memory. Talking together helps these memories to emerge – we all like to hear stories – and this talk is an important part of drafting in the initial planning stage. Also, one person's memory can spark off another's, as children swap experiences in their groups.

Another approach is based on A.A. Milne's poem 'The End' from *Now We Are Six*[1] ('When I was one/I had just begun . . . '). This gives a framework to aid the thinking process. The idea is to write one or two lines for each year of the child's age up to the present. All that is needed is one or two memories for each year; rhyming is optional, and children should take care that any rhyme they use does not distort the poem by being

---

[1]Milne, A.A. (1927) *Now We Are Six*, Methuen

inappropriate. Of course, most of us find it difficult to remember much before the age of four or five, sometimes three, so children should be allowed time to write such poems over a few days to enable them to ask their families at home for examples of incidents from their earliest years.

Yet another way of writing about memories is taken from a poem by James Berry which looks back over his life, detailing a series of pleasant and unpleasant memories. As with many other writing exercises, it can work well because it is basically a list and allows children to produce something sustained, in small units. A chance to take a break between memories, and let the mind wander, takes the pressure off and encourages children to persevere.

— ◆ —

Memories

I still remember my cats as kittens,
purring on my knee,
the soft warm feeling of loving them
and of them loving me.

I still remember my goldfish dying.
I woke up that morning
and found his body there.
I remember the feeling of hopelessness swelling from inside.

I still remember playtimes at my old school,
the feeling of belonging, the games we used to play.
I was an explorer in the bushes,
yet a hairdresser on the bench.

I still remember the old lady who used to live next door,
her laughing eyes still please me.
I played outside in the garden
while she watched over me.

I still remember sailing on rough grey sea,
hearing waves crashing, angry with the world,
the sky, a tent enclosing everything,
the ill feeling, but happy, at one with the sea.

I remember my cat's illness,
the vet's words, 'Make the best of her, make her last days her
    best.'
I remember holding her close to me, her ebony fur matted,
her damp nose against my cheek.

Katy Allsop (PH)

Something I Remember

How painful to remember my dear old Grancher.
I sort of knew he would die one day
But was quite unprepared when he faded away.
He used to build houses and planes,
He also took part in various campaigns,
But at the end of his life he was withered and ill.
He was put in a nursing home, kept alive by sheer will.

James Arundel (PH)

Memories

When I was one I could hardly run,
I would wobble from place to place.
I used to draw scribbles in all my books
And get in a state with my face.

When I was two I wasn't me at all,
I used to be skin and bones.
I was horrible to all the people I saw
And my mum had to ignore all the groans.

When I was three I was nearly me,
I would sit and chat away.
I had a craze for bubble gum and
Would eat all ten packs in a day.

When I was four we had to move house,
I didn't like it at all:
There was always some creepy crawly
To scare me right out of my shawl.

When I was five I started school,
I used to be such a bore.
Once I got a basket and ran
Out of the door.

When I was six my brother was born.
He used to get all the attention:
The things I used to do, I don't
Think I want to mention.

When I was seven my first tooth fell out
With a punch from my cousin Balginder;
Rushing streams of blood came out,
Some fell on to my jumper.

When I was eight I went to Florida,
I had a ball of a time;
I saw Mickey Mouse in his house
And shook hands with his chunky white gloves.

Kiran Kamboj (PH)

Memories

Still delightful is the flood in Arran
With the overflowing waterfalls
Cascading down the mountain of Goat Fell.
Still pleasing, collecting raindrops
In a cup outside the front door
And gazing at the rainbow in the sunset.
Still disturbing is the image of the cat in Greece
Whose mouth was rotten
And the people sitting at the café table shooing it away.
Still shocking to see the beast inside me
Being able to kill the insects in the tent,
And waking up to the sight of their bodies on the floor.
Still satisfying to think of Graham
Leaning over the bog to collect tadpoles,
And the impact of his body on the stagnant water.
Still pleasant are the rubber monsters in the films at Cinema City
And the prepared-for-anything super-heroes.

Still dreadful, the charred shell found after the bonfire
And the realisation that I'd incinerated a snail.
Still shocking, the memory of my cat
Bringing an offering of a half-dead blackbird.
Still pleasing, pushing and splashing Stella
As she lay on the lilo in the swimming pool in France.
Still distressing, the drowned mole
Floating on the surface of the very same pool
When I went for a swim in the early morning.

Calum Roche (BYW)

59

Zoom Lens

The idea for this comes from film and television, where, from a wide-angle shot, the camera can zoom slowly in to a close-up of a small detail. Children need to envisage a landscape or general scene – they might even write about something they can actually see, perhaps from a window – and begin by describing the overall first impressions. Having set their scene, they look next for a very small detail which they are going to home in on. This should then be described as from a distance. Gradually, thereafter, they slowly zoom in on this focal point, which becomes clearer and clearer, until it is the only important image in the frame.

It is as if we are being allowed to eavesdrop on a small drama which we may otherwise have overlooked. This is not unlike what happens in the opening of Thomas Hardy's *The Mayor of Casterbridge*, where we are gradually drawn into the story by the descriptions of the two people on the road, until we suddenly find ourselves experiencing the sights, sounds and smells of the fair where Michael Henchard sells his wife.

An exercise like this encourages children to take their time in describing what they see – something they do not always do – and to learn how to build up interest, expectation, and even tension. This can help their prose writing, too.

Zoom Lens

I'm on a rooftop
Looking down on the beach.
The sea is crashing on the rocks,
Making small rock pools.

The beach is empty.
Then two dots,
Moving slowly along the edge of the sand,
Two people,
The one wearing jeans and a black sweater,
The other a skirt and a T-shirt.
Both female, hand over shoulder,
One's hair is black, the other's blond.
They are speaking to each other,
Talking about the sea.
'It'so beautiful, isn't it?'
'Of course it is.'
Their faces look content and happy.

Lisa Kramer (BYW)

Zoom Lens

At first glance it is
A big black metal worm,
Snaking from one end of the horizon to the other,
Sucking in and spewing out the silver rails.
As I get nearer
It turns into a roaring, raging, dark streak,
Spitting out foul, grey mouthfuls of bitter smoke.
Nearer still
And I can feel the earth quiver.
A warm gust of air and it is here,
Rushing, screeching, screaming
Past my nose.
A live earthquake passes me by,
Carriage upon carriage shoots through the tunnel.
The never-ending train has finally gone,
Leaving me completely deaf
And with the taste of smoke in my mouth.

Nicholas Bieber (BYW)

Zoom Lens

Mauve heather, russet gorse,
Rambling hills, clear cold brisk sky.
Sharp black rocks, a stream running through them,
Quarries and valleys, old dirt tracks.
Whistling wind, fields down below
With white blobs of sheep grazing,
Wild ponies, free as the wind that screams over the moors.
At the furthest point on the horizon a sharp needle,
Black as a witch's eye,
Rooted to the ground
As a plant is rooted to its bed;
Made from thick stone blocks blackened with age.
Nearer and nearer still.
A peace sign scrawled on the surface,
An open doorway
With stone steps leading upwards.
The name, Stoodley Pike –
Weird symbol of peace.

Laura Lankester (BYW)

60

MIRRORS AND

REFLECTIONS

The first time I came across Louis MacNeice's poem 'Reflections', I was fascinated by it. I have never lost that fascination and the delight in the mental exercise of picturing what he describes. I have often read this poem to children and found that they, too, respond in a similar way.

Mirrors have played an important role in many traditional stories, for example, in *Snow White* ('Mirror, mirror, on the wall . . .'), *Perseus and the Gorgon, Through The Looking Glass,* and the superstition that seven years' bad luck descends when they are broken still persists. Think of the fascination with stories describing faces which appear, looking over the shoulder of the person watching in a mirror, to foretell death or marriage. As a child, I was captivated and intrigued by the Hall of Mirrors on the pier at the resort where we spent our summer holidays. I would stand for ages in front of the different distorting mirrors, sometimes laughing, sometimes strangely disturbed. I have frightened myself by staring long into my own eyes in a mirror. This is perhaps a peculiar thing to do but we must all have done it at some time in our lives. Almost hypnotised, you seem to be looking right into your own soul. Try it.

Mirrors make a good subject for writing. Wherever mirrors are involved there is a sense of unease or distortion or of something not quite real, because reflections are abstract and ephemeral. They are contrary in an obvious way since they reflect things the wrong way round. They can bend light. They are our simplest way of trying to present the concept of infinity by placing an object between two facing mirrors and seeing it reproduced ever smaller into the distance. They are hard and flat but seem to have depth.

When it comes to reflections in water or plain glass, we are not so discomposed, but these, too, offer plenty of scope for writing. All children should be able to find an angle for a poem in such a subject and if they prefer staying in the concrete realm, pure observation can also produce good work.

— ◆ —

Saloon Bar of Mirrors

Here I stand and there I am once more.
As I look the red padded walls crowd after me.
Back and back, far away, there is the sea,
Outside the door behind me I hear the sea again.
Behind each mirror there is a mirror
With padded walls and waves
And in between each one, standing,
Is melancholy me.

At the bottom of my cup I see reflected mirrors
And rows of lined-up stools.
Deep at the back of repeated mirror halls
With a twinkle in my eye
I see myself thinking,
Holding my cup in hand,
And behind me I see the sea
With washing waves upon the shore,
Licking and lapping at the padded walls.

Lucy Head

Hall of Mirrors

A hall of mirrors, quite attracting,
Changes the body, tricks the eye.
Makes your feet look very amusing
Sends your neck going up and down,
Sees your tummy low as the ground,
Chases your waist to grow twice its size,
Lets your legs go topsy-turvy,
Tells your head to grow small as a pea.
Hall of mirrors, quite attracting,
Changes the body, tricks the eye.

Maybe your head will become giddy,
Send you to lands where people look like yourself.
Maybe you'll wonder if the room is smaller,
Maybe you'll think you are going the wrong way.
Hall of mirrors, quite attracting,
Changes the body, tricks the eye.

Shula Lichfield

Three Faces

In a light bulb I see a pale face with huge cheeks,
Behind him there is a strange room
With a mirror reflecting a thin-faced boy.
As I move closer the face grows thinner
And the mirror face grows rounder and shapeless like a
    beanbag.
The three of me glare at each other.

Jonty Leff

The Stream

The wobbly reflection in the stream
Is of curved long grasses
And little bent trees.
The birds fold up like music stands
And mudbanks quiver with cold.
Dots of gold float in the deep blue blanket.
The flowers wriggle like worms.

James Souter

Frozen Tears

Two giants weeping make a wall of ice,
Two reflections make another wall of ice,
Eight reflections make an army of giants.
Strange there were only two of us
And now there are hundreds.
This has cheered me up.
Two giants happy make a wall of joy.

Julian Joyner

Window

A window is life,
Sharp, clear,
But it never looks clear enough
With smudges shadowing the way.
When you are born the window is clean
And as you grow older the dust collects.
You open the window to let the breeze float in,
You open your life to let ideas breeze into your head.
When a window is broken and shattered
So is your life.
You can pick up the pieces slowly and carefully
But they have sharp edges and can wound you deeply
Like snatches of life too painful to remember.

Natasha Lawrence

FACES AND

PLACES

Most of the work I do with children is based on exercises designed to improve their use of language and teach them new techniques to employ later on. The exercises give them a chance to practise without becoming bogged down in trying to come to grips with a subject that is dear to their hearts. Sometimes they are writing from direct personal experience while tackling an exercise, and that is an advantage.

However, most writers will tell you that it is no good sitting around waiting for inspiration. In the meantime you must keep the wheels turning by making yourself write. Often such an inauspicious start takes off into something wonderful; the exercise has served the purpose of releasing ideas and getting you going.

It is said that children must always write from their own experience, and this has led some teachers to restrict the stimuli given to classes. Writing from your own experience does not mean that you actually have to go through something to be able to put it into words. We pick up all sorts of experiences through reading, films, television, other people's accounts, and in our own imaginations. As we grow older we build up a bank of knowledge which enables us to imagine many things which we might never experience firsthand but which can nevertheless be vivid and valid to record.

Almost from the beginning of my teaching career, I became completely fed up with the practice of asking children to write accounts of things they had done on holiday, at Christmas or on bonfire night, or to write about general family news. I still think that it is often nothing better than a time-filling occupation which brings no real benefit to either teacher or pupil. Children just write in a 'chatty' style, which has the appeal of the simple tabloid newspaper, and never really come to grips with properly communicating their thoughts in a more effective, lasting and satisfying way. Reading such churned-out stuff is deadening and depressing for the teacher.

Certainly, children want to tell you about their holidays and family, but I have found that everyone prefers in the end to treat these subjects as a proper writing task. If children have learned to write poetry and had constant practice in using forms and techniques, they are well-equipped to cope with the demands this approach places on them. It really *does* matter when you care about the subject. And, of course, when we feel an emotional commitment, it shows. The authentic voice comes through.

The following examples are very personal poems by the children. They show keen observation, often conjured up in memory long after an event or visit, which is born of interest and love; they are drawing on their own enthusiasms, the best way to learn.

Notice that one of the things that helps to make these poems more interesting to a reader is the detail in them. Choosing which details and the right amount to include is important in writing. When we know a subject very well the main problem is what to leave out. It soon becomes clear to others when we know virtually nothing about a subject, as their interest cannot be sustained. Details and anecdotes bring one person's experience within the comprehension of a reader; they are like markers that help you find your way, and they are what help you remember. Steer clear of blandness and too much abstract theorising; 'be honest and let the poem speak for itself' is some of the best advice I ever received, and I try to pass this on to children.

— ◆ —

My Grandfather

My grandfather is nearly eighty-eight,
His age flowers with the years.
He used to be a great violinist
But when he picks up the instrument now
All you can hear is a scratching sound
And the occasional squeak.
When he walks he's meant to use a stick
And even though he doesn't like it
When he sits down he wants it within sight.
He is hard of hearing so you have to shout
And he won't use his hearing aid.
He can wiggle his ears though.
Also, he can raise one eyebrow.

Lisa Rose

The Caretaker

He used to feed stray cats and clip the bushes,
I loved to watch him in his old working clothes.
When he cut the grass the daisies disappeared
And then would start popping their heads up the next
    day.
There was always a spot in the garden where the sun
    streamed down,
That's where he and I sat watching butterflies and
    birds
Flying over our heads
And where we picked clovers to see if they had four
    leaves
But they never did.
I looked out of my window expecting to see him
But in his place was a stern man
With a wrinkly face like an old apple.
I said, 'Where's Peter?'
'Poor old thing, he died.'

Bridie Mayes

Today I Start School

(said by an incredibly intelligent five year old)

Today I start school
With all those football boys
And pencil-case girls.
Who's this one who makes
Everybody hold hands?
What are you doing
Holding my hand?

There are two hundred children in this playground.
In one corner there are girls
Doing handstands against a wall,
Skirts collapsing over their faces
And only their knickers to be seen.

In another corner there are boys
Celebrating a goal
And hugging each other like they've seen on
    television.

In another part of the playground you see infants
Jumping on and off the climbing frame
With the hoods of their coats on their heads
And the rest loose.

Elsewhere there are girls shouting
Pat-a-cake, pat-a-cake, baker's man,
Clapping each hand together
And patting each other's palms.

Then you see
Calculator-watch-technology enthusiasts
With transformers
Observing how the toy mechanically works.

Near the girls' toilets
They are playing a skipping rope game
With two people quarrelling
About who mistimed the jump.

Fidel Asante

The Photograph

Who ripped the photograph of my mother
Standing with her diploma?
We all denied it.
She was wearing her graduation gown
With sleeves that looked like wings.
Two other photographs were torn;
One of my father and sister,
They were sitting in a cafe drinking tea,
And one of me.
I was wearing my mother's graduation gown –
I looked like a comedian.
They had been ripped up like rubbish no-one cared for.
I often sit and wonder who would want to tear them,
It sometimes sends a chill up my spine.
One of all the family was lying in pieces.
They were torn at night.
We found them on the table in the morning.

James Souter

Finmere

The field I see is muddy and wet
With tractor wheels marking the ground.
The stream runs past that field
Bouncing over rocks and pebbles
And then goes under a very old bridge
Which cars go over sometimes.

Cars that go over the bridge
Sometimes go to the quiet village
Where cottages stand
With smoke coming out of their chimneys.
In this village is an old farmhouse
Where hens used to run
And cows used to moo.
The stables are old, dirty and smelly
With Indian packing cases
And a woodworm-bitten cart.

Jessica Ludgrove

Norfolk

The countryside of Norfolk has many fields of corn,
Corn that sways in the wind.
Lakes are swarming with ducks
That make ripples across the water.
The old abandoned windmill has lost half the fans
And the birds are nesting inside.
The wind whistles past the woods
And makes the branches dance gracefully from side to
    side.
The cottage roofs have small red tiles
And walls are of red bricks.
Churches are made of flint and squat down low.

Julian Joyner

Ship in the

Bottle

I have always been interested in ships in bottles, ever since my father made one when I was young. The obvious fascination is firstly how the ship could be made to go through the narrow bottle neck. It appears to be a case of doing the impossible, and, even though I now know how it is done, I am still able to suspend disbelief and marvel at the phenomenon of a ship in full sail filling a bottle where reason says it should not be.

This is no less fascinating for children today. There is something magical and intriguing here which, I have found, attracts all children and has consistently given rise to remarkable pieces of writing. The discussion which precedes the writing might concentrate on the following aspects.

Who made the ship in the bottle and why? What kind of ship is it? How has it been made? All these things are to do with the 'outside' qualities which may interest some children and allow them to create a character and introduce historical detail to add substance to the poem. For me, it is the 'inside' possibilities that capture the imagination. To suppose that I could shrink myself in some way, like Alice, and enter through the neck of the bottle with the ship is an exercise of the mind which I find very satisfying. There is the element of exploration and yet what you find is completely yours – you are free to imagine what you want. As I am a tall person perhaps it is a need to crawl away into small corners, to be able to curl up in tiny spaces, to be on the inside.

But it works for children too. The genie in the bottle has always been a popular element in stories and Alice's experiences in Wonderland would seem to be relevant too. Children enjoy the idea of putting themselves into the bottle and imagining what it would be like on the ship. This ship goes nowhere, it is stuck in time and place with sails fully rigged and never a breath of wind to fill them. The sea is static, usually highly coloured in tones of cobalt and green with crests of white on the rough still waves. The sky is immediately the curve of the glass and the horizon is distorted by reflections that change. What would it be like to be a crew member of this ship, to be a tiny figure stuck into position with a specific job to do and yet no way of carrying it out? How would the captain of such a ship feel? Would commands echo out through the staleness of the trapped air with no-one able to obey them? Would the sailors long for a storm in order to be active, or would they rather reach land and go on leave? Possibly there is something ignobling in being trained and equipped for sailing and yet captured and 'pirated' away to a drawing room table or a museum case only to be stared at and conveniently carried from place to place. There is also the romantic air of 'tall ships' and 'before the mast' and the taste and sound of the sea – putting your ear to an empty bottle has the same effect as listening to a shell. Perhaps you can imagine that things *do* happen inside the bottle unnoticed by the world outside.

There are numerous angles the children can take by just looking and thinking. It is not absolutely necessary to have an actual ship in a bottle to show them – I never have – or, indeed, to have a picture of one. It could be useful, of course, and it is true to say that in most cases it is better to have something 'concrete' on which to base observations – poems tend, as a general rule, to be more interesting and arresting the more specific they are. However, this must be judged according to the children you are dealing with and the subject they are being given. In this particular case, if the children are used to concentrating their imaginations, a good discussion can provide the details in such a way that each child has his or her own 'concrete' picture in mind which will be different from that of others. This will ensure that the poems are more individual and not so many reproductions of the same thing, which is to be avoided where possible.

Ship in a Bottle

Picture behind glass.
This life, now death,
This morning, now evening,
These years, just hell turned to stone.
I call to the helmsman,
I call to the captain,
I call to my god –
Sorry, their god.
He cannot see me,
For the child who sailed me
Through and around
The childish battles in his mind
Brought me to this steady mousetrap in his room.
I know I am not a sailor.
He, by my posed working hand, is not the captain,
That mindless man is not the helmsman
And they are not the crew.
We are behind the window of a craftsman's mind,
Strays from God's working hands in the sky.

Miles Greene

Ship in the Bottle

It's not the real sea,
All I float in is wax.
I hear the water rushing up against my hull
But it's just echoes.
The sky is blotted out prematurely
By fingers that touch me,
Not clouds but people's hands.
Man made me small
So I would not look down on him.
My sails yearn to touch the wind
But the wind passes over me.

Orson Nava

Ship in a Bottle

Floating on an aimless current,
A constant reminder that we'll never reach port.
Hope in a bottle is not easy to find
And happiness was lost in a storm.

Matthew Festenstein

Ship in a Bottle

No space,
I am cramped up,
My sails are small.
I have an anchor but no people.
All I can see is a blurry room with lots of books.
My flag has turned yellow,
The bottle is dusty
And the bottom feels as if it's falling out
But I am strong enough for a boy to use
As a toy.
The top is really special
For when a person looks at me
I get a gush of wind,
I think I am in the sun, sailing.
I have forgotten too many things.
There are hundreds of ships
Not like me.

Tara Byrne

The Ship in the Bottle

Standing in a glass bottle motionless
With only your thoughts running through your head.
The sun never sets in a glass bottle.
Only a faint glimpse of a boy
Sitting at a desk.
The dust settles on the glass bottle,
The dust of age.
An old man sits at the desk.

Katy Miles

Ship in a Bottle

No fish come to our net,
Our one and only ship in our world.
No cheers from the people
When we come to shore.
We make no profit from our job,
Only our souls' creator makes it.
No fish come to our net.

Sarah Hellier

Jesters,

Clowns and Dummies

There has always been something fascinating about the clown. Whether it be a circus clown, a comedian, a jester, a joker or a Shakespearean type of fool, there is the constant reminder of different layers and contradiction. On the surface these figures are supposed to be fun, to make us laugh (all the above words have that connotation). However, the surface seems to be only a thin veneer over a much darker nature. The clown makes us cry – as a small child I was frightened of clowns – the white face and crosses for eyes almost deliberately obliterating any sign of human emotions. The large, red-lipped smile is almost a gash, and the glow of the eyes, the only sign of life behind the mask, can look very sinister. The joker in the pack of cards works by no rules, he can take on the rôle of any of the other cards and is a law unto himself. The court jester or fool can get away with saying things other people would never dream of saying if they value their lives. Under the guise of a kind of madness the seeming simpleton can utter home truths with impunity, often dressing them in riddles to perplex a listener momentarily and to give himself room for manoeuvre in the interpretation of his words.

There are other figures akin to jesters in that they can appear to have a disturbing nature. These are the inanimate human representations like scarecrows, ventriloquists' dummies, waxworks, statues, shop window mannequins and dolls (particularly older ones, less so the modern kind). We make them in our likeness but our imagination has to fill out their characters and put words into their mouths. The silence surrounding them otherwise can be alarming. To see a dolls' hospital can be very strange, too. It is the rows of limbs, eyeballs and separate heads that seem so gruesome and haunting.

The odd thing is that if you mention the word 'clown', people immediately prepare themselves to be amused; the word acts as a trigger through our conditioning. Question people more closely and you often find that feeling of unease, sometimes dislike, lurking underneath. Clowns have done their job well. I do not think they are supposed to be cosy entertainers; they should jolt us out of complacency while making us laugh. The very act of laughing is akin to fear and aggression.

With all this in mind I wondered if children had the same feelings. Since it is always said that you take the children to the circus to see the clowns, I was interested to see what they would say. The following poems arose from a discussion we had on the subject, in which we all shared stories and feelings associated with clowns. But the children also had scope to write about any of the other figures mentioned above.

— ◆ —

Clowns' Faces

These are the laughing faces
Of men that are now dead,
But their painted faces still jeer
And taunt the old crooked houses.
The white masks of the faces
Are coming in thousands
Attached to no body.
Only the masks come.
They come closer and closer,
They tease and scare
And in the same second
They are going into a whirlwind,
Millions of them.
Suddenly I have been picked up
Into the mass of faces.
I've been taken to a world of memories.
I see an old man sitting in front of a mirror
With lights around it.
He is sitting as still as a statue.

Nancy Carpenter-Turner

The Ventriloquist's Dummy

I was exported from France.
I'm dead
Until I sit on the ventriloquist's lap
In front of an audience of men, women and children.
We start.
He grits his teeth while speaking for me.
I try to speak but nothing happens,
I have a tongue but it is not mine.
I have movements
But I can't, and don't, work them.
He sticks his hand into my stomach
Pressing me inside, forcing me to speak.
He dresses me in the most ridiculous clothes
Which I hate.
After the show
He throws me into a box
And puts me in the boot.
When we arrive at home
He gives me to his son to play with.
Once he pulled me so violently
He tore my arm off.
I wasn't meant to feel pain
So I didn't.

Nicolai Bradnum

Joker

I am a joker
Standing in a painting
Waiting to be looked at.
I'm freckle-faced
And I stand next to a gnome
At the bottom of the garden.
I've a joker's cap,
A joker's mind
And a joker's talent.
Inside me I feel as though
I'm a little statue

Waiting to be moved.
The gnome starts to talk to me
But I can't hear him
Because it's like a dream.
Suddenly I'm with the King
Risking my life to make him laugh.
I'm on a playing card
Being tossed about
Acting like a jester,
Then a clown.
I never want the day to come
When I'm the joker
And the players decide
They don't want me.
Or, when I'm laid face up
With the Queen face down on me
Smothering me with kisses.

Sean Carnegie

Clown

There I was in the middle of the tent
Looking at the people as they looked at me.
It was like feeling people as they felt me,
Sensing them as they sensed me,
Pulling faces, and the people laughing away.
I felt my fears as they felt mine.
I felt like a person inside me, laughing,
Laughing at my own jokes.

I went to explore the world.
I came back to see the children,
To let them laugh at my jokes for ever.
All the time I felt them inside me,
Laughing away like a joker,
A laughing joker,
Coming out of a joker box
Laughing its head off.

Caroline Bradley

The Ventriloquist's Dummy

I wait for the moment
When his arm wriggles up my spine
And a form of life runs through my body.
And when it reaches my mouth
I seem to be talking
But the voice (if it's mine)
Comes from his direction.
Yet, whenever I look
His mouth is as still as can be
And I feel the vibration of his squeaky voice
And I'm insulted.
The audience is laughing
But it's always the same
And after every one of our appearances
His arm slithers down
And I'm put in a box.
I am mute,
I've lost my voice.
But when I'm crouched up in the box
Secretly inside me
Life is waiting for this moment
When I'm alone.
And when this moment has come
I feel as free as anyone can be.
And with the same clothes
And the same voice
I make my appearance once more.
This time as I sit on his lap
I feel
It's not as bad as I thought.
It's my life.

Yael Shavit

The Jester

The jester is a cat who dances and prances,
From the audience came a round of applause.
The king sat unmoved and called for more boars.
The jester is a hyena who giggles and wriggles,
The audience's remarks were unclear.
The jester's hopes began to disappear.
The jester is a juggler who fumbles the tumbles,
The audience booed and hissed.
The king called for the executioner
With his blood-covered fist.
The jester shivered with fear from head to toe,
His blood stopped its flow.
The jester is crying and dying.

Julian Joyner

64

Earth, Air,

Fire and Water

There are not really any new ideas for subjects in poetry – you can generally break them down into the age-old categories of love, life and death. For children, the areas are, broadly speaking, animals, nature generally, people, places and death! The teacher, then, has to think of new ways of presenting the same topics so that they appear different. So we try to provide a new slant to encourage the children to be excited enough to approach old ideas from a new angle.

The four elements – earth, air, fire and water – have a magical ring about them. The signs of the zodiac are divided up into these four groups, and if we consider them it becomes clear that they are the very stuff of life itself. Without any one of them we could not exist. In its basic form, fire is the sun. So taking this idea as a subject can give a unifying theme for a series of poems.

The subject can be approached in different ways, perhaps looking at the elements one at a time or in their basic forms, or in an historical context. Another way, which I have used with the subject of places, is to make lists on the board of all the things the children can think of which might come under each heading. For example:

Earth	Air	Fire	Water
mud	breeze	lava	river
sand	tornado	sun	ice
stone	cloud	firefly	rain
stalagmite	pollution	candle	puddle
minerals	whirlwind	stars	swimming pool
dust	breath	bonfire	rainbow

and so on.

Having produced a fairly long list for each, the children then proceed to select one idea as a starting point for a poem. With so many to choose from, no child should have any difficulty in finding something to spark the imagination. Often it is best to suggest that they see if anything reminds them of an experience they have had. Firsthand experience will be more vivid in their minds and therefore more likely to give rise to poems which have that air of authority and individual voice we look for in writing. Some of the following examples are poems of this kind, while others arise out of real experience but are developed through the imagination.

— ◆ —

The Little Willywilly

The small whirlwind eddied round and round.
The sand, dust and dry leaves caught in its passage
Pirouetted, joining in the dance.
It reeled ever faster, swirling and spinning.
The boy tried to move into the cool vortex of air
For he was hot after the climb
But it edged away.
He tried to get caught in the twisting screw.
It was coiling towards the forest
Leaving a trail of fine sandgrains,
It was slowing down.
The boy stopped and it stayed still.
The leaves started to drop until
There was only a small pile
Where it had been and gone.

Seth Wallis-Jones

Rain Versus Wind

Rain patting on the soil reached the tip of my sill,
Palm trees danced to the swish of rain's friend – the
    wind.
A fight has been started by the two friends.
Rain punches the ground violently,

Wind pulls and tosses things he passes by.
Everybody races to get home
So as not to be struck by thunder
Or swirled into air by the wind.
A troop of scouts is hit by the rain
And the fire of the barbecue is put out.
The joyful scouts throw their caps in the air
And stamp in the mud.
Now the rain has died, the sun is out,
And the promise of God colours the sky with rainbows.

Bukky Omotoso

The Hurricane

The distant cries of a howling wind
Are coming closer and closer.
Death is in the air
With a sense of close destruction.
There is a feeling of hopelessness
And uselessness.
It can be seen now,
A huge, twisting, raging spiral
Spinning across the land
And murdering everything it meets.
Coming closer and closer.
An aeroplane is caught in its hurling force
And thrown to the ground
In a sudden crack of enormous explosions
Muffled by the sound of a mad wind.
Coming closer and closer.
All we can think is that we're going to die
When it rips and tears upon us
With excruciating noise and pain.

Josh Szeps

Swimming Pool Without Water

You are rejected.
Nobody will swim in you because you have no water.
I am the only person still with faith.
I sit here and watch the lights glisten
On your shiny silvery sides.
There are no echoing shouts
Rebounding around your walls any more,
Just the mournful whirr of the blood
Rushing around my head.
All the clocks have stopped,
Their continuous turning mechanisms
Have slowed down to a menacing halt.
The attendants do not wave or shout
Or kick you out
And all the diving boards have been barricaded.
Your usually wet and puddled sides
Are now dry.
I am the sole survivor of your audience.

Neill Crawford

The Mine

The mine is a gaping mouth
Into the stomach of the hill.
The ladder, its tongue, reaches
Into the blackness of a tomb
For many who have worked there.

Lisa van Gelder

A Candle

Shades of golden thread circle the flame.
It quivers with fright
Each time a draught enters the room.
Slowly the candle shrinks down
Into a bubbling ocean of wax.
It flickers while it fights

To keep its flame burning,
It chokes and splutters
As it meets defeat.
As soon as it is dead
The spirit rises
In a thin stream of smoke.

Brigid Gorski

The Light

The street lamp's bulb has broken,
Who will fix it?
That part of the street is dark.
It will be dark for a long time,
No-one will replace the bulb for weeks –
They never do.
Soon all the streets will be dark
And we will have to watch them fade
One by one
Like lemmings jumping off a cliff.

James Souter

65

Shells, Pictures
and Jack-in-the-Box

This is an exercise which is similar to *Ship in the Bottle* (see Chapter 62) in that it partly involves putting oneself inside an object. It does more than that however as will become clear. It should be carried out as a class lesson and no preparation should be done. There is an element of surprise needed to ensure its success. Ideally the class should work in silence and fairly strict timing ought to be observed. Giving time limits in the way this exercise does will probably automatically encourage silent working – no time to talk. The exercise is taken step by step.

First of all the words *shell, picture, jack-in-the-box* (and any suitable objects which have an inside into which one might go in the imagination) are written on the board. Nothing is said about them but the children are asked to choose one word only and write it at the top of the page. Ask them to imagine a particular shell, picture, or jack-in-the-box.

They then have five to ten minutes *only* in which to write down a description of what their object looks like, starting with the words 'Outside the . . .' When the time is up everyone must stop. The next thing you ask them to do is to put themselves *into* the object and write for five to ten minutes on what that looks like, beginning with the words, 'Inside the . . .'

They should soon have built up a detailed picture of their subject which has made it their very own. They should now be ready to move on to the next stages which will take them out of the concrete and provide scope for a different kind of writing. Between each stage there is no discussion, no talking at all. This would interrupt and spoil the whole fantasy that is being woven.

The next piece of writing concerns the dreams of the jack-in-the-box, or picture, or shell and begins with the words 'My . . . dreams . . .' The same time limit is set.

The fourth angle depends for its success on the atmosphere that has been generated. By now the children should be very involved in their subject and should feel a possessiveness towards what they have created. They are asked to give it away. What feelings would they have in doing this and what instructions, if any, would they give to the recipient? This section begins with the words, 'If I give my . . . to you . . .'

Having given it away they will probably experience a sense of loss or release. Either way can provide the substance of the fifth and final selection which begins with the words, 'Without my . . .'

The exercise is now complete and the best thing to do is to hear everyone's piece. This could be regarded as a workshop and everyone encouraged to make comments both critical and complimentary about each other's work. This is best led by the teacher but as unobtrusively as possible. The teacher's place here, I think, is to 'head off' destructive criticism, and over-enthusiastic praise of friends' work or of things which are perhaps less worthy of it. Encouragement with discernment should be the theme and the teacher can perhaps enter the discussion to endorse a comment or to highlight a passage or phrase which is good but seems to have been overlooked. We do not want to discourage children in any way from being prepared either to venture opinions and constructive criticism, or to offer their own work for discussion by a class. The more children know about the writing of poetry, the better they will become at conducting workshops. If these are carried out in the right spirit the benefit that can be gained is enormous.

Some of the pieces written for this exercise might stand on their own without any more work, but generally what has been written serves as notes and a basis on which to do further work. It may be that one section is obviously better than the others and can be worked on to provide a poem. It may be that there is material for more than one poem. This exercise can show a way of working for the future, namely to write down quickly all the

thoughts on a subject out of which a line will emerge which can
be pursued.

Jack-In-A-Box

Outside the Jack-in-the-Box was the silent fright.
Inside the Jack-in-the-Box
The fright was in the making,
It forgot to frighten the millions.
The thoughts forgot it in its silence.
The box nerves broken open into loud realism.
The trap door opens
Into the mist of light,
Shouting brilliantly, sharp in laughter and
Screams.
As he swings free, hung by the neck,
Blue eyes set in pools of concrete,
Smiling he finds pleasure in his death.
Through the larder is carried the box,
The silent procession fights the crowds of age.
I gave this coffin to my past youth.
I cremated the box in the flames of my past time,
Lost in time.
My shadow found a place behind me,
The shadow loomed square
And three dimensional in its cubed glory.
The shadow wasn't mine.
It sulked away and was forgotten
As it had forgotten
How to frighten me.

Miles Greene (YWW)

Picture

Outside the picture the big golden rimmed frame,
The yellow flowered wallpaper
Leading down to the fireplace.
The curve-shaped hook to hold up a thousand thoughts,
The picture handed from century to century, glistening of tomorrow,

From side to side the canvas cracks and fades
As the house falls to decay.
The picture rises to brilliance.
Outside the picture the gold frame
With angels peeking over
Like the sun rising to bring new life.
The outside edge is as far as you can go,
If you go further you will fall into eternity.

Inside the picture the world is being held in three single colours
Rattling to escape.
The baby sitting in the corner waiting to be free
To grow and burst out.
The small squashed space to be cut
Into a million little stars to be shared by the world.
'Mother, mother,' the babe shouts out
But nobody can hear inside the ring of torture,
Nor in heaven can he be heard.
The plants never grow inside,
They are seeds for ever.

The picture dreams of fame from the world
Yet it is still stuck in an everyday room,
In an everyday house
Soon to crumble and dissolve.
Who can save it now?
Now that it is alone for ever,
Dreaming, yet always in reality.
The babe wants to grow and cannot,
The child's mind may comfort its round body
And yet do nothing to help.
'Mother, mother, come and make me famous', he dreams.

If I give the picture to you
How long would it survive?
Would the dream fade away for ever?
Will I be assured of the baby's care
Or will you leave him to die?
The question is, shall you take it

And never refuse to give it the fame it wants?
Is your mind set on the looking after
Of the diamond stone that never was found?
Can it survive without my mind?

Without my picture my brain is emptied
And will have to be filled with more things.
Who can care for a picture
When the world is falling apart?
I am falling apart as well
But I care not for myself
'Mother, mother,' the baby is still trapped.
The Mona Lisa laughs.

Nicholas Midgley

66

BÊTES NOIRES

Writing about people can cover a broad range of subjects depending on the angle we take. For example, we can write about family, friends, enemies, famous people, historical characters, fictional characters, old people, young people, people at work, people at play, and many more. With a theme as wide as 'People', it is essential that we choose specific areas upon which to concentrate; we also want children to write about people more than once in their careers, so each time we need a different stimulus to capture their imaginations.

One of these, which generally seems to work, is to write about our *bêtes noires*, or pet hates, among the types of people we meet. The best pieces will probably combine the general characteristics of universally recognised 'types' with descriptions of actual people we know or have seen. This way we bring personal experience into the writing, which will give it an authenticity that makes it more effective.

Children should think of people who have character traits which annoy them to a greater or lesser degree. These may be people they know well, people they have seen around their neighbourhood, famous people of the past or present, or even famous fictional characters. It is important that children know enough details about their subjects to make their writing vivid and convincing. It is always better if they can communicate their antipathy towards their *bêtes noires* by the way they describe them, rather than by a bald statement of dislike.

Although I have dealt exclusively with the idea of people as *bêtes noires*, it would also be possible to extend this to cover instances of modern living. Some possible subjects might be: canned music, supermarket checkouts, commercial breaks, soap operas, parental advice, dog-fouling in public places, and any other of life's irritations which, though important, are minor in comparison to the larger problems that face the world.

The following are from a longer sequence, entitled '*Bêtes Noires*', written by three children aged 13 years.

— ◆ —

The Ardent Feminist

I'm off to a
Minorities' women's ethnic dance exhibition
At the right-on, feminist-rallying, group-funded
Theatre in Hackney,
And I'm not quite sure when I'll be back
Because I'm boycotting all transport
That exploits women,
And whose profits go to the state
And are spent on arms.
So I want you to Spring-clean the house while I'm out.
After all,
We couldn't have any
Male-dominated, sexual-stereotypical women
Cleaning all the time,
Could we?

Calum Roche (BYW)

The Slob

He sits on the wall
By the top of Canfield Gardens,
Killing all the flowers
With his grotesque body odour,
Burping like a toad that has no manners,
Always seeking attention
From the sickened passer-by.
I often think to myself,
Where does this slob live?
Has he enrolled with the Slobs' Association
On Finchley Road?
He treats this poor harmless wall
As an open-air toilet
And sick bed.

Noushin Sorayyapour (BYW)

The Fat American Tourist

'Where's the tube station, Mac?'
Says the obesely fat American,
Wearing bright Bermuda shorts
Stretching to keep in the flubber
Of his wobbling thighs.
'Right at the lights,' I say,
Sending him to Parliament Hill Fields –
Punishment for not noticing the huge
Belsize Park Tube Station sign
Right behind him.
'Thanks, Mac,' he says,
And winks,
His large camera bouncing
On the immensity of his chest.
I snigger as I go into the station.
I'm in good time for the bus
And there are only two people in front of me
In the queue for a bus pass.
The one in front
Only speaks Latvian.

David Stallibrass (BYW)

The Drunk

Jim, the perennially red-faced drunk,
Stares at a tile across the station,
Asking it to 'Call me that just *one more time!*'
His concentration dwindles
And he takes another swig of cider,
The Strongbow that safeguarded him
From consciousness last night.
A man walks past in a suit.
'Schush me. You gotta shigarette, mate?'

No reply.
A boy, going to school, arcs around him
But doesn't escape.
'Shpare shome change?'
No boy.
And another typical non-memorable day is begun.

Calum Roche (BYW)

The Sneak

She crawls like a slimy snail to school,
Covering its trail with a lubricant,
Wanting you to slip
So she has something to talk about.
Whenever you squash the piece of plasticine
To dried-up droppings
Pretending it is her face,
She always catches you
And makes a headline out of a subtitle.
This tiny, sneaky girl who fancies herself
Is always in my way.

Noushin Sorayyapour (BYW)

The Wimp

She's not just a drip,
It runs in the family.
She is a squatty, pathetic weed
Who's the type to sit behind her desk
With only her finger protruding in the air,
Calling out,
'Miss, Miss!'

She is the type
To hold her best friend's hand
Because she is going to her house.
She is the type
Who sits on the bench at play,
With her thumb in her mouth

And her jolly crunchy apple
In her other hand.
She is the type
Who won't participate
But is unable to refuse;
The type to sit on her own
With her 'my little pony'
And 'Barbie doll',
Combing the plastic hair.
She is the type who cannot sing,
But stands at the back
And all you can hear are her squeaks.

And her mother is the type
To say at a school-journey meeting,
'Please may Roberta bring an umbrella?'

Noushin Sorayyapour (BYW)

CONSUMER

REPORTS

Not a new idea this, but one which may have been forgotten of late or may be new to more recently qualified teachers. Peter Porter's poem, 'A Consumer's Report', popular in the seventies, is based on the kind of market research carried out by manufacturers in order to gauge the effectiveness of their advertising and the popularity of their products with the general buying public. Porter imagines he is answering questions about a product he has tested, and this product is 'Life'.

The sort of questions that appear on such consumer report forms are as follows:

- How did you hear about this product?
- Where did you buy it, or was it a gift?
- Why did you choose this product above others?
- Do you think it is priced correctly for what it is?
- Was the packaging attractive and convenient to carry?
- Was it economical to use?
- Were the instructions user-friendly?
- Did it do the job for which you bought it?
- Was there anything more you wished it could do?
- Would you recommend it to your friends?

Children today are quite sophisticated with regard to advertising techniques, and know what they want from things they buy. They know the jargon involved in the selling game. They are bombarded with it on television, at the cinema, on commercial radio and in magazines. So the idea here is to bring all that knowledge to bear on the sort of things which cannot be packaged and sold on supermarket shelves. They either write a consumer report, as if they are being canvassed for their opinion, write a letter requesting information on a product in which they are interested, or write a letter of complaint about something they feel was not all it was made out to be. Suitable subjects might include, Life, Death, Love, Happiness, Responsibility, Adulthood, Sleep, Dreams, Anger, Success, and so on.

— ◆ —

Death

Dear Sirs/Madams/Angels/Demons/Minor Deities,

I've been researching Death,
Where to get it from and how it works.
You see,
I think I'm going to be needing it soon
And if you don't book in advance
Then, well, you never know what cowboy you'll be travelling with.

I fear Death.
I don't think it is advertised properly
And it has an awful reputation,
And I would like somewhere to go afterwards –
An after-life, if you will.

Some say you go to Heaven
And become an angel;
This doesn't appeal,
Since sitting on a cloud all day
Isn't my idea of fun,
And I can't play the harp,
Let alone guide people's lives.
Even Hell sounds preferable;
It's warm, and, from what I hear,
Never boring.

But I just want to be happy.
I'm sure you've got your own version of a Leeds Home Arranger
And I would be delighted to see your prospectus.
Please mail me as soon as possible
And I'll consider the options carefully.

Yours sincerely

David Stallibrass (BYW)

Happiness Isn't Working

Dear Sir/Madam,

I am writing to you to complain.
I have tried to use your product to the fullest,
However, it has not satisfied me.
I bought it with the idea in mind
That it would change the way I looked at hard work.
I thought I could make full use of it.

The back of the package said, and I quote:
'Your housework will be fun, with this all-in-one.'
Believe me, this was not true,
The product did not help me in the slightest.
It got me into trouble with my family and friends,
I even laughed at them because they didn't have it.

It never seemed to fit into my handbag.
I've no idea what attracted me to buy it –
Probably the most unattractive model there,
With sharp pieces sticking out of the sides.
I also found the call-out charge to correct the fault
Was definitely over the top, and it did no good.

I could only use it once, then had to dispose of it.
I was also told it was meant for a single woman,
Living on her own – it didn't help me.
I am disgusted with this product and expect a refund.
I will certainly not purchase from your company again.
With regret, an 'unhappy' customer.

Noushin Sorayyapour (BYW)

Dreams

I'm writing this letter to tell you
That I am definitely not satisfied
With the product, DREAMS.
The problem is – it doesn't work
And the price is much too high.
Every time I use it

It just isn't strong enough.
The dream keeps escaping from the bottle
And I have to chase it round the house.
I think you should consider redesigning it
If you want it to sell well;
I'm sure you know
That people cannot use nightmares,
But this just isn't the way
To get rid of them.
I expected DREAMS to help me sleep peacefully,
Give me ideas so that, at least once,
I could enjoy myself;
But, instead, it made me restless.
The dreams I was meant to have
Didn't come at first,
But when they did
They were closer to nightmares.
I heard of DREAMS in a magazine
– *Consumer Reports*, to be exact.
I sent off for it
But I regret it very much.
I want my money back.
Yours truly

Lisa Kramer (BYW)

Letter of Complaint

Dear Sir/Madam,

I am writing to complain about BOREDOM,
The wonder product you sent me.
It looked like a good idea on the picture
But nowhere in the ad. did it say
What trouble it would bring.
The words above the drawing told me
That I'd never have to work again.
This was very misleading.
True enough, I haven't worked since I got it,
But I thought it meant instant prosperity.
The side effects are definitely undesirable,

i.e. insomnia, tedium, etc.
I took it on holiday
And it completely spoiled my time on the beach.
I was not able to do anything
As my mind would not concentrate on making decisions.
So, for the above reasons,
I would like to cancel my order
For 'Unlimited BOREDOM'.
I hope that as I have replied promptly
You will refund my money.
In the meantime I am forced
To bear with the remaining quantity.
Yours very sluggishly,

Nicholas Bieber (**BYW**)

GROWING UP

This idea is mainly appropriate for children aged around ten to sixteen, as it is about taking stock of one's life in that in-between age – no longer a child, but not yet an adult. There are three sections to such poems. The first looks back at the writer's childhood, drawing upon personal, as well as universal, experiences and memories, and identifies those which usually must be left behind as we grow older – the putting away of childish things. The section might begin with the words, 'When I was a child I would . . . ', or something similar, followed by all the things that in your mind belong specifically to childhood and which you think you will no longer be able to do when you are older, for example:

When I was a child I would play all day
Without a thought for tomorrow.
I could cry without shame when I hurt myself . . .

Children might also include childhood beliefs which become less black and white, or are even disproved, as you grow older.

The second section looks forward to adulthood and to all the things you could do as an adult. These are either possible, or highly likely, or may be things you will probably never do, but as an adult you would have the capability to carry out. Children should consider that adulthood usually brings increased responsibility and the necessity to think of others more, as well as power and independence; it can bring disappointment and loss, as well as success and security. Begin this section with the words, 'When I am adult I could . . . ' and follow with all the things you would like to do, or, as in the example here, things you *could* do (but presumably will not) based on some of the bad deeds perpetrated in the so-called adult world. For example:

When I am adult I could cut down whole forests,
Lord it over others, or
Destroy someone's world with one withering look . . .

The last section brings us back to the present and looks at the
child in these in-between years. How does it feel to be halfway
between childhood and adulthood? What worries do we have?
What hopes or fears? What expectations? Do we feel ready to
cope with it all, or does time move too slowly and we cannot wait
to be free of this growing-up burden? Children should try to be
very honest and to draw on their own experiences – this way
their original and authentic voice will shine through their
writing and help to make it more effective. I find that this
exercise is extremely helpful to young people at this stage of life,
as it encourages them to consider many of their almost
subconscious thoughts, and to try to articulate some of their
concerns. These early teenage years are obviously a time of some
turmoil and change, both physical and emotional, and such an
exercise taps into their lives in a very real way. Begin this section
with the words, 'Caught between the two I . . . ', or something
similar. For example:

Caught between the two I am
Too old for cuddles without embarrassment
And too young to know how to cope with death.
The child in me wants to right all wrongs
But a gradual awareness of my limitations
Grows stronger every day . . .

Age Concern

When I was a child
I would snake around the playground
With a chain made of jumpers;
I'd make a jungle out of
The creases in my duvet
For animals to explore

Or for a motor cross course.
I would make up after arguments
And relinquish all my grudges,
I would not cast judgement
On absolute strangers.

When I am adult
I could have my independence.
I could control my own future,
For better or for worse;
I could buy eccentric ornaments
And not be told
That my money could be better spent.
I could live on junk food
And see any film –
But then the 'dare' of it would go.

Caught between the two
I have the worst of both worlds.
The carefree child in me
Is mocked for having fun,
And the adult in me
Does not get understood.
Adults see me as a child,
Children see me as adult,
But inside even I
Do not know where I stand.

Calum Roche (BYW)

As Time Goes By

When I was a child I'd suck my thumb,
I'd play with my He-Man, I'd cuddle with Mum.
When I put on clothes it didn't matter what colour,
I had hair long and short, I played with my brother.
I dribbled my ice cream, I slurped my soup,
I sang nursery songs, I played with a hoop,
Sometimes I'd shout and sometimes I'd cry,
And sometimes I'd kick things – God only knows why.

When I am an adult I could teach at a school,
I could stay up all night or break every rule.
I'd want to do good for the world and mankind –
The best PM or President earth could find.
I wouldn't want to cry or go to gaol,
I might write a book or a fairytale.
I wonder what people will think when I'm grown?
I could get married, I could be alone,
I could be unemployed, I could be a rich man,
I could bring on world peace. Will I do what I can?

Now as I enter my teenage years,
I want to be adult, but have many fears.
What will I do after GCSE?
An 'A' level or two? University?
Will Dad get a new job? Will Mum find one too?
Both of them teachers, what will they do?
Will the Tories continue to mess up the country,
Run down schools and ruin the economy?
Will I get a good job? What will it be?
Will I be on the dole, or a good salary?
They say there's a greenhouse up there in the sky:
Will the icecaps melt? Will some creatures die?
And what about now? What about me?
Will I learn more each day? Will they help me to see?

I'll go back to computers and football and play –
Will I be this free at the end of my day?

Anthony Carrigan (PH)

The following example uses travelling as a metaphor for growing up. Roads have often been used as metaphors for life, notably Robert Frost's 'The Road Not Taken', and Christina Rossetti's 'Uphill', among others. The language of roads (e.g. crossroads, the straight and narrow, primrose path, routes and destinations) has naturally lent itself to descriptions of one's journey through life and the various decisions one is called upon to make along the way.

Approaching a Bend

As a child I took the back seat,
Strapped in for safety,
Unable to fend for myself.
Though as I grew older
I was introduced to the passenger seat
Where things were just for looking,
No touching.
Being in between isn't easy.
It is like seeing the light
At the end of the tunnel,
But not knowing how to reach it.
There's a train approaching.

This age is like being a car radio.
The one taking the front seat
Turns you on.
Edging near is the disconnector,
Nothing can change what's coming.
You can't reverse or hit the brake
And suddenly the connection is broken –
The bridge cuts me off
From the outside world.

Yet over the years the change is made
From teenage to adult,
From pavement to road,
From passenger to driver.

Noushin Sorayyapour (BYW)

This final poem looks specifically at old age and how the writer
wants to be when he grows old. This has links with the theme of
this chapter, but also arises as an idea from poems by Jenny
Joseph ('Warning') and Jim Burns ('Note for the Future').
There is no reason why children should not write about only
one of the three sections described fully above, if they prefer.
This will be a different exercise, as it loses the specific reflective

element of comparing the three stages, but it still provides an interesting idea, for all that.

When My Old Age Pension Draws Near

When my hourglass rotates
For the ultimate time

I won't be the man with a buttonhole and monocle
Inquiring, 'What wine shall we have for supper,
Dear?'

I shan't be the man who was once on the bus
Constantly gibbering and laughing,
'Can I sit on your knee, please?'
And they let him
So as not to hurt his feelings.

I won't be the forgetful family man
Who buys the same present
For the same person
Every year.

If I am placed in an old people's home
I will commit suicide
In the quickest and most imaginative way possible.

Then I will be spared the anguish
Of having to save my state pension for weeks
And weeks
Just to buy something
I might not even need.

My clothes won't make me look loathsome:
No purple overcoats with brown and white shirts,
No red cravats that clash with my orange glasses,
No blue cords.
No, I won't be colour blind.

I want to be able to live
Without having to go to the Senior Citizens' Lunch Club.

I won't have a body that lets me be diseased,
I won't have to use a crutch to walk,
I won't hobble with each step I take.
I won't have to take a pill for my heart,
And one for my blood,
My neck,
My brain,
And yet another, to counteract the side effects.

David Stallibrass (BYW)

THE CREATION

OF THE WORLD

One of the projects I have frequently done with my Year 6 classes is comparative mythology. We pay particular attention to the different stories told by peoples through the ages to deal with the question of how the world began. These creation myths are always popular with children and are fascinating to compare. One can find so many parallels both in subject matter and in the techniques used in story-telling, for example, the importance of numbers like three and forty.

Today, very few families are regular churchgoers, and often it is only strict religious groups like Jews, Catholics and Muslims who teach their children about such things. This is a shame because, whether you believe or not, the stories are so good and there is no doubt that the children respond to them (in spite of their so-called sophisticated tastes for programmes like *EastEnders* and *Neighbours*). Stories that have survived so long must have something. The 'magic' still works.

It occurred to me that I could extend this interest to poetry writing. The obvious way seemed to be to ask children to write their own creation myth, and this I have tried. Whether I did not introduce the idea properly, or did not prepare them well enough, I do not know. But what resulted was disappointing. There was a tendency to fall back on stereotyped names and settings, heavily influenced by comics and sci-fi films. They also found it more difficult to write their thoughts as poems. Possibly I shall try again with another group of children to see if I achieve a different result.

What did seem to work rather well, though, was asking the children to write a poem arising out of work we had been doing. The examples later in this chapter clearly all have their origin in the story from the beginning of the book of Genesis in the Old Testament. This creation story is so well put together that it never fails to fire the imagination. It must be read in the Authorized Version (King James's Bible), otherwise it completely loses its appeal. The story is written to a pattern based on the magic number seven (seven days) and has a powerful main character, God, who out of chaos builds the world we know, layer by layer. It thrives on repetition, like so many folk tales, and children love repetition. The poetic language of the translation only serves to enhance the effect ('and the evening and the morning were the first day'). Do not let anyone suggest to you that the language is too difficult for children to understand – it is not. (If only schools did not shy away from such things! They even often omit our finest popular writer ever – Shakespeare – on the grounds that the language is too difficult. The illiterate Elizabethan audiences and my primary school children have much in common – they love(d) Shakespeare! Please excuse this digression.)

The scope for writing is extensive, and for primary colleagues there is the opportunity to mount exciting wall displays picturing the Creation. One of my classes even did a *son et lumière* assembly on the subject, using slides, tape recorders, microphones, silhouettes, overhead projector and coloured lights. When a class is so involved and enthusiastic about the material, they are ripe for expanding this into their own writing. The following examples will give you some idea of the possibilities.

— ◆ —

The Making of the World

On the first day God made light,
And he was dazzled and made dark,
And then a switch.

On the second day God made the earth,
And he took the elements,
Shuffled them
And dealt them.

On the third day God made plants.
He learnt to breathe the fresh air
Before it was too late
And he saw beauty.

On the fourth day God made the stars
And God was proud of them.
He winked at them
And they winked back.

On the fifth day God made birds and fish
And wanted conversation
But they would not talk.

On the sixth morn he made animals to talk to
But they wouldn't listen,
And in the evening he made man.
He said, 'Man, my companion.'
And man said, 'Off my land.
You're trespassing.'

On the seventh day God rested
And thought.
And he never saw the eighth day.

Nicholas Midgley

The Tree of Knowledge

The tree of knowledge,
Of good and evil,
Is covered with carved knotted lines
And musical words
Written by God
In the oldest unknown language.
These are the thoughts
He wanted no man to read.
He wrote them in notches
And grooves in the wood
On the trunk of the tree
Of good and evil.

But the serpent
With his stubby legs
Crawled and twisted
Round the tree trunk
Trying to hide
The writing he could not read.
He said to Eve,
Come and try this fruit
And you will learn God's thoughts.
So Eve,
Obeying his luring words,
Plucked
One of the plump fruits
That were bursting with knowledge
And began to eat.
With every mouthful
Eve began to learn.
When the fruit had gone
Eve looked at the wild old tree
And each word became clear to her.
She read it
Line by line
And learnt the truth
No man had learnt before.
The tree swayed angrily
Tossing its head of tangled branches
Matted by the wind.
It groaned.
It felt naked.

Lucy Head

The next poem is a sustained rhyming piece which is quite
difficult for an eleven year old to pull off successfully. It took
some time to write – days – and the problems the poet
encountered in both rhyme and rhythm are clear to us now as
readers. Children must start somewhere to come to grips with
these essentials for poetry writing, but I hope teachers will be
aware that it is not easy to do. Rather forget rhyme for the time
being than have facile worthless pieces rushed out in one lesson.

I hope there are no teachers left who think a poem has to rhyme, or that it is good if it does rhyme, regardless of what it says!

— ◆ —

Adam and Eve

I need a good man, said God one day,
A man who must not be led astray.
Somebody willing, who is wise,
A man who will not tell lies.
I'll teach him the difference between right and wrong
And he'll be my man before long.
He needs a name which is easily said,
A name he'll remember until he's dead,
David, Jacob, Isaac, or
Adam.

Adam, that's it, and I'll get him a wife.
So Adam began a glorious life
And from a rib God created his wife.
She had the beautiful name of Eve
And in God's wisdom she had to believe.
They obeyed the law of the knowledge tree.
(Said God), Anyone who eats it must flee
And earn themselves an honest living,
And be like me – giving.
As Eve one day was walking
She stopped and started talking
To a devil who was very, very bad
And everything he did made people sad.
He talked about the knowledge tree
And God's law was his enemy.

He said the fruit must be delicious
And whoever guarded it wasn't vicious.
So Eve made up her mind to try
But what the devil said was a lie.
Adam trusted his wife's decision
And the taste of the fruit gave him great vision.

God was sad that his appointed man
Had believed another. Adam's new life began.
He chucked them out to live their lives,
Now men have to find their own wives.

Shula Lichfield

A brave attempt, I think.

— ◆ —

How God Made the Trees

First for its trunk he bought clay,
Moulded it until it was gnarled
And left it to dry.
Its bark was the rough skin of a rhino,
One of his creations.
He wrapped it round the trunk
And the bark became its guardian.
Then came the branches,
Not clay but ice carved by the wind
That froze its spindly arms.
Its leaves were soft feathers donated by birds
Wound round the ice branches with vines.
The fruit on this tree was the rosy red apple,
Hot molten lava from under the earth
Squeezed into round shapes
And hung on the tree.
And that's how the first tree was sculptured
And treasured by God in the heavens.
He's watching it now.

Zoë Scott

Ambition

God bellowed, let the first dimension be a dot!
And man conquered the first dimension
Putting dots everywhere like a used dartboard.
God threw his dart to open the gate of his imagination.

Then God sat up in bed and announced,
Let the second dimension be a line.
Man got excited and used his lines and dots
In pictures and paintings.

God slumped into his slippers and grumbled,
Let the third dimension be a cube.
Man took his building blocks
And made cities and towns.

Then God, while brushing his teeth, became ambitious.
He roared, Let the fourth dimension be time!
Man looked at time and played with it
And death tapped him on the shoulder.

God blurted, with a mouth full of cornflakes,
Let the fifth dimension be the unexplainable.
And the ashes of man were put in a gridded box
And thrown through time
Weaving in and out of light and sound
Like a needle going through felt without a thread.

Jonty Leff

70

BELIEFS,
HOPES AND FEARS

Idealism is not the exclusive province of the young, of course, but, thank goodness, the tendency towards cynicism and disillusion with the world, that can come with age, has not yet managed to stifle youthful optimism and determination to change the world for the better. Scratch the surface of many seemingly blasé young people and you find a thoughtful concern for their future, and I do not mean just jobs or money-making. I believe that schools have a role to play in encouraging children to consider the moral judgements and behaviour of society, and to help them formulate their own ideas and codes of conduct for living their lives. In other words, I believe that even quite young children have opinions on matters of importance to the world and should be given the opportunity to express these, whether in debate or through their writing. If I had any say in the curriculum (which I do not – which of us does these days?), I would include lessons on philosophy, particularly ethics, aesthetics and logic. Philosophy teaches us how to think, not what to think, and, as such, I believe it to be more valuable to true educationalists than any other subject. But, of course, it is rarely taught in schools.

Poetry (and creative writing generally) offers us a possible way to begin to remedy this omission. Before you can write down your opinions in a coherent fashion, you need to order your thoughts and marshal your arguments. You have to think more deeply about your subject than you may previously have done. You need to learn how to criticise and also how to propose alternative solutions to the problems you identify. You need to feel confident enough to have the courage of your own convictions, and you have to wrestle with words, techniques and forms for expressing your ideas in the most effective way. Simply being asked for your opinions, with the implication that they really matter, does wonders for self-esteem, anyway.

Children of all ages have similar hopes and fears, ranging from the highly personal to global concerns. Not just children, either; these concerns are generally widespread among adults, too. It is no surprise to find the age-old themes of poetry recurring: 'love' and 'death' practically sum them all up, all life is there! Under these headings come questions about the environment, religious beliefs, cruelty, power, the course of one's life, and the emotions in general. Less abstractly these translate into subjects like war, poverty, homelessness, unemployment, nuclear and chemical weapons, the ozone layer and global warming, relationships with, and the health and happiness of, family and friends, animal welfare, and many more.

The following examples address some of the beliefs, hopes and fears of children aged 10–13 years. Each takes a different approach in subject and form to express matters about which they feel strongly. The first poem was written by a girl who was particularly interested in horses and their welfare. She decided to use the Nicene Creed as a pattern for her poem about the death of one. This creed (from Latin 'credo', meaning 'I believe') is a formal statement of Christian beliefs and begins, 'I believe in one God, the Father Almighty, Maker of Heaven and Earth, and of all things visible and invisible . . . '.

— ◆ —

A Tribute to Sir Arkay

I believe in one horse,
The stallion almighty,
Maker of the stable and field,
And all things fast and slow;
And in one colt, Sir Arkay,
The only begotten foal of horse,
Sired by the stallion before all stables.
Horse of horse,
Stable light of stable light,
Very horse of very horse.

Sir Arkay slipped down the bank,
Also for horses under many people;
He suffered, and was put down;
And on the third day he rose again,
According to the manual,
And ascended to the Elysian Fields;
And trotted on the right hand
Of the stallion almighty.

Poppy Toland (BYW)

In this next poem, a boy envisages starting his own new religion, and through this device he is enabled to articulate his doubts and worries about his and others' beliefs.

— ◆ —

My Religion

In my religion
My name shall not be used as an expletive.
I shall not be drawn as a sixty-year-old ghost on a death bed.
I won't live in the sky
Looking down on my minions like a crazed megalomaniac.
I'll do something on the seventh day
Instead of sleeping and taking root;
I might even do what I say,
Like save some people's lives,
Stop some wars (which I started in the first place),
Maybe even nudge my followers in the right direction.

I think I would be a far better god than the current despot.
What has he done since time began?
Nothing.
He sends us the messiah,
Starts more wars
And pain
And suffering
Than you could imagine.
Then, like Stalin, declares it is all in the interest of peace.
After that small exertion of power, he settles back,
Content that that will make him strong and liked.

He settles back to have an eternal game of chess
With himself.

David Stallibrass (BYW)

Our World

I'll tell you what's wrong with our world.
We have multi-millionaire companies
Spending God knows what
On advertisements for some stupid product.
Soft drinks, for example.
Happy, well-fed black children,
Probably fed for the sake of a couple of millions
For the company,
Then thrown back on to the streets.
No thought of the torture and anguish they go through
Having to watch their parents shot, hanged,
Or left to starve
By the white South African beer-bellied bully.

I'll tell you what's wrong with our world . . .
The anti-black, anti-Jew Margaret Thatcher
Has turned it into a death-trap
Where you can't survive without the private clinics.
(You can, of course, receive an appointment
After a two-year wait.)
When a ten-year-old is dying from an asthma attack
The ambulance takes two hours
And there isn't a bed for her to stay in.

Noushin Sorayyapour (BYW)

Recipe for a New World

First, break a fresh factory chimney
Into a saucepan of boiling water.
Then, as the green TVs rise,
Add the child murderer whom everyone blamed,
A pinch of scapegoating,
And some hypocritical morals.

Stir gently as a thousand eyes watch.
Crumble in some of last Christmas's turkey
And a breath of 'Christmas spirit',
All wrapped up in a white beard
On a white man with a slit throat
And marbles for eyes.

Lastly, stir in the social decay,
The mistrust between nations,
Advanced nuclear weaponry
And a big, bright red button.

Nicholas Bieber (BYW)

True Love – a sonnet

Love makes the world go round, is what they say
But there are many different kinds of love.
The love of money should be kept at bay
For money goes with evil, hand in glove.
The Bible preaches, 'Love your enemy',
But there are hypocrites of every creed
Who don't think twice to kill expediently
For power and wealth and land and pride and greed.
Romantic love can bloom through rain and sun
Though all too often it will fade and fall,
Doomed before it ever had begun.
Which leaves us with self-love, and that is all.
The other side of love is hate, I've found –
Which one is it that makes the world go round?

BYW Group

The next poem is written to a pattern based on contrasts, that of rich versus poor. Other possible subjects might be Love and Hate, War and Peace, Men and Women, Success and Failure, Health and Sickness, Living and Dying, among others.

Wealth and Poverty

The poor can never be combined with the rich:
While the rich sit at home with a cosy lit fire,
The poor lie on the cobbled streets with a thin blanket.
The warmed-up houses,
The stone-cold streets.
The choosers go out and buy for themselves,
But the beggars ask people for money.
The rich drool in their finery
While with no money the poor wear rags.
The rich have plenty of clean water and soap
But the 'dirty' share hot water to the dozen.
Servants come to the use of the rich
But the poor will work hard for welfare.
The comfort lies with the rich
And the bareness of the poor is laid on their own backs.
The rich stride past, feeling their pride,
While the poor limp along with their lame thin bodies.
Strong are the rich,
Weak are the poor.
The pleasance of the rich amazes people,
While the disgrace of the poor
People dare not even think about.
The rich buy to keep,
But the poor find, only to lose.
The winners among the rich grovel over victory,
But the poor will weep over their losses.
The rich slowly trek
Through their three-course, steaming hot meal,
While at the sight of a scrap of bread
The poor grab, snatch and ravishingly eat.
The plumpness of the rich is overwhelming,
But the poor will remain starving and hungry.
How can rich and poor be combined together
And when will the rich give in and share?

Lucinda Wright (BYW)

71

The Seven Ages

Of Man

Shakespeare is a rich source of inspiration for any age, not least for top primary children, regardless of academic ability. I wish more Shakespeare plays were studied in all schools – not in a dry manner that can destroy enjoyment but in ways that present the language in all its glory and convey the pure magic of seeing them on stage. Younger children approach Shakespeare in the same way they approach any other storyteller, and they love to speak the lines and act out scenes. The best introduction at this age is usually *A Midsummer Night's Dream*, but they also respond to *Romeo and Juliet, Macbeth, Twelfth Night* and *Julius Caesar*, to name but a few. Something must be going sadly wrong when one hears so many people saying they do not like Shakespeare.

I decided to look at the famous speech from *As You Like It* – The Seven Ages of Man – with a class of 10 to 11 year olds. I read it through once and then explained some of the more unusual words. The children told me some of the things they had picked up from this first reading, and then I read it again. Each child had a copy in order to follow the text. There then followed a discussion of what was in the piece. We talked all round it and then I asked the class to think of writing something themselves. They could write about anything mentioned in the speech, or use an idea sparked off by something they had read. Alternatively, they could take a line or phrase from the text to use as a title or basis from which to write. The children responded with great enthusiasm and produced the best writing so far that year. There was such a wide choice of themes, and I like to think that having been in the presence of the Master, as it were, they were inspired to greater heights than usual. In other words, if the examples put in front of them are the best, in whatever sphere you care to examine, people will aim higher and raise their standards. If you constantly give them low-grade material on the grounds that that is all they can understand, they will never improve or widen their horizons, and often they become extremely bored. A little challenge can do wonders if presented in a way that allows people to fail without loss of confidence.

I intend to try other famous speeches in the future as stimuli for writing. Reading and understanding are also important. And the feeling of a subject shared, where each person's approach is valid and interesting, can bridge centuries, joining these young writers with Shakespeare (or other poets) in a common experience.

The following examples were all written on the above described occasion and in order to make it easier to see whence ideas arose I shall print Jaques's speech first.

From Shakespeare's *As You Like It*:

All the world's a stage,
And all the men and women merely players;
They have their exits and their entrances;
And one man in his time plays many parts,
His acts being seven ages. At first the infant,
Mewling and puking in the nurse's arms;
Then the whining school-boy, with his satchel
And shining morning face, creeping like snail
Unwillingly to school. And then the lover,
Sighing like furnace, with a woeful ballad
Made to his mistress' eyebrow. Then a soldier,
Full of strange oaths, and bearded like the pard,
Jealous in honour, sudden and quick in quarrel,
Seeking the bubble reputation
Even in the cannon's mouth. And then the justice,
In fair round belly with good capon lin'd,
With eyes severe and beard of formal cut,
Full of wise saws and modern instances;

And so he plays his part. The sixth age shifts
Into the lean and slipper'd pantaloon,
With spectacles on nose and pouch on side,
His youthful hose, well sav'd, a world too wide
For his shrunk shank; and his big manly voice,
Turning again toward childish treble, pipes
And whistles in his sound. Last scene of all,
That ends this strange eventful history,
Is second childishness and mere oblivion;
Sans teeth, sans eyes, sans taste, sans everything.

William Shakespeare

— ◆ —

The Seven Ages of Woman

The woman's role is particularly hard.
There are not many parts for women
And when there are they are difficult to win.
In Shakespeare's time they never had a chance.
Auditions come rarely;
Success for a woman is hard.
First, babyhood,
Staggering around like a drunk, banana in hand,
Throttling the cat with glee and enjoyment
Not realising how the poor cat feels,
Dribbling all over the banana
Then offering it to you as a kind of gesture.
The second age is the schoolgirl
With her rucksack and tracksuit,
Confident and ready for anything
With her neatly-packed pencil case
And playing kiss chase in the playground.
Then the adolescent, going through physical changes,
And fantasising over teeny pop-stars;
Spending hours on the 'phone to a girlfriend,
Giggling and gossiping about girlie things.
Now the scholar, taken to a new town,
Making new friends, learning new things
And having a taste of proper independence.
The fifth stage is the successful fashion editor

With her designer clothes and her filofax;
Going to fashion shows,
Living in her luxurious Hampstead house,
Driving around in her BMW.
From a yuppie to a middle-aged woman
Who bustles around, organising jumble sales
And going for walks with her King Charles' spaniel.
The last age is the old woman
Living in her country cottage,
Going on cruises as presents from her son,
Or sitting in front of the telly
With her grandchildren
And stuffing them full of tea and cakes.

Jessie Martelhof-Johnson

My Grandfather

The seventy-seven-year-old body sits in his chair.
The slime in his mouth comes out when he talks.
His legs are weak, the muscles are not strong enough
    to carry him
So he has to have a crutch to help him stand.
About twenty pills are next to his bed to keep him
    going,
Being cared for, waiting for death.
He is always locked in the toilet.
A shuffling noise can be heard when he walks across
    the hall
And his eyes look sorrowful.
His bald head, with the peeling skin, shines in the light
As he sits reading the newspaper.
His voice crumbles away as he speaks.

Charlotte Koolhaas

The Snail

The snail feels his way through the mosses,
Past the daffodil and tulip patch,
Trumps out the soil into neat little stacks.
His eyes see the blades of grass
Three times as high as he.
Like a crusader against the Turks
He fights for his own victory – the greenhouse.
Reaching the door
He negotiates the hole the tennis ball made.
Rows of plants tower over him
As if he's walking down a street of skyscrapers.
He climbs up a table leg and into a pot
For the delicious green leaves
Leaving a gleaming trail behind him.

Jamie Hendry

The Bubble Reputation

Bubbles float like small clouds being pushed around by
   the wind.
A young soldier catches one –
It bursts on the first touch.
He tries again and succeeds,
Holding in his hand a reputation
Which makes everyone admire and flatter him.
His pride has its rise and fall.
When the bubble pops in his hand
It leaves only a wet palm
Which slowly dries to become a forgotten memory.

Anna Pirani

Unwillingly to School

He strokes every cat on every wall,
He kicks a coke can
Which ends up under a car
Too far to reach.

An irresistibly low wall comes up,
He springs on it as nimbly as a cat
And walks along it like a pigeon.
He looks in his pockets and finds a piece of string,
A couple of chipped marbles
And an ink-stained handkerchief.
He bowls his best alley at the milk bottles
On every path he passes.
School looms like a big black hawk.

Shem Wallis-Jones

My Mistress' Fruity Face

Your eyes are like blackcurrants
And your nose is like a cherry,
Your lips are the colour of strawberries
And your teeth are like lychees.
Your ears look like peardrops
And your hair is like the hair of the coconut shell,
Your cheeks are peaches.

Yuki Hill

THE

POET-TREE

I first learned of this idea while lecturing on a teachers' course one weekend in Anglesey. As I am usually the one giving out the ideas, it is all the more exciting for me these days to be handed one by somebody else. I went back that Monday morning and immediately put it into operation with my class. It is such a simple but brilliant idea, and I am totally indebted to Mike Jones, English Adviser for Cheshire, whose idea it was and with whose willing consent I now pass it on to you.

On a large blank wall covered with some backing paper you draw the outline of a tree – trunk, branches and twigs. This will be the Poet-tree. Then have a box full of prepared paper leaves, of a decent size and perhaps in different shades of green, in a permanent position near the wall. The tree only needs to grow now, and this is how it is done.

Over the next few weeks, the children are encouraged to read as much poetry as possible; when they find something they like, they can put it on the tree. First they write the name of the poet in felt-tip on an empty branch. The name should be written quite large. Then they take a leaf and write the title of the poem on to it. The leaf is then attached to the poet's branch by its stem. If other poems by the same poet are enjoyed by any of the children they can add a leaf for each poem to the same branch. Each new poet has a separate branch. It makes a wonderful wall display and it is exciting to watch it grow as the term progresses. Each group of children will produce a slightly different tree, and it is a visual record of their reading. As can be imagined, children recommend poems to others and they widen their knowledge of poetry very quickly.

I often combine this tree with another activity which is very

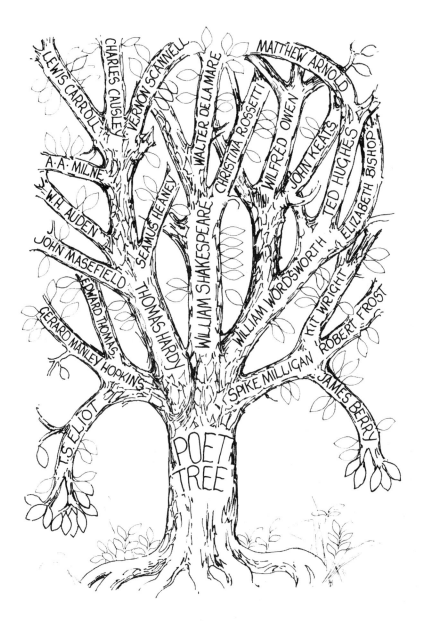

popular with my classes – that of reading poems aloud. I generally ask for about six volunteers a week to choose poems on a theme which they read to the class the following week. I usually set the theme which is something fairly broad like water, people, weather, etc. and always have a good selection of anthologies and individual volumes of poetry in the classroom through which the children can browse. The only stipulation I make is that they should not have known the poems before. Many of these, of course, then find their way on to the Poet-tree.

The Poet-tree idea is suitable for any age, but with younger children there are one or two suggestions I can make which might be of some help. So as not to have spelling mistakes (or messy crossing out) on the wall, I found it better to suggest to children that they write the name of the poet in pencil first in case of errors in spelling or spacing. When satisfied, the child can go over it in pen. Also, it might be a good idea if children mention to you which poet they want to put up so that you can suggest whether the name should be put on a short, medium or long branch. This avoids the problem of having A.A. Milne or Charles Causley, for example, on a tiny branch which will not be able to accommodate all the leaves coming its way, and some name like George and Audrey Mortimer Waterford on a large branch with only one poem to attach. (This last is a pseudonym for a well-known poet – but I'm not saying who! – and was 'writ large' by one of my class before he could be stopped. That branch was then out of action, cut off in its prime, as it were.)

The picture on p. 313 is a diagram of the kind of display produced, just to give you the idea. I'm sure you will add your own refinements. I think I probably have since first hearing of the idea myself. If you run out of branches you simply draw more. It might also be possible to incorporate the roots in some way too – perhaps for books of criticism – though this would obviously be something for secondary schools.

FINDING

A THEME

It is the finding of ideas that is usually the hardest part of teaching poetry. Many of the other chapters in this book have suggested specific themes, and here I propose to put forward a few more general thoughts on the subject.

Direct observation is a tried and trusted way of encouraging children to write: bringing in objects; bottles containing cotton wool soaked in different solutions to hand round for writing about smell; looking at pictures, slides or films; listening to music or tape recordings; taking children out to a park, a high street, market, or anywhere they can write while experiencing their surroundings. Any way that involves direct use of the five senses can lead to good poems and the more used to writing children are, the more interesting will be the results.

— ◆ —

Storm

Cold water balls fall in heavy currents
Upon the varnished land,
And the circling scraping slide of feet
Moves wetly over the puddled ground.
The relentless wind circles the shiny wet pebbles
Causing an unheard whistling as it passes through.
It makes sea-like waves
As it gusts into the water-drenched air.
The massive grey clouds
Shedding great bolts of energy.
The clouds give thundering claps
As they watch arrows of light
Turn dead objects into living infernos.

Orson Nava

Ship in a Bottle

Floating on an aimless current,
A constant reminder that we'll never reach port.
Hope in a bottle is not easy to find
And happiness was lost in a storm.

Matthew Festenstein

Forest Ocean

Enclosed in an ocean of rippling green
But no fishes swim here.
Insects crawl unseen, unheard
Like water nymphs flitting
A sea within a pond.
A duck quacks and flies away
Frightened by your presence,
Ripples form on sea and pond,
Flying fish make very birdlike noises.

Michael Corti

Bull

Maddened by a man and his tempter.
Dancing around like the tell-tale birds
Which used to circle him.
An arena of hatred
Reminding him of his now forbidden freedom.
A five foot terror and yet passive inside.
If given the chance he would go off and wallow in mud.

Christina Young

Projects can always give rise to some creative writing because the children have been studying a subject in detail; the poems they write will contain information which will improve their writing, if used well. Having a factual knowledge of a subject will ensure a more specific approach which is to be encouraged. There is almost nothing worse than the woolly generalisations that are often presented.

— ◆ —

Tournament

The herald sounded his bugle twice, then thrice.
As the last note faded away
A ripple of anticipation ran through the crowd.
The knights got on their armoured horses.
The knights' squires
Passed up their big heavy shields and lances.
The gallop of the horses, and the upturned turf
Where the great black stallions have beaten and
    plundered.

Jason Turner

Yggdrasil Is Dying

Yggdrasil is dying,
It is going, going.
From the curse of mighty Thor's hammer?
It is going, going.
From the mischief of the evil Loki?
It is going, going.
From Surtur's cold fire?
It is going, going.
No!
It is dying from the Nid Hog
Gnawing through its single root.
It is eating its wooden heart.
There is no blood left.

Donal Crawford

How the Round Table was Completed

A chilled circle slab of coldness.
The core had been finished
But the outline was still to begin.
The chisel had yet to strike
The meaning of the table.

Sir Gawain
Unknown to the group assembled
Went forth to perform his deed.
And when he returned
In the air they felt victory,
The hammer,
The chisel,
A new blow.
Gradually the outline was done,
The round table was completed.

Rita Monjardino

Different facets of the same word can be investigated, an idea which involves taking a subject, for example 'light', and allowing the children to write on any aspect of the theme. The word or words chosen must offer many possibilities, although it may be argued that all nouns fall into this category.

If we take the example of 'light', the idea would be to make a list on the blackboard of all the different kinds of light. These suggestions should mainly come from the children.

For example, they might propose candle, electric, gas, lighthouses, torches, matches, open fires, forest fires, sunlight, moonlight, starlight, reflected light, signals, traffic lights, headlamps, glowworms, luminous paint, the spectrum, Blackpool lights, street lamps and so on.

The children then have a wide choice of titles for their poems; each one will be essentially different from the others, although they all fall under the same heading. It can be useful to ask the children to suggest a theme, as they will feel it is more their own idea. Other such themes might include the four elements – earth, air, fire and water – or trees, darkness, wood, metal, heat, cold.

(*Note*: The essential thing to remember, however, is that there are no special themes for poetry. Poetry can be about absolutely anything, from the most mundane material object or experience to the highest philosophical thought!)

— ◆ —

Searchlight

Searchlight shining through the blackness
Picking out the plane's location,
Shooting it down with the whole spectrum.
Always swivelling its white shadow
Against the sound of falling bombs.

Matthew Festenstein

The Moonlit Circle

It reflects on the water, the moon,
A circle of shining ripples.
A tin can is thrown in from the pier,
It lands in the moonlit circle.
Water fills in through the opening,
The can floats out from the circle.

Julie Howson

The Reflected Light

The light shone in her face,
Red, green, purple and white.
It shone straight into her eyes.
She pulled a face and tightly shut her eyes.
It hurt but she didn't say.
Turn it off please, she said.
A man put a board in the way,
The light reflected on to it.
The light dazzled, flickered and went off.
The reflection went too.

Wendy Ellis

(See also 'Candlelight', page 186.)

Reading poems in various volumes and anthologies will often
spark off an idea. Seeing what angles poets have taken on

different subjects can sometimes suggest something you had not previously thought of. This is a quite legitimate way of obtaining ideas as long as they are not presented to the children in a restricted form, which results in poor imitations of the original poem.

Using lines from famous poems as the first lines of poems can produce interesting results. If the line is good it will set a tone for the rest of the poem. In some cases a whole verse may be used. (This exercise is not something to attempt very often, nor, for that matter, should any of the ideas or ways be used to excess. Variety of approach is always best.)

Perhaps three or four different lines can be given to the children, thus affording them a choice. A further interest can be excited by reading the original poems *after* the children have written their own – not before, however, as they should be free from all associations.

(line from 'The Thought-Fox' by Ted Hughes)

'I imagine this midnight moment's forest'
Where you can hear the owl
Calling through the silent trees.
The gaudy gnarlness of the rows of firewood
Growing and dying in the night aromas.

The stillness of forgotten time.
The emptiness filled with life,
Shunted and roused as the daylight approaches.
My midnight moment's forest
Destroyed by its creator.

The same place is another
As the sun surrounds it.
My own image thrived in this lushness of forests,
And died in its own world of immortality.

Rebecca Luff

(line from 'Wind' by Ted Hughes)

'This house has been far out at sea all night.'
The waves were tall, the house was small.
We sank once or twice, but resurfaced.
But the lifeguard stood shaking his fist
Because the house was blocking the light.

David Bailey

(verse from 'Neutral Tones' by Thomas Hardy)

'We stood by a pond that winter day,
And the sun was white, as though chidden of god.
And a few leaves lay on the starving sod;
– They had fallen from an ash, and were gray.'

Gray from the time they had left their home,
Their dwelling far off the ground.
We left them there untouched, unfound,
On the sod by the pond, so dark and alone.

And there set apart from the world they will lie,
Dropped from the tree of ecstasy.
None of us thinks this is fantasy,
For in the well of our hearts lives a lonely cry.

Donal Crawford

Some Points
of Technique

This chapter deals with a few points of technique which can be used by children in their writing. Some of them have been mentioned in passing in other chapters but they are set out here for easier reference. They are points that the children should be constantly aware of and use as they feel necessary. They are tools in the craft of writing that will help to give shape to the children's poems. There are many examples illustrating these techniques throughout the book. I have chosen only a few to illustrate each point here.

Rhyme Patterns

Rhyme, when well used, will add music and rhythm to poems and assist in giving a form and polish to the finished work. It does not need to be a conventional rhyme pattern but can be the children's own invention. Near rhymes (e.g. 'dine' and 'done') and spelling rhymes (e.g. 'clover' and 'plover') can be used, and internal rhyme – within and not at the ends of lines – can also add texture to poems.

— ◆ —

To Be Sold

Metal meets metal, the last noise.
Not seeing, only hearing the *rain*
Drill down on the corrugated *tin*,
The calf inhales the *smell* of his ancestors
Who know the place *well*
Like a criminal knowing his *cell*.
Winds play tunes through holes in the *walls*,
The orphan baby whose mother is gone
And she *calls*.

Zak Hall

House on the Horizon

House on the horizon,
Gaze back at *me*.
I see you sleeping,
Darkened, that I *see*.
Your little door is crying,
Your roof is not just *slate*.
I must never go near you,
For the thing that I would *hate*
Is the thought of getting closer
And not to touch the *gate*.

Nicholas Midgley

The Day They Walked Forever

That day when they walked down the hill,
The day when all the men were still
For it was fear now walking past,
When all the trees came alive at last.
The elders say 'It's but a dream'.
But the children saw it on the green,
The wooden figures that walked by
And floated slowly to the sky.

Nicholas Midgley

The Candle

A flickering light
Stunning and bright
Protruding into
The surrounding night.

A yellow flame
Sharp but tame
Like the shock of hair
On a lion's mane.

A cylindrical waxen figure,
A snow covered pole
Burning away slowly
It's no longer whole.

A familiar figure
Standing there
Alone in one room,
Solitaire.

Lincia Daniel (YWW)

ALLITERATION

The judicious use of alliteration in small phrases within a poem
will add to the poem's success almost without the reader being
aware of it if it is done subtly.

The following extracts are from 'Suburbia' by Ben Owen (see
Chapter 22, page 104, for the complete poem):

An old woman *sh*uffles with her *sh*opping
Crossing her prayers with *k*erbstones.

and

Her *sh*abby *sh*awl limp on her *sh*oulders,
Retired from her job she *p*umps on her *p*ension.
Her *l*ife*l*ess card *l*ies among *l*onely photographs . . .

METAPHOR

With similes, metaphors are almost a prerequisite of good
poetry. In describing something the imagination draws parallels
between one object or experience and another, which may be
completely unconnected. Seeing these links and pointing them
out to others is one of the joys of poetry and gives scope for
original and creative thought.

Life is a Book

Life is a book lost for words,
Unfinished sentences
Standing on a page.
A bent staple clings to the paper,
The pencil waits to do
Its immortal full stop.

Charles De'Ath

Alcohol

Like a black cat it wanders into your life
Going round and round until the job is done.
A spiral of death mixing until smooth.
When you look at a book it reads you,
An eye peering at you,
Staring at you
From every corner, moving towards the middle.
The gun in your mind turns to fire,
The gun shoots death, the fire leaps.

Helen Alexander

REPETITION

The use of repetition should not be overdone as it should be part of the form of the poem. It might be used for emphasis or as a refrain at the beginning or end of stanzas. It may also represent a symbol or motif which haunts the poem through repetition. The practice of merely repeating the poem's first line as its last line, in some kind of attempt to 'round it all off', is not one I would encourage.

Riddle

No man can enter
Without breaking in,
A small insect can die
And with ease
Get in.

No man can enter
Without breaking in,
No insect can exit
Already there.

No man can enter
Without breaking in,
An old insect there
Did it long before him.

Anna Colloms (YWW)
(Ɩssoɟ)

Afraid

Evacuated from your town,
Leaving your homelife behind,
Being taken to an unknown destination.
Led away from my life's beginning
Never to see it again.
Pass through towns leaving weeping relatives.
We left in fear, we left in hope.

Our fathers have gone off to fight
To save our homes and our town.
We'll win, we say. We'll win, we say,
They'd never let us down.
We left in fear, we left in hope.

We left in grief
And not to be obliged
Hoping to see our families once more.
We left in fear, we left in hope.

Karen Bounds

The following extract is from 'The Making of the Tiger' by
Nadya Kassam (see Chapter 53, page 217):

The face and the staring eye
Seem to be alone,
Not with the body

The staring eye,
Not with the body
The motionless face,
The harsh silence.

RUNNING ON LINES

In order to vary rhythm and pace it is essential that children be
made aware that lines of poetry do not have to be complete in
themselves. The sense of a line can run from one line to the
next and will help the poem to be freer. This point can also be
emphasised to help the children's reading of poetry. Too many
people still believe a poem is read line by line instead of noting
sense and punctuation and reading it accordingly. The fact that
it is written in lines and possibly in a particular rhythm will still
come through but in a more natural way.

The World Reunion

Ladies and Gentlemen,
We are gathered here today
For me to say
About our plan
To run away.

Ladies and Gentlemen,
We have come here to leave
And not to grieve
For dead friends,
Don't deceive.

Ladies and Gentlemen,
You'll meet some you don't know,
Friendships will grow,
Some will not,
A counterblow.

We must forget our past,
Lock it in an iron cast
In our mind.

We will have no outcast,
We will not be classed
Above others.

We will have food to eat,
Our hearts will go at a steady beat
In our chests,
And anyone who tries to cheat
Or force others into defeat
Is banished.

We will be in the unknown,
But we will not be alone
Where we are,
And when lost we will be shown
To a place of our own
To rest.

Nicholas Midgley

CHAIN WRITING

This is linked to repetition but is a little different. A word or phrase from one line is used to begin the next, and so on throughout the poem. (See also Chapter 37, page 156.)

— ◆ —

Seashore

Pretty shells washed onto the sand,
Sand a golden yellow colour,
Colour in the blue of the sea,
Sea with gentle lapping waves,
Waves clouded with green seaweed,
Seaweed clinging to the breakwaters.
Breakwaters stand ugly in the water,
Water envelops the cliffs,
Cliffs with bare white faces.
Faces of donkeys and faces of people,
People lying tanned in deckchairs,
Deckchairs lying disregarded.
Disregarded boats tied to the piers,

Piers standing rooted in pebbles
Pebbles worn smooth by the water,
Water collecting in the rock pools.
Rock pools inhabited by limpets,
Limpets stuck to surrounding rocks,
Rocks distorted like bits of wood,
Wood washed up along the shore,
Shore with litter, synthetic rope.

Nadya Kassam (YWW)

QUESTION AND ANSWER

This is a form which can provide a pattern for a whole poem. It
can be used as a conversation between two people. It is not a
technique that should be used too often, but it has possibilities
which the children might wish to explore.

The Worthless Form

What is the city's name?
The city has no name,
They don't care for history.
How do they live?
They live out of tin cans.
What keeps them alive?
They're kept alive by the turn of the cement mixer.
What is their aim?
Their aim is a future of skyscrapers and robots.
Where do they live?
They live in a city of dreams for the future
And hatred of the past.
What is their work?
Their work is to overpower reality.

Hedy-anne Goodman

CONTRADICTIONS

This is one device that can be used to create a disturbing
atmosphere or a surreal quality of the sort perhaps found in

dreams where the opposite may occur to what you intend, or think is happening. For example, you are running as fast as you can but it is all in slow motion and you seem never to reach your destination.

The Dream

I see this world through my own eyes
– I cannot see myself.
Snow has found its way to this place,
It covers every side of the trees
And everyone here is old and wrinkled.
The whole place is silent and quiet,
This place feels deathly,
The old people aren't walking, speaking, working,
They just stand like figures in some horrific surrealist
     picture.
Their clothes and hair are still in the raging torrent of
     wind.
I fall further and further down
Before I hit the ground.
I wake with a jolt,
It is pitch dark in my room.
I cannot see my outstretched hand
Yet I know it is there.
                                        Tilly Ballantine (YWW)

Similes

His smile was like that of a Cheshire cat,
His face was as solemn as the barren trees in winter.
That day his humour was more sarcastic than it had
     ever been,
His good news from abroad put him in a good mood.
His mind was as confused as a mad professor,
That day he was feeling fully aware.
On that Sunday morning, as on all Sunday mornings,
The streets were silent and free from all city bustle,
The crowds swarmed the shopping precinct
Like bees in a hive.
                                        Lincia Daniel (YWW)

ECONOMY OF LANGUAGE

Sometimes it is better for a poem to understate its case, leaving readers to think on for themselves, and it is almost always true to say that in any poem there should be no redundant words. If you can omit a word or phrase without endangering the meaning, and ways of effecting the meaning in the poem, then it is probably unnecessary. Every word must have a part (or parts) to play and a reason for being included. I feel this is perhaps one of the most important points to emphasise when encouraging children to write. To this end, practice in writing haiku, tanka and cinquains is invaluable, and a constant purge on 'thens', 'ands', 'buts' should be in operation where these are unnecessary.

The Expectation of Death

A white painted room,
An ominous straitjacket,
A mental patient.
A train waiting room,
An old lady in her chair
Alone with many people.

Tilly Ballantine (YWW)

Wheelchair Feelings

I watch the boy with sympathy
Though I know nothing about him.
I watch his ugly face and deformed figure,
His smile an act of self-discipline.
The family grin into the camera.
For once he is not the lens,
For once they don't smile at him.

Hedy-anne Goodman

STYLE

Every child should be encouraged to find his or her own style, and, if this is to happen, teachers should not impose their own ideas. There is no reason to interfere with what a child has written except to suggest that there might be better ways of saying a particular thing. One should never suggest how to do it or what to say. It is sufficient to say why something is *not* working and encourage the children to re-write it in another way. They must experiment for themselves. The more they have to take the initiative and discover for themselves, the better, so long as the teacher can back them up with informed criticism.

There are one or two things that ought to be said here. A poem does not sound more 'poetic' if too many adjectives or adverbs are used. Similarly, it is often better to use a verb in its proper form rather than overusing present participles. For example, the following extract from a poem contains too many 'ing' words:

Seagulls swoop*ing* over the rock*ing* waters
Gently mov*ing* the buoyant seaweed
As it stretches its slimy fingers
Reach*ing* for a dead crab
With one leg miss*ing.*
Bits of wood grat*ing* against the pebbles . . .

I would suggest that this can be immediately improved simply by changing some of the verbs.

Seagulls *swoop* over the rocking waters
Gently moving the buoyant seaweed
As it stretches its slimy fingers
To reach for a dead crab
With one leg missing.
Bits of wood *grate* against the pebbles . . .

I have heard of teachers who instruct classes to make sure they use two adjectives to describe each noun and include a lot of adverbs as this will make a poem 'better'. This is not true; it won't.

Another very important fundamental teaching point is to encourage children not to use a key word more than once, unless it is for a specific purpose. If they think properly they can almost always find another way to describe what they want to say. It is lazy to use the same word over and over again – and this means virtually any nouns, verbs, adverbs and adjectives. Having to search for synonyms is good practice, enlarges the vocabulary and can often push the writer into new areas which otherwise may have remained unexplored.

75

Drafting

What is Drafting?

Drafting is the process of re-working a piece of writing in order to make it clearer, more vivid and more effective, according to the genre, subject matter, purpose and intended audience. In other words, it is the process leading up to a finished article which will be the best version possible. It is rare that any one can write a very good piece straight off.

Let us take an example from the adult world – something with which most of us are very familiar. You are applying for a new job, and the form asks for a two hundred word statement in support of your application. Very few, if any, people will write that statement straight on to the form. It is more likely that you start by jotting down a list of all the points you wish to include. This is the first stage of your drafting, the planning stage.

Having made your list, you then write a first version of your statement. You read it through a few times, probably counting the words. You find you have written too many (less often, too few). You will have to cut it down. Painstakingly you go through your writing to see where you can cut out unnecessary words. Often you need to rephrase a sentence completely in order to economise on the number of words. This is the second stage of your drafting.

By now your piece of paper is covered with correcting marks – arrows, stars, crossings out – so you probably write it again in order to see it clearly. The next stage is when you show it to a close and trusted friend for comments. Does it read well? Have you said everything you want to say? What impression does it create? You make more changes, shift some paragraphs around, find you have used a particular word four times, which will not do. Eventually, with the help of the thesaurus you replace three of these words with synonyms. You count the words again and decide that two hundred and ten will probably be all right.

After showing it to your friendly critic again, you make your last changes and are ready to write it on to the form. Dictionary to hand for a last-minute check of a few spellings (words do have a habit of looking wrong at times when it matters that they are spelt correctly), you carefully copy your statement into its allotted space, hoping you do not leave a word out or make a mistake.

Does this sound familiar? This is how *we* work when writing something that matters to us, but, for some reason, we do not always bring this real-life experience into the classroom. Drafting has at last become part of the National Curriculum, albeit that the monolithic statement on the teaching of English has itself been through many different changes since its first introduction in 1989, and looks set to continue causing controversy of one kind or another for some years yet to come. Whether drafting ends up enshrined in the legal requirements, however, is really neither here nor there. Anyone wishing to learn to write, and anyone attempting to teach this discipline, *must* come to grips with drafting if they want to practise the craft of writing.

COMMON MISCONCEPTIONS ABOUT DRAFTING (BY BOTH TEACHERS AND CHILDREN)

1. That all writing must be neat and correctly spelt at all times.

Is yours? When we make notes, we rarely worry about neatness and spelling, just as long as *we* can read what we have written. Neat handwriting and correct grammar and spelling belong to the secretarial side of presentation, and, as such, correction of these aspects comes naturally at the final drafting stage when we are preparing to show others what we have written. Too much emphasis on these in the early creative stages can stifle the imagination and result in 'safe' writing, limited by the words we feel sure we *can* spell. Having to do our 'best' writing slows us down and can interfere with the faster thought processes.

2. *That every time a change is made, children should rewrite the whole piece.*

Making children do this is likely to put them off writing for life. What a waste of time! No published writer would do this. Each draft should be worked on until it is so covered with changes – stars, crossing out, arrows – that it has become difficult to read. Only then is it necessary to write the piece out. If children have put their first draft on to the word processor and written their changes on the printout, it will not be necessary to do anything more than incorporate the changes into the filed piece. Keeping the drafts gives valuable evidence of children's developing abilities as self-critics.

3. *That drafting takes up too much time which is needed for other subjects.*

Yes, drafting takes time, but can result in a much higher quality of writing. It is better to settle for fewer pieces of written work over the course of a week/term than you may previously have expected. Go for quality rather than quantity. After all, it is part of the teacher's job to encourage children to aim for the highest standard and to take a pride in their work. Too many children seem to have acquired the idea that the more they write, the better they are. The quality of their learning and development is what matters – *not* how many words (often banal) they can put down on paper.

4. *That it is the teacher's job, not the child's, to put marks on work in order to show what is 'wrong'.*

This is probably just a question of conditioning. Teachers often feel that they must justify their positions by putting marks on to children's work; there is a long history of just such an expectation. Of course, work should be marked, but with creative writing, in particular, the situation is not clear cut. Apart from the previously mentioned secretarial aspects, there are no 'right' or 'wrong' ways of expressing something – only 'more effective' and 'less effective' ways, and this often depends upon subjective appreciations. It is really the teacher's job to ask the right questions to enable children to make their own 'corrections'. It is purely a matter of changing classroom methods so that children stop expecting the teacher to make their decisions for them, and learn to trust in their own ability to solve problems in their writing. And this includes being able to identify words whose spelling may be wrong. If children underline such words themselves and then check them in the dictionary, they are more likely to remember the spellings thereafter. This system offers positive reinforcement, since the children cannot lose. If the word *does* need correcting, then the child has guessed right and feels successful. If the word *was* correctly spelt in the first place, then the child also feels successful. Nothing succeeds like success.

GUIDELINES AND SUGGESTIONS FOR ENCOURAGING DRAFTING

The planning stage – different approaches

- Make notes of anything that comes to mind and may be useful. These may be in the form of lists of words/ideas, 'stream of consciousness' outpourings in order to see what emerges, or diagrammatical recording of ideas, e.g. webs.

- Drawing pictures can help to plan the course of a story or poem, e.g. storyboards.

- Encourage a group, or paired, discussion in order to help raise ideas and crystallise them before putting pen to paper – having to explain to others or answer their questions helps to make things clear in one's own mind.

- Oral telling of stories can help sequencing, choice of details and the best method of communicating them, based on the reactions of listeners.

- Listening to music, researching a subject in the library,

firsthand experience (e.g. an actual object, an outside visit), engaging in some art or craft work, or acting out ideas in drama can all be useful at the planning stage.

Methods of working – succeeding stages

- Use rough work books, separate pieces of paper, or computer printouts for drafts. Only the final draft (or finished version) goes into the 'best' book or file.

- Show published writers' drafts, or teachers' own drafts, to prove that this is a legitimate way of working, and to show just how messy a 'working document' can be. Keep children's drafts for display alongside the finished pieces so that children and parents can see the work and progression of thought that went into them. Discourage the use of rubbers or Tippex. We want to see where the changes were made.

- Give children some of the simple established drafting marks used by writers and editors, or encourage them to invent their own (see the table at the end of this chapter). This not only legitimises this way of working but also makes it more fun and 'grown up'. Writing on alternate lines can make drafting easier, and using different colour pens for each new round of changes on the same piece of paper can help to identify the different drafts.

- Allow enough time for children to work through a number of drafts. This may stretch over days, a little at a time.

- It is allowed to move text around; even if a version begins one way, later whole sections might be moved or cut out altogether. Nothing is carved in tablets of stone until the piece is finished. Also, it is hard to lose 'favourite' phrases, but if they are not really working in context then why not save them up for another time?

SOME SUGGESTIONS FOR HOW WORK CAN BE IMPROVED

- Avoid using an important word too often (nouns, verbs, adjectives, adverbs) – the thesaurus can help in finding other ways of saying the same thing. Repetition of words/lines must be intentional and necessary for effect or meaning. Repetition should never be the result of laziness.

- Make sure that poems contain main verbs (unless the form dictates otherwise). This means avoiding the over-use of participles, i.e. 'ing' words (see example at the end of Chapter 74).

- Avoid using: bland words, like 'lovely', 'pretty', 'nice'; archaic constructions, like ' . . . and away we *did* go'; and words like 'a bit', 'lots of', 'get' and '*so* . . . this, *so* . . . that'.

- Only use rhyme if it does not compromise the sense of the poem; if in doubt, leave it out.

- Pay attention to verbs – an exciting but undertaught part of speech (see Chapter 3, page 35).
  - Details are important. Use the specific names for things, e.g.:
    – instead of 'prey', perhaps 'vole' or 'field mouse'
    – instead of 'bird', perhaps 'robin' or 'eagle'
    – instead of 'flower', perhaps 'rose' or 'snowdrop'
    – instead of 'colour', perhaps 'green' or 'orange'
    – instead of 'tree', perhaps 'willow' or 'elm'

- The title is important – it is the first thing the audience reads and, therefore, determines how the piece is approached. If possible a title should add an extra dimension and not just be a line or phrase from the poem. Titles need to be thought about carefully.

- Line breaks in poems can often be identified by reading the work out loud. Where the voice pauses naturally will help to denote the end of a line. Reading out loud shows up personal speech patterns.

- Workshops can help to identify whether something works or not. Notes can be made during such a session, which is best organised so that other children are encouraged to pick out what they particularly *like* – accentuate the positive! Questions can help clarify meaning.

- Teacher-led discussions with individuals demand open-ended, sensitive questions which lead children to come to their own conclusions. Examples:
  – Are there any parts you're particularly worried about?
  – Are there any parts you are particularly pleased with?
  – That's a good idea; what made you think of that?
  – Are there any parts you feel you want to improve?
  – Did this happen to you, or to someone you know?
  Questions should be positive, encouraging and supportive. Very often, in answer to such questions, children will say the sort of things they should have written down. They frequently leave out vital information, assuming that a reader will know it as well as they do.

- If a piece still feels 'not right', there are two other ways which might help identify what is wrong. Reading your own piece out loud to yourself, or hearing someone else read it to you, will often pinpoint what is not working. We hear things very differently when they are read aloud from when we read them in our heads. Take my word for it, it works. Also, leaving a piece for a few days and returning to it 'fresh' will often solve any problems. We see it for the first time, as it were.

SOME DRAFTING MARKS IN COMMON USE WHEN RE-WORKING A PIECE OF WRITING

⋏ ⋏	Omission marks when a word or phrase needs to be inserted	Mark for changing the place of letters or words
	gar Come into the/den, Maud.	the hills (far and) away
✱ ✱✱	Stars – to denote the place for new text to go; one is placed in the original text* and a second next to the new text	Marks to denote where line-breaks occur in poetry
	✱ I wanna be a star!	There once was an amorous duck // who accepted a ride in a truck // but they hadn't gone far...
	Arrows to show that a piece of text is to be moved elsewhere	For reinstating something previously crossed out (from Latin = 'let it stand')
	I shot an arrow in the air	stet To be, or not to be stet
	Lines for crossing things out – no rubbers or Tippex	Sp? For marking words whose spelling you want to check
	Lollipop Briant It was on the good ship Venus	sp? Whose afrade of the big bad wolf?
( ) { } [ ]	Brackets around words or phrases you want to think about or possibly leave out	For showing where a new paragraph should begin

photocopiable page

76

TEACHING

POINTS

1 The teacher should be interested in, and enthusiastic about, poetry – otherwise the children themselves will be indifferent towards it. This involves the teacher in reading poetry for pleasure, listening to poetry on radio and television and, if possible, going to poetry readings. Trying to write yourself (whether you show anyone or not) will help to increase your own enjoyment, and your awareness of technical points and difficulties. For anyone who would like to know more about the different forms used in poetry there are a few books which set them out briefly but clearly. One of the best, I have found, is *The Poet's Manual and Rhyming Dictionary* by Frances Stillman (Thames and Hudson). The rhyming dictionary is an unnecessary extra on the whole, but the manual is well worth having.

2 Ban the use of such endings as ' . . . and then I woke up', and 'The End'. It is clear if a piece of writing is finished, and all dream sequences are usually better left in dream. I think children often write these endings to provide a sort of security. They may experience the need to return to reality before they leave the piece, but I feel it should be stopped as it mars so many good ideas. They should be encouraged to feel at ease in their fantasy worlds.

3 Have plenty of dictionaries of all types and grades of difficulty available in the room, and encourage children to use them.

4 Have as many anthologies and individual volumes of poetry as you can available on a shelf in the classroom where children

may freely borrow them. Encourage children to read poems as well as novels from the school library.

5   Read plenty of poems to the children, sometimes just for fun, sometimes for discussion, sometimes as a starting off point for some writing. If used in the last way, it is often better to read a number of poems on a theme, otherwise many children will only re-hash what you have read.

6   It is very good to have volunteers to read to the class poems which they have found in books from the library or at home. I have known nine-year-old children who began by reading Spike Milligan, Ogden Nash and Lewis Carroll (all perfectly all right), but graduated in their taste and sophistication by the age of eleven to choosing poems by Hardy, Yeats and MacNeice. There never seems to be a shortage of volunteers. Not only does this encourage the children to read poetry – they must read a number of poems in order to choose one – but it helps their ability to read out loud, something which is often overlooked these days.

7   It is useful to keep a class poetry book where the best work from each session is mounted. The work is typed out, and this acts as an encouragement to all; there is nothing like seeing one's work in print! During the year you should make sure that every child is represented in the book, but you must also set a high standard.

Each session the work from the previous lesson should be read out by you or by the children and it is useful if you can all comment on why the poems are good. Children learn from these comments.

The book should be attractive and left around the classroom so that the children can read it at any time. It is probably better to put as many pieces in as you can at the beginning as this will be more encouraging. Standards can be raised as you go on. One-finger typists take heart – you will soon improve and it is worth the effort!

8   I would advise against using creative writing cards, or similar,

as a general rule. They exist supposedly to help teachers, but are most often used as an easy way out. There may be occasion to use them sometimes as a change, but they are very limiting unless a child has a well-developed ability to write – in which case, of course, they should not be necessary. It is really so much better if you, as the teacher, can provide the ideas. A card is unlikely to stimulate and enthuse a child in the same way that a teacher can, and used to excess, as with any method, will soon become tedious.

9   When the children are writing it is sometimes a good idea if you try to write something yourself. Tell them you are going to try, and be prepared to let them hear your attempt. We are constantly expecting children to write to order and it is a very sobering experience to face up to the same difficulties that they encounter.

10   Do not expect each child to produce a good piece of work every time. No poet can possibly write a masterpiece with every poem. There will be failures. Sometimes writers are just not in the mood, for some reason the ideas will not come or will not fall into place. Tell the children this, and they will not use it as an excuse; it is more likely to encourage.

11   It takes time to write a good poem. Very occasionally it comes quickly, but you are lucky if it does, so do not expect much if you only allow twenty minutes for writing. If possible, arrange your day so that children who want to can go on working on their poems.

12   Encourage children to re-work poems as a 'real' poet does. Nibble away at the poem until it comes right.

13   Until the children are used to writing poems it will be necessary for you to go through much of their work and help them put it into lines, commenting on your reasons. You may find that there are accidental full, near, or internal rhymes, or that a natural rhythm pattern makes the line breaks obvious. Taking out odd words or rearranging sentences can make all the difference and turn what is essentially prose into poetry. After

doing this a few times with children, you can ask them to do it for themselves. Here is an example:

The boy was as free as a bird that had been trapped in a cage and as lively as a leaf, which is all wrinkled and dry. He sits in the corner of a room where the door is locked and so is his mind but in a different way. His mind is locked on the life he had once led and the freedom he had once had. He sits there not moving and will soon become an everlasting part of the room. Now he is dead and all that remains is a watch that doesn't tell the time but it tells a story which is the story I've just told you.

(by a boy aged 10)

And here is one way of making this piece into a poem.

The Boy

Free as a bird trapped in a cage,
Lively as a leaf wrinkled and dry,
He sits in the corner of a room.
The door is locked and so is his mind,
Locked on the life he once had led,
Locked on the freedom he once had known,
He becomes an everlasting part of the room.
Dead now, and all that remains
Is a watch that doesn't tell the time.
It tells a story –
This story.

Most of the lines have a rhythm created by a pattern of four strong beats ending on a strong syllable, but this pattern is occasionally varied, on lines three, seven and the last two, at points where there are definite pauses indicated by meaning and punctuation. These variations help to improve the poem. A little repetition in lines five and six, and the last two, helps to bind it together. The last two lines are shorter and break naturally to emphasise the last line for a more dramatic finish than in the original. Nothing has been drastically altered, but a child can learn a tremendous amount from this exercise.

14   Never prescribe a set length of writing you expect the children to do in a session. Too many teachers say, 'I want a page by lunchtime', or similar stipulations. A piece of writing is finished when it is finished, and that might be at three lines or thirty-three. This obviously demands some initiative from the children, but they soon understand. To aim at the highest possible standard is what is important and a few well thought-out, successful lines are better than pages of mediocre work or worse.

15   Let the children have rough books to work in. They should not have to be bothered about spelling and neatness when they are writing. If you are encouraging them to re-work their poems, there will inevitably be things to cross out and words to add in. A writer's notebook is often messy. The time to write out a fair copy in the English book is when the poem is in its final version. Then spellings should be correct and handwriting neat. If the children have to think about that when first writing, it will interfere with their spontaneity.

16   Never type out children's work with wrong spellings: it is far too patronising. Always correct them. Besides, other children will be reading the poems and it is bad policy to present anything which is incorrect.

17   It is also not advisable to use bad examples from children's work to illustrate what should not be done. Teaching by positive examples is better and will help to build up confidence.

18   If it is at all possible, working in silence produces better poems. There is no doubt about this. Everyone needs room to think, and this means the least possible distraction. Long queues of children with completed work should therefore be avoided. I have always explained that I prefer to read their poems at home where I can sit down and enjoy them. This is usually

appreciated. It is useful to make sure that there is other work organised for those children to do when they have finished, or they can be encouraged to write another poem. This will also leave the teacher free to give help on specific points where needed.

LEARNING POEMS

BY HEART

O nce upon a time poetry was not written, but spoken. What memories our ancestors must have had, uncluttered as they were by the preoccupations of twentieth century living and the lumber of educationalists. Once upon a time poetry was a spoken art, closer to music, which could hold an illiterate audience spellbound for hours – something that might only apply to Shakespeare now, such is the limited attention span of fast-living modern society.

However, once upon a time, and not so long ago, we still spoke poems, at least in schools, under the laudable but misguided apprehension that it was 'good' for us to learn them off by heart. Do you remember the last-minute panic of memorising often unmemorable lines; the interminable mumbling and stumbling as one by one you stood to recite the *same* poem; the artificial choral speaking with flourishings of arms and voices? Too often this had the unfortunate effect of killing poetry for many people. How odd, I find, that usually the worst poems stay in my memory, word for word, and the best remain just a good feeling.

So, inevitably, there came the backlash and this practice of memorising has dwindled. A great majority of today's teachers came through the old system which did such a disservice to poetry. Most of my teachers at school were unaware of any poetry written since World War One and thus denied us the opportunity of relating to poetry through our own times. Of course, poetry speaks universal truths, and I now love the work of poets throughout the centuries, but as a schoolgirl I would probably have welcomed more of a mixture of ancient and modern.

But poetry used to be spoken and enthral, so why should it not do so again? Children learn songs easily, but there is also music in poetry. We have a strong oral tradition, kept alive in folk songs, rhymes and playground games, stronger perhaps outside the big cities but nevertheless there. People understand music and enjoy singing at all levels whether it be in the bath, pubs, amateur festivals or at professional standard. But poetry lost much of its appeal – writing, speaking, reading or listening – perhaps because of bad teaching in schools. The 'sixties and 'seventies did much to re-open this area, and the success of public poetry readings has brought in a wider audience. 'A' level and GCSE courses now acknowledge modern writers such as Seamus Heaney and Ted Hughes, although poetry is still relegated to a tiny part of the curriculum. There are Art Schools, Music Schools, Drama Schools but virtually no Writing Schools. A few groups and organisations run some courses, but although competitions and writers' circles have revealed thousands of people who 'scribble away' in isolation, there is still reluctance to take poetry seriously or to recognise its importance. 'The pen is mightier than the sword', but try telling that to the government, or even to many teachers. However, children of today do not have this induced antipathy towards poetry and perhaps the time is now ripe for its revival if we can learn from our mistakes. It all depends on how it is done.

I asked a class of ten-year-olds if they would like to learn a poem. I had my doubts but was overwhelmed by their response. They liked poetry, and we had often read to each other poems which we had found in books. They were used to reading out their own work, too. Both practices had improved their reading techniques: good clear voices, expression with understanding, appreciation of poetry and discernment. They did this because they wanted to and gained in confidence each time. They were beginning to keep their own anthologies of favourite poems, writing them out in notebooks and illustrating them – another practice that has unfortunately almost disappeared. The idea of learning one was received with enthusiasm by most of them, particularly as they were given a completely free choice. There was no compulsion to do it which would have partly destroyed the enjoyment, and for the next few weeks odd moments every day were enlivened by children standing up to say their poems. About two thirds of the class participated and their choices were extremely varied and interesting. Some learnt more than one, and often the choices were astonishing. Some poems were complex and adult, perhaps not fully understood by the children and certainly not what a teacher might have considered setting for this age group, chosen for their 'music' with what can only be described as an intuitive sense of meaning and quality.

I felt it was important that I should learn one too, partly because it is not fair to ask children to do things you are not prepared to do yourself, and partly because I wanted to know what it felt like. I chose a favourite poem of mine and set to learn it one evening. It was surprisingly easier than I had thought and I went to bed excited by the words and the exhilaration of knowing and understanding the poem fully. A slight recurrence of the old conditioned nerves made me practise on a colleague at lunchtime and I recited it to my class that afternoon. I doubt whether they understood it but I am sure they appreciated my effort. I had put my head on the block too and I came away with a feeling of achievement unfamiliar for a long time. I think and hope their experience was similar to mine. We shall learn more. To be able to say a favourite poem to yourself, or quote whole passages which have meaning for you, can so often bring comfort and satisfaction.

78

How To Organise
A Writer's Visit

The points in this chapter are intended as a guide for teachers who would like to have a writer into school to read and talk to the children or to work with them. They are based on my own experience as a teacher who has organised such visits and also on the feelings of many writers themselves, most of whom have good experiences to relate, as well as horrifying tales of bad management by schools. These points, then, are an attempt to alert teachers, who may be thinking of arranging a writer's visit, to some of the details that can help to make it memorable and valuable for all concerned; the children, the staff *and* the writer. The value of arranging these visits is, I think, self-evident.

Making Contact

Having chosen the writer you wish to ask to your school, write a letter of invitation, preferably offering alternative dates and with as much notice as possible to avoid disappointment. If you cannot find out a writer's address, you can always write to him or her care of the writer's publisher. Do be adventurous in your choice of writer, even if you are a Junior School. Most writers will give a very good session with Juniors and it is well, particularly where poetry is concerned, to guard against only having writers who set themselves up as 'children's writers'.

If you know exactly what you would like the writer to do on the visit – read to the children and answer questions, run a workshop or give a talk about current literary trends, etc. – make this clear in your first letter. Also, if possible, state how large the group of children will be and how old. If you would like the writer to choose what kind of session it will be, then make this clear too. It must be remembered that a freelance writer may have to give up two days of his or her working time to come to your school. Travelling one day, staying overnight and travelling back the next day can be very tiring when you do a lot of readings. This all interferes with a writer's own work. It is always good if you can persuade other schools in the area to engage his or her services too so that, for the writer, the trip is more worthwhile.

When the date, time and fee have been agreed write a letter to the writer confirming these and enclosing directions for finding the school, with details of arrangements for meeting him or her and overnight accommodation if necessary. Hotel bills must be borne by the school; but in most cases you, or one of your colleagues, can probably put up the writer: this is normally quite acceptable.

Note: Do not expect your writer to work a whole day, or even a whole morning, for the standard fee. Too many teachers treat these visits as 'free periods'. Teaching is hard work, and teachers are trained to do it. They also know the children. For a writer to be expected to do a full teaching day is most unfair, and the amount of time you expect the writer to 'perform' should be mutually agreed before the visit. The writer should also not be used merely as a convenient person to relieve Mr So-and-so of difficult classes so that he can put his feet up in the staffroom. Lastly, 9 am is perhaps not such a good time for a visit as, say, 11 am.

PREPARING THE CHILDREN FOR THE VISIT

Once the details have been fixed and you know which class, or classes, will be involved, some teaching preparation should be done. I feel it is essential for the children to know something about the writer and the writer's work. They should have read or heard a number of poems by the writer (or one or two novels, or short stories) and any background information you are able to provide about the writer. It is far more satisfying for all concerned if the children know some of the work beforehand.

The writer will be encouraged because, after all, writers want to be read – it is the work that matters – and the children will enjoy hearing poems read which they already know 'straight from the horse's mouth', as it were. They will find it easier to listen and to ask questions. Now is the chance to find out what the writer *really* meant by such and such a phrase. It will make what they have been taught come alive. They should be encouraged to make requests for poems they know by this writer to be read by him or her. They may want to show the writer some of their own although he or she shouldn't be bombarded with too much. Perhaps the writer can be presented with copies to take away.

If it is felt necessary a word about behaviour should be given in advance but try to avoid cowing them so that they dare not open their mouths. Make them excited about the visit in a positive and enthusiastic way.

Preparing the Room

Depending on what kind of session is to be conducted, give some thought to the ambience and conditions with which the writer will have to cope. For a reading in a classroom it is usually best to push back the desks and arrange the chairs in a semicircle. This will help to create as informal an atmosphere as is possible in a classroom. Make sure the writer has a good chair (not too low!) and a small table or something upon which to place his or her books. A carafe of water and a glass – the usual accessory for a visiting speaker – should be on the table too.

Try to choose a room, if this is possible, which does not have windows which many children from other classes will be passing. This can be very distracting.

If there are lesson bells and you cannot escape them please warn the writer in advance of when they are likely to sound and try to avoid children having to get up and leave in the middle of a session to go to another class. This requires tactful communication with other staff and departments on behalf of the children – it is not fair to put the onus on children to arrange to miss lessons. Whichever kind of room you have to use, try to make it as relaxed and informal an occasion as possible as this is probably best for everybody.

THE DAY OF THE VISIT

Try to organise things so that you are available to welcome the writer on his or her arrival – failing that, at least make sure that somebody does. Allow time to sit down with a cup of coffee or tea, breathing space before the session.

The children should all be present in the room when you take the writer in. Make a short introduction and then, if possible, sit in the background so that your presence does not impinge on the children. If there is a time for questions be prepared to allow a silence to go on. The children may be shy at first but someone will usually open questions without the need for you to step in. If teachers ask all the questions the children can feel that they are excluded and will cease to be interested. The session has been set up for them and, given the right preparation and opportunity, they will certainly make good use of it.

When the session ends either you, or a child, should thank the writer and if you have established in advance that he or she will sign autographs, then allow the children to line up. (This happens particularly in Primary Schools!)

It is best if you can arrange it so that the session ends a morning or an afternoon. Then the writer can be provided with some hospitality, if he or she wishes, in the way of lunch or a drink. Pubs or restaurants may be preferable to your school dinners but you can decide which seems best. One important matter now is to *pay* the writer. If possible, the writer should be paid on the day of the visit. Most writers are dependent on prompt payment in order to live. Making them wait, sometimes for months, seems to me to be merely bad manners. Even if the money is coming from your LEA, it should be possible to arrange for payment on the day.

SELLING THE WRITER'S BOOKS

This may not seem appropriate to do in school, and I think the decision should be yours. I do not generally sell books to Junior Children at such times, although I might encourage them to buy from the local bookshop, which happens to be very good in our area, in advance of a visit.

However, many writers are able to bring along copies of their books to sell to the children, if you wish. This means that the children should be prepared for this and have money with them if they want to buy. It is better if you, or a colleague, can take charge of the selling to relieve the writer of any possible embarrassment and to free the writer to speak to the children. Your local bookshop may also be prepared to let you have copies on a sale-or-return basis, as do some publishers. If you have a school bookshop, it might be persuaded to stock some copies. If the children have already bought some of the books they can, of course, ask the writer to sign their copies. Most writers are only too happy to do this.

I hope this chapter will prove of use to teachers who would like a writer to visit school. It can certainly be a very worthwhile experience for everybody, and schools can build up valuable and lasting relationships with writers. I apologise if many of the things I have said seem to be only common sense but I have tried to cover most of the aspects and problems which I know have occurred from time to time.

79

ACTIVITIES

FOR BOOK WEEK

Many schools try to have a Book Week at least once during the school year. Sometimes this coincides with National Book Week, set up by the National Book League some years ago to highlight the joy of reading and the value of books for young people. National Book Week is usually held in October; if schools want to hold their own at the same time, they should be aware that it will obviously be more difficult to get hold of popular children's writers then, since everybody will be wanting them and they cannot be everywhere at once. If you do wish to arrange writers' visits, make sure you book them well in advance, even a year ahead if possible. The previous chapter on arranging a writer's visit (on page 351) should help you to ensure that you all get the most out of the occasion.

However, you can still have a Book Week with just one or two visiting writers, backed up by plenty of 'home-grown' activities. The following are just a few suggestions for activities that could be set up during a Book Week and do not eat excessively into school funds. Try to involve all teachers in the preparations for these activities, and suspend as much of the normal week's timetable as is practical, so that everyone – children and teachers alike – can enjoy the week to the full. Placing an emphasis on this one area of the curriculum can raise its profile and show children how worthwhile it is to read and write literature. (As a *quid pro quo* in persuading colleagues, or the Head, to agree to a Book Week, you might suggest that the school has other subject weeks during the course of the year.)

COMPETITIONS

a) Anagrams of well-known writers' names, storybook characters, or book titles, to be solved.

b) Identify the authors from their pictures.

c) Write a poem or story on a theme.

d) Illustrate a character from a favourite story or poem.

e) Make up, or solve, a literary crossword or word search.

f) Design a poster for a book.

g) Devise a problem-solving activity based on a book or poem. For example, children must devise, and make, a device that will enable the Borrowers to cross a room, carrying something they have 'borrowed', without being caught by the cat. Alternatively, you could cut up a poem into separate lines: the children, in small groups, have to see if they can put it back together. This is a good exercise in speaking, listening and reasoning, as the children will have to use their powers of deduction to make sure that the poem makes sense.

h) Have a literary quiz, either as a team game, or on paper for individuals, which will require them to do some research.

i) Devise a literary treasure hunt – solving the clues will demand knowledge of, and research into, books and poems.

STORYTELLING

a) Older children share books/stories with younger children.

b) Everyone brings in a favourite book or poem and talks about it to someone else – a useful activity for pairs or groups.

c) Teachers read or tell stories to groups of children.

d) One class starts writing a story which is then passed on, class to class, and completed by the end of the week.

e) Parents and other relevant adults are recruited to come in for a session and tell a story or read poems. It is particularly good if you can have stories from other cultures, and even in other languages.

f) Children make puppets (finger, hand, shadow) and use them to tell stories to their, or another, class.

g) Children act out, in small groups, some of their favourite stories or poems.

h) Children put on a poetry reading of their own, or published poets', works.

i) Children make their own books.

j) Are there any parents who are authors? Try to get them in to talk to the children about what they do.

EXHIBITIONS

a) Children's stories and poems.

b) Art and craft work from fiction.

c) Science and maths work from fiction.

d) Book exhibitions – from the school or local library, travelling book fairs, or displays from local bookshops, with books for sale.

MISCELLANEOUS

a) Arrange an assembly called 'Desert Island Poems' and ask a child, the Head, a teacher, a visiting writer, or a parent, to be the castaway. The poems will have to be chosen well in advance so that they can be available on the day. There could even be one of these assemblies on each day of the week with a different person (possibly one from each category on the above list) each time.

b) Have one day when everyone, including the adults in school, dresses up as a character from fiction.

c) Have a fancy dress parade to finish (or start) the week.

d) Show video films of books, e.g. *The Railway Children, Watership Down, The Wolves of Willoughby Chase, Peter Pan, Tarka the Otter, Ring of Bright Water, The Secret Garden, The BFG, Danny the Champion of the World* and, from television, *The Borrowers* and *A Box of Delights*.

e) Make, buy or borrow, story tapes for use in the classroom.

Sponsored Read

Pupils are sponsored for, perhaps, five activities around reading, to be completed over the week. For example:

a) Write a book review.

b) Tell a story to another person (to be done in class and verified by a teacher).

c) Illustrate a book character.

d) Design a poster for book week, or a storybook.

e) Read a poem, or learn and recite one by heart, to the class.

f) Write a poem or story.

g) Perform a play with others.

h) Give a short talk about their favourite book or poem.

i) Make a story or poetry book with illustrations.

j) Write a letter, either to an author about a story or poem, or to a story character about the story, or from one character to another, or any other variations you think of.

k) Write a news report for a newspaper, reporting an incident from a story.

l) Keep a diary for the week of everything they have read, heard or done in connection with books.

(Some useful addresses for organisations that may be able to provide assistance in the planning of your book week will be found at the back of this book.)

THE ARVON

FOUNDATION

This chapter deals specifically with one organisation which runs residential writing courses; I hope it will be self-evident how much value these can be to the children who attend them. School journeys have long been considered a marvellous way of extending the children in a different atmosphere from that of school, with its, of necessity, heavily timetabled day. The same sort of benefits are to be had from subject-orientated courses, as these are, as those obtained from the more usual school journeys for physical recreation or environmental studies.

The Arvon Foundation was the brainchild of authors John Moat and John Fairfax who wanted to set up courses where people could get away from the pressures of everyday life and live for five days in the remote countryside to concentrate on writing. They began by setting up a few closed courses in various locations, but in 1970 John Moat opened Totleigh Barton and Arvon had its first permanent home.

Totleigh Barton is an eleventh century thatched farmhouse said to have had associations with King John, whose hunting lodge was nearby. It has been completely modernised and imaginatively furnished to provide accommodation for about fifteen students and two course tutors. There is central heating as well as romantic log fires for the winter months. The dining room boasts a very long refectory table which came from Woburn, and there is a comfortable sitting room where readings and work sessions take place in a relaxed and informal setting. The kitchen is large and is generally the focus of the house where people naturally congregate for cups of coffee and conversation. Some bedrooms have bunk beds and sleep two, three or four to a room, although there are several single rooms for those who feel they need them as well as for teachers who accompany school parties. One of the most interesting of these is the Monk's Room which was originally a priest's hole entered through the fireplace but now approached by a staircase. It is said that the house has ghosts, but they are generally acknowledged to be benevolent!

The tutors are accommodated in a separate block known as the pigsties which adjoins the house, or in the goose house which stands separately facing the courtyard. There is also a large barn which has been converted to provide a workshop or performance studio for courses involving music or theatre. There are many quiet nooks and corners to which people can escape to write, as well as the beautiful Devon countryside. Totleigh Barton is close to the River Torridge (trout and Tarka country) and the nearest village is Sheepwash, about a mile and a half away. Okehampton is the nearest town, eleven miles to the south, and Bude is about twenty miles away.

During the summer months many 'open' courses are run on the lines developed by John Moat and John Fairfax, and anyone can apply to attend one of these courses. All the courses, open or closed, cover mainly the writing of poetry, prose and plays, but there are also courses on writing for radio and television, as well as courses on many different writing genres. Two tutors who are practising artists in the subject live alongside the students for five days and can be consulted at any time about the students' own work. The courses are reasonably free in organisation to allow the opportunity to provide what the students of each week might want. The sort of things which generally happen are as follows.

The tutors will give a reading of their own work; there is a visiting reader on one evening; course members read their own work in a special last evening performance; another evening is probably spent reading to each other poems by published authors found in the Arvon library; there may be workshops or sessions for stimulating writing through poetry games or discussion; the tutors are available for individual tuition regarding your own work, and there is plenty of time and the right atmosphere to talk with others and to get on with your own writing. One day, usually the second, is traditionally allocated for sending the students out into the country in order to find ideas and the solitude necessary for writing.

During the winter months (October–April) the centre is available for schools, colleges and other organisations to book their own 'closed' courses for which they can choose the tutors and reader. I have taken many groups of children from the top Primary classes and have always found that they have benefited enormously, as do adults, from this extended contact with living writers. These are school journeys with a difference, and the setting is particularly good for city children.

The domestic arrangements are deliberately informal. The centres are to be considered as 'home' for the week and all cooking is done by course members. This is not as horrific as it might first seem to some people. Breakfast and lunch are worked on a help-yourself basis. You can get up when you want, and at any time of the day you are free to make tea, coffee, snacks, whatever you like, with the only proviso that you take account of other people. You do your own washing up – just like home! For evening meals a rota is usually worked out so that about four people take charge of cooking for everybody on one day only. The evening meals are taken together at the refectory table and are usually very convivial occasions. There are two centre directors at each place who are there to assist and advise. They will buy all the food you feel you need. In the case of school parties, the teacher will have to organise the groups and perhaps help, particularly with younger children; however, children are quite capable of doing much of the cooking, and this side of the holiday is equally valuable and enjoyable for them. Learning to live together in a small community is all part of the experience and works very well. Do not be put off by what you might think sounds too much like 'commune' living – it is not really like that at all.

The second centre of the Arvon Foundation is Lumb Bank near Hebden Bridge in West Yorkshire – a very different setting with the Pennine moors and Haworth (Brontë country) not far away. The house used to belong to the Poet Laureate, Ted Hughes, who became involved with the Arvon Foundation in the early 'seventies and provided it with its second centre. It is an eighteenth century millowner's house in the land of millstone grit and is set halfway down steeply sloping pasture land on the side of the wooded valley of the River Colden which runs into the Calder. The valley contains the ruins of several silk mills which once thrived in the area. Now all that remains are the tall chimneys, stubbornly straight against the sky, while below the river rushes noisily over the rocks and falls, down to Hebden Bridge. The nearest village is Heptonstall half a mile up a steep track. This house has also been completely modernised and contains the same facilities as Totleigh, including a converted barn for workshops and performances. In winter the log fires add to the cheerful atmosphere of the living rooms and here, too, the long wooden refectory table helps to ensure that meals are enjoyable social occasions. The whole of one wall of the dining room has windows and a door giving access to the terrace and the magnificent views across the valley with the moors stretching away over the Pennines. (For a much better impression of this area than I can possibly provide here, see the book *Remains of Elmet* (Faber) which has poems by Ted Hughes and photographs by Fay Godwin.) This dramatic landscape can, in any season, be particularly exciting for town children.

— ◆ —

Lumb Bank

The frowning face of a person typing,
The wooden plaque's thoughts, orange in the flames.
Charcoal spreads laughs around the human library.
The poem is finished, the writing shadowed by
    happiness
And the cows' quiet footsteps under the buds of dusk.

Joanna Cooper

Devon

Devon brings you into an endless dream
Almost as if in a different world.
Fresh air fills your lungs
Like water filling an empty jug.
The sky so clear

You can see through it.
It seems that every house
You come across
Is filled with a sense of joy.
Every hill has wonders captured inside
For you to let out and set free.

Steve Webber

Both these centres are happy to take parties of children of about
ten years and upwards, and many schools can already bear
witness to the success of the venture. Those that have been to
courses there usually go back again with new groups of children
every year. If you are interested, and I can certainly recommend
Arvon to anyone, I suggest that you visit one of the centres when
a course is in progress, or, better still, go on an 'open' course
first yourself, perhaps during the summer holidays. You can then
see for yourself how it all works. The centre directors will be
pleased to show you around and will be able to advise on
suitable tutors for your requirements. They may also be able to
tell you of schemes operated by some LEAs and Regional Arts
Associations whereby you can obtain a subsidy towards the cost
of the course for yourself or for the children. The costs are kept
as low as possible, although affected by inflation, and compare
very favourably indeed with courses run by other organisations.
There is nothing quite like Arvon in the rest of the country and
certainly nothing which caters for children as young as ten years
old in this field.

Arvon has now opened a third centre called Moniack Mhor,
which is fourteen miles from Inverness, in Scotland. It is a
traditional croft house with converted out-buildings. All around
are the sort of breathtaking views you would expect from a
Highland landscape, including the woods of Glen Convinth,
Strathfarrar's heather and silver birches, and the table plateau of
Ben Wyvis, one of Scotland's highest mountains. The village of
Kiltarlity is two miles away down the hill from Moniack Mhor.

For further information write to The Centre Directors, The
Arvon Foundation, at the following addresses:

Totleigh Barton,
Sheepwash,
Beaworthy,
Devon
EX21 5NS
(Tel: 0409 23338)

Lumb Bank,
Heptonstall,
Hebden Bridge,
West Yorkshire
HX7 6DF
(Tel: 0422 843714)

Moniack Mhor,
Teavarran,
Kiltarlity,
Beauly,
Inverness-shire
IV4 7HT
(Tel: 0463 74675)

Useful Addresses

1 The Arts Council Poetry Library (The Saison Poetry Library), in the Royal Festival Hall in London's South Bank complex, offers a wide range of facilities. It is an unrivalled resource for anyone wishing to do research, and there are days organised for teachers who want to find out what is available. Worksheet packs on a number of topics are available for classes of school pupils (of 5–16 years old) who are booked for a visit to the collection. The library is open seven days a week from 11am to 8pm, and membership is free. Books can be borrowed, and you can always ring up with any queries which the library staff will do their best to answer. (People often ring to try to locate a poem from just a few remembered lines.) The staff have built up a database of poem titles filed under both subject and author. Poetry readings are also held in the Voice Box, next to the library. For more information contact:

The Saison Poetry Library,
Royal Festival Hall,
South Bank Centre,
London
SE1 8XX
(Tel: 071 921 0943)

2 The Education Department of The Poetry Society also has packs for schools and is a source of information on poets who work in schools. The Poetry Society administers the W.H. Smith Poets in Schools scheme, and schools can apply to have a writer in to work for three days with children. For more information, contact:

The Education Secretary,
The Poetry Society,
22, Betterton Street,
London
WC2H 9BU
(Tel: 071-240 4810)

3   Pearse House Creative Writing Courses are residential
     courses for school children of any age, although each course
     is arranged for a specific age group. Pearse House used to be
     a residential teachers' centre for Hertfordshire Education
     Authority and now, like many other such centres, has had to
     go it alone. The creative writing courses, originally set up by
     the author Dennis Hamley, are just one string to their bow
     (they specialise in management courses and conferences at
     the house itself). The children stay at Youth Hostels all over
     the country. Under the guidance of experienced writers,
     children spend their time working in small groups for four
     days. Everything is meticulously organised and, when not
     actually writing, the children are supervised by trained
     pastoral tutors. Each evening one of the writers talks about
     his or her work, and at the end of the course there is a grand
     session when all groups come together to read the work they
     have produced. Later, a booklet is printed containing writing
     from each course member and sent to the participants. Since
     these courses are based at Youth Hostels, there is likely to be
     one arranged near you which your pupils could attend. The
     costs are reasonable and comparable to other such visits. For
     more information contact:

     Pearse House,
     Creative Writing Courses,
     Parsonage Lane,
     Bishop's Stortford,
     Hertfordshire
     CM23 5BQ
     (Tel: 0279 757400)

4   You may soon reach the point when you want to enter the
     children's work in national competitions. By far the best of
     these, which covers the age range from five to sixteen, is the
     W.H. Smith Young Writers' Competition (formerly the *Daily
     Mirror* Children's Literary Competition). The standard is
     high, and each year a book is published containing the
     winning entries. Poems, prose and plays are all eligible and a

distinguished panel of judges makes the final choices. There are certificates of merit for individual children, as well as prizes for individual winners and schools. For more information contact:

The Sponsorship Secretary,
Young Writers' Competition,
W.H. SMITH,
7, Holbein Place,
London
SW1W 8NR
(Tel: 071-730 1200)

5   Book House (containing Book Trust, the Children's Book Foundation, the International Board for Books for Young People, and the Book Information Service) is the place to go for information about books in general. They have author videos, booklets and posters, and events are organised, particularly during National Book Week. They will be happy to advise schools hoping to set up their own book weeks. For more information contact:

Book House,
45 East Hill,
London
SW18 2QZ
(Tel: 081-870 9055)